PAINTED DIAL
CLOCKS

PAINTED DIAL
CLOCKS

BRIAN LOOMES

Antique Collectors' Club

British Library Cataloguing-in-Publication Data
A catalogue record for this book is available from the British Library

*Frontispiece: Eight-day dial of a longcase clock of about 1830 by John Ablitt of Ipswich (see Colour
Plate 17). Courtesy Derek Roberts Antiques.*

Title-page: Detail from the arch of a longcase clock of about 1840-50 (see Colour Plate 20).

Printed in England
by the Antique Collectors' Club Ltd., Woodbridge, Suffolk
on Consort Royal Satin paper
supplied by the Donside Paper Company, Aberdeen, Scotland

ANTIQUE COLLECTORS' CLUB

The Antique Collectors' Club was formed in 1966 and quickly grew to a five figure membership spread throughout the world. It publishes the only independently run monthly antiques magazine, *Antique Collecting*, which caters for those collectors who are interested in widening their knowledge of antiques, both by greater awareness of quality and by discussion of the factors which influence the price that is likely to be asked. The Antique Collectors' Club pioneered the provision of information on prices for collectors and the magazine still leads in the provision of detailed articles on a variety of subjects.

It was in response to the enormous demand for information on 'what to pay' that the price guide series was introduced in 1968 with the first edition of *The Price Guide to Antique Furniture* (completely revised 1978 and 1989), a book which broke new ground by illustrating the more common types of antique furniture, the sort that collectors could buy in shops and at auctions rather than the rare museum pieces which had previously been used (and still to a large extent are used) to make up the limited amount of illustrations in books published by commercial publishers. Many other price guides have followed, all copiously illustrated, and greatly appreciated by collectors for the valuable information they contain, quite apart from prices. The Price Guide Series heralded the publication of many standard works of reference on art and antiques. *The Dictionary of British Art* (now in six volumes), *The Pictorial Dictionary of British 19th Century Furniture Design, Oak Furniture* and *Early English Clocks* were followed by many deeply researched reference works such as *The Directory of Gold and Silversmiths,* providing new information. Many of these books are now accepted as the standard work of reference on their subject.

The Antique Collectors' Club has widened its list to include books on gardens and architecture. All the Club's publications are available through bookshops world wide and a full catalogue of all these titles is available free of charge from the addresses below.

Club membership, open to all collectors, costs little. Members receive free of charge *Antique Collecting*, the Club's magazine (published ten times a year), which contains well-illustrated articles dealing with the practical aspects of collecting not normally dealt with by magazines. Prices, features of value, investment potential, fakes and forgeries are all given prominence in the magazine.

Among other facilities available to members are private buying and selling facilities, the longest list of 'For Sales' of any antiques magazine, an annual ceramics conference and the opportunity to meet other collectors at their local antique collectors' clubs. There are over eighty in Britain and more than a dozen overseas. Members may also buy the Club's publications at special pre-publication prices.

As its motto implies, the Club is an organisation designed to help collectors get the most out of their hobby: it is informal and friendly and gives enormous enjoyment to all concerned.

For Collectors — By Collectors — About Collecting

ANTIQUE COLLECTORS' CLUB
5 Church Street, Woodbridge Suffolk IP12 1DS, UK
Tel: 01394 385501 Fax: 01394 384434
——— or ———
Market Street Industrial Park Wappingers' Falls, NY 12590, USA
Tel: 914 297 0003 Fax: 914 297 0068

OTHER HOROLOGICAL BOOKS
by Brian Loomes

Antique British Clocks, A Buyer's Guide
British Clocks Illustrated
Clocks – Guide to Dating and Valuation
Complete British Clocks
The Concise Guide to British Clocks
Country Clocks and their London Origins
The Early Clockmakers of Great Britain
Grandfather Clocks and their Cases
Lancashire Clocks and Clockmakers
Watchmakers and Clockmakers of the World (Volume Two)
Westmorland Clocks and Clockmakers
The White Dial Clock
White Dial Clocks, The Complete Guide
Yorkshire Clockmakers

OTHER TITLES
by Brian Loomes

Bird Gardening
The Concise Guide to Tracing your Ancestry

CONTENTS

Introduction and Acknowledgements   9

Chapter 1   The Years of Neglect   10

Chapter 2   The First Painted Dials   13

Chapter 3   British Dialmakers   23

Chapter 4   Names and Identification   35

Chapter 5   How the Clockmaker got his Dials   48

Chapter 6   Dials, Period One (1770-1800)   66

Chapter 7   Dials, Period Two (1800-1830)   89

Chapter 8   Dials, Period Three (1830-1870)   104

Chapter 9   Original Prices of Dials and Clocks   119

Chapter 10   Long Cases: General Considerations   127

Chapter 11   Cases, Period One (1770-1800)   142

Chapter 12   Cases, Period Two (1800-1830)   161

Chapter 13   Cases, Period Three (1830-1870)   175

Chapter 14   Dials in Scotland   188

Chapter 15   Casework in Scotland   208

Chapter 16   Special Clocks   223

Chapter 17   Spring-driven Clocks   235

Chapter 18   America   248

Chapter 19   Is it genuine?   259

Chapter 20   Care, Handling and Research   268

Longcase Clock Dial Features   276

Longcase Clock Case Features   277

Index   279

INTRODUCTION AND ACKNOWLEDGEMENTS

This book deals with antique clocks with painted dials, also known as white dials or japanned dials, the terms being used indiscriminately. The origins of the book are complicated and perhaps need explanation. In 1974 I wrote a small book titled *The White Dial Clock,* being the first and only book on this topic. It was reprinted in 1977 and then re-published in 1981 in a greatly enlarged and revised form, re-titled *White Dial Clocks, the Complete Guide.* Both books have been out of print for some years now.

This present book is a completely new book covering painted dial clocks in greater detail incorporating all essential facts on the subject known to me including the latest researches and up-datings of the lists of dialmakers. The great majority of the photographs are new, mostly being of clocks I have handled as a dealer – I use these as I know what is inside them as well as what can be seen externally.

The photographs were taken by myself and my son, Robert. They were developed and printed by my wife, Joy, who has acquired the skill of making good prints from our terrible negatives.

In the preparation of this book the following people helped in varying ways, and it would be unfair to single out any for special mention as all helped to the best of their abilities – some with research, some with advice, suggestions or encouragement, some with photographs or details of clocks: Birmingham City Librarian W.A.Taylor; Peter C. Nutt; the late E.L. (Larry) Edwardes; Ken Roberts; Brian Morison; David Barker; Messrs. Manby of Skipton; former Archivist in Charge at Westmorland Record Office, Kendal, Miss S.J. MacPherson; A. Ankerson; Eric Benton; John Coker; Jeremy Evans; the late Bernard Mason, OBE; Dr. J.M. Plowman; Chris Bailey; Ed. La Fond; Stacy Wood; Tom Spittler; Roy Gault; Patrick A. Hewitt; John Daniell; Felix Hudson; Bill Seaby; Leicester Record Office; Leicester Museum; Robert W. Snyder Jr.; Stephen E. Kramer III; Granville Barrett; John Morris; P. Custers; Ian Haigh; Bob Hill; Dick Barder.

To anyone overlooked I offer my apologies.

Brian Loomes
Pateley Bridge
North Yorkshire
1994

CHAPTER ONE

THE YEARS OF NEGLECT

Until the publication of the first version of this book (known as *The White Dial Clock*) in 1974 it was very difficult to find any information on clocks with painted dials. Most people refer to this type of clock as having a 'painted dial', though the original makers called them 'white dials', made by a process known as 'japanning' and therefore they are sometimes termed 'japanned dials'. All three terms refer to the same type of dial and today are used indiscriminately.

The most respected textbooks on clocks at that time (the 1970s) were mostly written at the end of the nineteenth century, though a few were produced in the first half of the twentieth century. F.J. Britten, for example, in his massive work *Former Clock and Watchmakers and their Work*, devoted barely one page to them. Authors of this period had little time for a type of clock which had not long gone out of production (they were made until the 1870s). They were not regarded as of a collectable nature and indeed were very cheap to buy because they were largely unwanted.

In the early years of this century such clocks could be bought for as little as £1 each. Even in the 1960s, when I first began to deal in clocks, we sold the large type, often known as a 'Yorkshire clock', in working order for between £7and £10 each. Those which were thought unsaleable on account of their sheer size, or damaged ones not considered worth the cost of repair, were bought by dealers like myself at between £3 and £5 each and were broken up to use as spares, the cases being plundered for their veneers, which could be used to repair more worthwhile examples.

So, little was written about them, and what was written was mostly inaccurate. There were several reasons for these inaccuracies and some of them will emerge in due course. Principal amongst them, however, was the fact that the Birmingham imprint, left by the dialmakers inside many such clocks, was mistakenly thought to indicate that these clocks were made in some sort of Birmingham factory as mass-produced items. Students and collectors therefore ignored this kind of clock and their Birmingham imprints, which ironically were the very factors which would have revealed their true origin had anyone taken the trouble to study them.

From the beginnings of British clockmaking the dials had been made of brass, and brass dial clocks had been written about at great length, almost always with a heavy emphasis on those made in London which led the world in the manufacture of longcase and bracket clocks throughout the seventeenth and eighteenth centuries. Those who wrote about brass dial clocks failed to recognise that the same excellence of clockwork often existed alongside them in the form of the painted dial versions. In fact research has shown that a painted dial longcase clock would have been more costly when new than a brass dial equivalent, but we shall examine these factors in detail later.

Today clock enthusiasts appreciate painted dial clocks in their own right, and clocks tend to be judged on their intrinsic qualities of excellence or style regardless of whether the dial is made of brass or is japanned. This consideration can only apply, of course, where clocks of each kind are from the same period, for it would be foolish to compare a brass dial clock of the 1690s with a painted dial one of the 1790s. In terms of prices, however, we seem still to be stuck with the fact that brass dial clocks will often outrate painted dial ones of a similar period and nature, probably because of a lingering of past attitudes which supposed that brass dial clocks were somehow better.

Pendulum clocks were made in Britain from 1658, though in the first thirty years production was confined almost entirely to London. The majority of London-made brass dial clocks we are likely to come across (and virtually all those of British provincial origin) will date between about 1690 and 1790, a span of about a century. Painted dial clocks cover roughly the period 1770 to 1870, also a span of a hundred years of production. In the history of British clocks, then, this type is every bit as important as the brass dial.

From the point of view of the collector or student in Britain the painted dial type is probably more important because it is more readily available. They were made in far greater numbers and have undergone a much lower destruction rate by virtue of their relative youth. Their greater availability often also means that they fall into a lower price category and so are more easily within the range of affordability of the potential buyer.

For the collector or student in America the painted dial clock assumes even greater importance. The majority of longcase (known as tall) clocks in North America were British-made clocks taken there by immigrants or shipped there by relatives or dealers at a later date. Of those clocks actually made in North America few were made with brass dials, and those with painted dials were often made using dials imported from England by the clockmaker.

The same applies too to clocks in Canada, Australia and New Zealand. So for all these countries a knowledge of British painted dial clockmaking is essential.

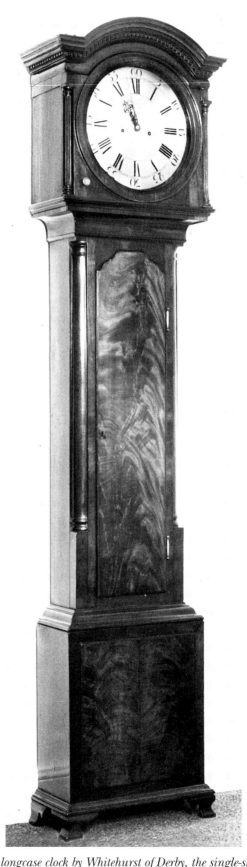

PLATE 1. *Mahogany longcase clock by Whitehurst of Derby, the single-sheet silvered brass dial engraved with the year of making, 1761, an unusually early date for this type of dial.*

CHAPTER TWO
THE FIRST PAINTED DIALS

Until the introduction of the japanned dial, all British clocks had dials made of brass. About the middle of the eighteenth century this situation began to change, but before that time the traditional clock dial consisted of a brass dial sheet proper, to which were attached certain separate brass fittings such as the chapter ring (the circle containing the numbers, which were strictly known as 'chapters'), perhaps a seconds chapter ring, usually a calendar disc or ring, and usually brass spandrels for the dial corners or arch or both. For convenience of description such a dial is often known as a composite brass dial. On such a dial engraved areas were normally silvered by the application on the surface of silver chloride for greater clarity and legibility. The dark (blued) steel hands stand out better against this silvered background for time reading.

Shortly after about 1750, at a date as yet uncertain but predating 1760, a different type of brass dial appeared. This was in the form of a single sheet of brass on to which all the necessary information and decoration was engraved. Today we know this type of dial as a single-sheet dial or sometimes as a one-piece brass dial. The single-sheet dial was silvered over its entire surface to increase legibility, and therefore gave a steely-white appearance.

It is very difficult to date the first appearance of the single-sheet dial as a regular style, since the dates of clocks having such dials are usually only estimates and therefore unreliable. Over the years different authorities have each expressed individual and often very varying opinions, and these usually set the appearance of the single-sheet dial between about 1750 and 1770.

A single-sheet longcase clock by Whitehurst of Derby (Plate 1) bears the year of manufacture of 1761,and for our purposes serves to establish that this form of dial was in use by that date, though most single-sheet dials met with will prove to be later in period (Plates 2 and 3).

The single-sheet brass dial is relevant to our discussion of painted dial clocks in so far as it has a bearing on the nature and perhaps also the development of the latter. The prime purpose of any clock is to tell the time in a legible manner. The origin and persistence for some years of the single-sheet type of dial can be attributed to the fact that it was believed to be more clearly legible than the original type of composite dial. A silvered dial has a steely-white appearance, at least until such time as the lacquer goes off, when the dial needs to be re-silvered, a process which needs performing at least every twenty years. It is by no means uncommon to see single-sheet silvered brass dials described in ignorance as 'steel' dials. In the past lacquers were of poorer quality than those of today and this probably involved more frequent re-silvering.

The single-sheet dial was not universally popular. There appears to have been a certain amount of regional fashion in so far as it was more popular in some areas than in others. In the North of England it seems to have been less popular than in the South, though it was popular in Scotland, whilst not so in Wales or Ireland.

As a very general guide the single-sheet brass dial was not used by all clockmakers, but those who did use it fell largely into the period 1770-1800 with its strongest popularity between about 1780 and 1790. In certain areas, notably London and the West Country, it was used for a considerable period beyond 1800, and West Country examples as late as even 1840 are not uncommon.

The single-sheet dial was for many clockmakers the last stage of brass dial clockmaking, and most clockmakers had changed over to the painted dial before the end of the eighteenth century. There are exceptions to this, where some clockmakers opted to use it for some considerable time after the white dial was universally popular, notably in certain regions and in certain types of clock, such as regulators.

The reasons why the single-sheet dial persisted with some clockmakers may be no more than a matter of chance preference, but it is possible that some dialmakers/engravers saw the single-sheet dial as a last haven of employment. The clockmaker who could perform his own engraving may have tried to prolong the single-sheet fashion rather than be forced to buy his white dial from the specialist japanners. In other words some may have continued with the single-sheet engraved dial to preserve the work of the engraver, as the switch to japanned dials must have meant a considerable loss of work to hundreds of engravers throughout the land.

Other forms of dial were also known before the appearance of the painted (japanned) dial. Wooden dials were sometimes made, and in Britain these were almost always confined to a type of weight-driven wall clock known as a tavern clock, sometimes called an Act of Parliament clock. Tavern clocks usually had very large dials which exceeded 3ft. in diameter and it is perhaps for this reason that wood was used. Rarely if ever was a brass or a japanned dial made to this extreme size.

Dials of true (vitreous) enamel were made for watches from very early times and long before the introduction of pendulum clocks (1658). Vitreous enamel fused on to copper was far less suitable for clock dials by virtue of their larger size, which risked buckling or cracking during firing. True enamel *was* used for bracket clocks and occasionally for longcase clocks, though the latter very infrequently. So few enamel dial longcase clocks exist that a search through the published books on clocks would probably fail to locate more than half a dozen. White (japanned) dials were sometimes erroneously described as 'enamel', but of course were not true enamel. In fact when they were first advertised, japanned dials were described by their manufacturers as being 'in imitation of enamel'. This description implies not only that the new japanned dials looked like those of enamel, but also clearly indicates that enamel dials were already in use.

True enamel dials were usually fired in sections of suitably small size, then assembled to form the whole dial. This might be done in a variety of ways such as enamelling the dial square separately from the arch, the dial centre separately from the square (even, for example, as an enamelled centre on to a brass surround as happened occasionally with longcase clocks but more frequently with bracket clocks).

True enamel dials are usually fired on to a copper ground and are very light in weight and consequently very delicate. Longcase clocks with such dials are especially prone to damage in handling, when the heavy movement can put great strain on the fragile dial.

A longcase clock with a true enamel dial is featured in Plates 4 and 5. The clock is signed on its dial front (traditionally the area where the clockmaker placed his name) by W. & C. Nicholas, Birmingham. William and Caleb Nicholas were brothers, born at Almeley in Herefordshire in 1760 and 1761 respectively. They set up in business in Birmingham about 1785 and worked together at least during the period 1785-87, after which they seem to have worked separately. They are known principally as dialmakers of the new type of (japanned) dial. However they also appear to have worked as clockmakers as clocks are known bearing the name of each individually and of both jointly.

PLATE 2. *Eleven-inch single-sheet silvered brass dial on a thirty-hour clock of about 1780 by Daniel Dickerson of Eye. This keeps the tracked minute markers of the earlier composite brass dial style. The original hands of blued steel are non-matching at this period. Note the engraved corner decoration is of a style seen on some early japanned dials.*

PLATE 3. *Eleven-inch single-sheet dial of about 1798 from an eight-day clock by Reynolds and Earl of Oxford, who were in partnership between 1797 and 1799 when Reynolds died, thus defining the period unusually accurately. Note corner decoration of a style found in goldwork on some early japanned dials. Note also the single-track minute band, a feature found late in the century.*

This particular clock with a true enamel dial can be dated to about 1785. It is therefore at least ten years later than the first known japanned dials and offers interesting evidence. It might reasonably have been deduced that the japanned dial ('in imitation of enamel') would have post-dated the true enamel one. This is clearly not always the case

We know that true enamel dials were made as early as about 1760, at least in bracket clocks if not in longcase examples (see Anthony Theelke, *Faces of Mystery*, 1983). The japanned dial offered a more robust item with the benefits of the appearance of enamel. Yet oddly enough we find examples of true enamel dials, such as this one, being made some years after the japanned version was well known. The implication of this must have been that the delicate and impractical true enamel dial was still a preferred choice of some, though probably very few, customers even after the japanned alternative was commonly available.

In short we can summarise that true enamel dials were made, apparently for very few clocks; that large size was a problem for such enamel dials and that because of this their suitability seems to have been more for bracket than longcase examples; that whilst we would imagine these to have largely preceded japanned dials, exceptions appear to have been made later too; and that true enamel dials for clocks seem to have been largely of an experimental nature and failed to achieve wide popularity, perhaps because they lacked robustness or were too costly, or both. For clarity of understanding we usually refer to enamel dials as such and the term painted dial or white dial is used to refer to the japanned iron dial which forms the major topic of this book.

The enamel dial illustrated here has its enamel fused on to copper, as was usual. The enamelling was done in sections, as was the case with most enamel dials, presumably to keep down the size of individual parts. Hence the arch section was

PLATE 4. *A very uncommon dial of true (vitreous) enamel from an eight-day longcase clock of about 1785 by William and Caleb Nicholas of Birmingham, who were also makers of japanned dials. The arch was made separately from the square, as was the dial centre which is of engraved copper. Dotted minutes are the regular style on enamel and japanned dials. The coloured corner and arch decoration is in pink. Note firing cracks in the dial edge.*

made separately from the square and joined after firing, as was usual. In this particular clock dial the copper centre with its engraving was made separately from the surround, which was an unusual procedure and may have been done to give the dial feet a firm grip against the copper; to have fitted them to the enamel area would have risked chipping.

The coloured decoration on this dial is of a pink/brown colour and is of restrained nature, typical of this type of dial. Its numbering system of Roman hour numerals and Arabic minutes marked at every fifth unit using dots for individual

PLATE 5. *Movement of the clock in Plate 4 showing how the dial feet fit directly to the movement with no intermediate falseplate, which is achieved by fixing the feet to the stronger copper dial centre, not to the enamel area. The arch section is attached by a lead joining strip, camouflaged by white paint on the face side.*

minutes is exactly the same as found on most late composite brass dials (after about 1770) and most, though not all, single-sheet brass dials. It is even possible that later brass dials (of both types) using dotted minutes do so because they are copying the numbering system used by the first japanned dials.

The clock has neither seconds dial nor calendar feature and most eight-day clocks (which this of course is) normally have both. This is very unusual and may have been because of the delicate nature of enamelwork and the reluctance to fit any additional items such riding lugs for a calendar, or a reluctance to weaken the dial centre by cutting any apertures into its surface area.

There is an unusual form of dial midway between the traditional brass dial and the true enamel type, where a brass dial has an enamelled circular area, such as a whole enamelled dial centre (with its numbers) or an enamelled circular disc in the arch for, for example, strike/silent work. These clocks are not commonplace but exist both in bracket and longcase form. This was perhaps an attempt to keep the rigidity of the brass dial with what may have been seen as the greater clarity or even delicacy of the enamel dial. It was a passing fashion, or at any rate one adopted by very few clockmakers, and most decided that the japanned dial offered legibility and attractiveness in a form sturdy enough to survive the years.

In the early years of the white dial an occasional clockmaker might experiment by producing dials which were a mixture of the old brass dial form and the new white (japanned) dial in just the same way as had been done with the brass-and-enamel dials mentioned above. For example, I have seen clocks with a japanned dial sheet on to which were imposed traditional engraved brass chapter rings. Sometimes too one sees a traditional brass (composite) dial with its dial centre neither matted nor engraved but instead painted as a complete centre zone scene. Both approaches seem to be attempts at combining the choice features of brass and japanned dials. Neither was regular practice, but apparently just done at the whim of a maker here or there, or perhaps even at the direction of the customer, who probably had over-riding say on most occasions.

The white (or painted) dial term is correctly used today to refer only to a japanned dial. Sometimes the inexperienced will describe a dial as being an enamel dial, a porcelain dial, a Battersea enamel dial, or a china dial, when often that person is trying to signify what we know as a white or painted (i.e. japanned) dial. Such terms used loosely must be taken as an indication of the style of the dial rather than its true nature.

Misnomers were also used in the past to describe white dials. In 1799 the cabinetmakers Gillow of Lancaster ordered a thirty-hour clock dial and movement from clockmakers Newby of Kendal to fit into a case of their making. The cost was £2.11s.0d. They described this as a 'china dial', but what they were ordering was in fact a japanned dial, probably made in Birmingham, which, as we shall see, is where the great majority were made. Whether such incorrect descriptions were used intentionally to make the dials sound more desirable, or whether it was just careless terminology, we may never know.

A japanned dial was basically an iron sheet with its face surface treated with paints. It appears to have been dipped into one or more baths of base paint, normally white, though in fact most are an off-white colour having a faint hint of blue or green about them. Coloured decoration was then applied in oil paints by hand to the white surface, as was the black numbering for hours, minutes, etc. This treatment was known as japanning and was used for other items as well as clock dials – such things as tea trays, trinket boxes, etc., known generally as japanware. A dial could have been made in any shape, but conventionally they were square or arched, sometimes round, occasionally oval.

Many dials were marked by the manufacturer with his name, often on the back of the dial, but sometimes on a plate behind the dial. We shall examine dialmakers' marks later, but the fact that many dials were so marked means that we can establish a date for them. Some, however, were not marked with the dial-maker's name, and these can only be dated by style or by some other evidence, often of a circumstantial nature.

It is difficult to date the first white dials of this japanned type. A few white dial clocks do seem to date from the 1760s, and yet our first factual evidence does not appear till 1772. Nevertheless, there do appear to be a few examples where the evidence suggests the dials predate 1772 by a mere handful of years. Such examples are very few and far between, and often they have some feature about them which suggests they are of a prototype nature. These prototype features will be discussed later, but the owner of an early dial (unmarked on the back as to its maker) should not leap to the conclusion that it pre-dates 1772, as the likelihood is that it does not.

On 28 September 1772 the following advertisement appeared in the *Birmingham Gazette:*

PLATE 6. *Cast iron falseplate from a dial by Osborne & Wilson of Birmingham (1772-1777) from the dial in Plate 27 by Waren of Thirsk. The falseplate feet, seen facing camera, fit into the frontplate of the movement. The dialmakers' names, put in during casting, are clearly visible*

White Clock Dials

Osborne and Wilson manufacturers of White Clock Dials in Imitation of Enamel, in a Manner entirely new, have opened a Warehouse at No3 in Colmore-Row, Birmingham, where they have an Assortment of the above-mentioned Goods. Those who favour them with their Orders may depend upon their being executed with the utmost Punctuality and Expedition. N.B. The Dial Feet will be rivetted in the Dials, and such Methods used as will enable Clock Makers to fix them to the Movements.

This is the earliest dated evidence I know of regarding the makers of japanned dials – though, as I said earlier, there is indication that a few may have been made before this time by unknown manufacturers.

It can be assumed that painted dials cannot have been made for long before this advertisement appeared, as Osborne and Wilson specify they are 'in a manner entirely new'. The year 1770 seems a reasonably safe round date, therefore, for the start of white dial manufacture, bearing in mind the occasional earlier prototype.

The last line of the advertisement is an interesting and most important one, in that an explanation is given that the dial feet will be riveted into the dials (during manufacture and therefore before delivery) yet in such a way that they can be fitted to the movements by the clockmaker without difficulty. Clearly the dial feet *had* to be fitted before they were japanned so that the dial feet ends would be hidden by the surface finish of paint. But there was a potential problem inherent in any dial with pre-fixed feet, as any clockmaker could anticipate, and the japanners are keen to point out that any such problem has been avoided by their particular 'methods'.

On a brass dial clock the dial feet could be fitted by the clockmaker anywhere into the dial at such points as they best suited the movement frontplate. Very often the clockmaker would choose to site them behind the chapter ring, so that the riveted ends, which could be potentially unsightly, would be hidden.

With pre-fixed dial feet the possibility existed that the feet themselves might meet up with the movement frontplate at some awkward point, such as where they might foul the wheelwork or other mechanical features. Osborne and Wilson set the clockmakers' minds at rest by asserting that this problem would not arise, and they achieved this by means of what we now call a 'falseplate' (and which at that time was sometimes known as a 'backplate'). The falseplate is explained more fully on pages 24-26 but briefly was an intermediate plate, which fitted between dial and movement on to the pre-fixed dial feet. Secondary feet could then be fixed to any desired part of the falseplate rim in order that these falseplate feet

PLATE 7. *Eight-day clock with rolling moon feature by Osborne and Wilson of Birmingham made between 1772 and 1777 showing the first phase style of Period One with heavy, asymmetrical gesso corners in gold, short-mouthed calendar and seconds dots inside the numbers. Note absence of winding collets typical of this early style, the winding holes being gold-painted instead. Original non-matching hands in blued steel: the seconds hand is probably a replacement.*

PLATE 8. *Unusual, perhaps unique, moon dial disc 10in. diameter from a thirteen-inch eight-day painted dial longcase clock of the early 19th century by George Muscroft of Sheffield. Note one is a normal moon 'face' but the other is a naturalistic representation of how the moon appears, termed a 'scientific' moon by American horologist Tom Spittler, who provided this rare photograph.*

would meet the movement in a mechanically convenient location (Plates 6 and 7).

Not all dialmakers who followed on after Osborne and Wilson used falseplates, though many did. But at all periods a good many clock dials are seen without them. Those (unknown) dialmakers who preceded Osborne and Wilson seem not to have used falseplates, and it looks as if these two men invented the falseplate system.

Five years later Osborne and Wilson decided to part company. On 29 September 1777 they announced that the partnership was to be dissolved:

Birmingham Sept.29 1777.

The Partnership lately subsisting between Messrs T. Osborne and J. Wilson, Manufacturers of Clock Dial Plates, was on 27th Instant dissolved; of which the Public are requested to take Notice; and also that this Branch of Business will be carried on by Wilson alone at No 11, Great-Charles-Street, Birmingham, who hopes for the Continuance of the Favours of his Friends and the Public...All Persons having any Demands on the said Partnership, are desired to send an account of the same as above: and all Persons who stand indebted to the aforesaid Partnership, are desired to pay the same.

Clock Dials

The Partnership between Thomas Hadley Osborne and James Wilson, Manufacturers of Clock Dials, is this Day mutually dissolved – They have authorised Mr John Walker of Colmore-Row to receive and discharge all Debts due to, and by, the said Partnership.

Birmingham Dec 24 1777.

On 19 January 1778 we read:

> T.Hadley Osborne thinks it necessary to acquaint the Public that he intends to carry on the Manufactory of Clock Dials as usual, when the Favours of his Friends will be punctually attended to and gratefully acknowledged by their Obedient humble Servant
>
> T. Hadley Osborne
>
> No.20, Cherry Orchard,Birmingham.
>
> James Wilson respectfully informs his Friends and the Public That he continues the Clock Dial Manufactory (late Osborne and Wilson's) at No.11 Great-Charles-Street, where Orders will be grate-fully received and executed in the most expeditious and complete Manner by their obedient Servant, Birmingham Jan 5 1778.
>
> JAMES WILSON

It seems possible that Osborne was failing in health for he appears to have died in 1779, after which his widow, Ann, continued the trade for some years, followed by his son, James.

James Wilson seems to have prospered and traded on until his death in 1809. Some years ago I traced his will dated 20 March 1809 and proved in London 15 June 1810. In it he described himself as a clock *dialmaker* (not a clockmaker). He appears to have been a widower, mentioning no wife but two daughters and one son, who were then minors. Among the trustees was one Edward Simpson, japanner.

The partnership of Osborne and Wilson revolutionised the clock world with the new japanned dial. We cannot say with certainty that they were the very first to produce these dials, but they are the first we know about by name. Instead of becoming famous their names were forgotten the year they died, and at the time of the first version of this book (1974) it is doubtful whether one clock enthusiast in a hundred had ever heard of them.

Today the position is very different. These names are now well known, as is the falseplate system they apparently invented. The increasing popularity and understanding of painted dials has meant that not only are names such as Osborne and Wilson much used by collectors but their names are sometimes even used to indicate a *style* of first period dial. Much misunderstanding persists, however, about the nature of 'Birmingham dials', but in the history of British clockmaking Osborne and Wilson represent just as important a landmark as did Ahasuerus Fromanteel when he introduced the pendulum clock in 1658.

That I was not the first to write about Osborne and Wilson was pointed out to me by Mr. Ken Roberts of Bristol, Connecticut, himself author of several works on American horology. In *Antiques* in September 1931 Penrose Hoopes published an article entitled 'Osborne & Wilson, Dialmakers', written with particular reference to the use of these dials on American-made clocks. Hoopes makes a point, with which I disagree, that he believes falseplates to have been introduced to prevent chipping on the dial feet ends (explained more fully on page 25). An article by W.A. Seaby in *Apollo* Vol. 48 (1948) also refers to them briefly.

CHAPTER THREE

BRITISH DIALMAKERS

A clockmaker was a worker in metals. He was not normally a woodworker and so it is obvious that he made only clocks and not the cases which contained them. There are rare exceptions to this general rule, where a clockmaker might also have made his own cases, but this was highly unusual and in all probability such examples would go unrecognised anyway. The wooden case was the product of a country joiner, carpenter or cabinetmaker (depending on the region and period involved) and not of the clockmaker whose name appears on the clock dial.

What is less obvious is that for the most part the clockmaker did not make his own dials either. Brass dial clocks involved engraving work for the dial, or at least a part of the dial. Some clockmakers *could* engrave, and in those cases (which we may or may not be capable of recognising anyway) the clockmaker may well have made his own dials too. Many clockmakers were unable to perform engraved work, and they would have had two options: either to buy the brass dial ready-made from a dialmaking specialist, or to make what parts they could and buy in only the engraved work. When the japanned dial appeared the clockmaker was faced with the situation whereby he was *obliged* to buy the finished dial from a dialmaking specialist such as Osborne and Wilson.

When we look at a white dial clock, therefore, we are looking at a combination of the work of three craftsmen: the clockmaker, the dialmaker and the cabinet-maker. The clockmaker was the instigator of the whole and it was his name which appeared on the dial front for all to see. The cabinetmaker/casemaker did not as a rule leave any evidence of who he was, and clock casemakers are normally unidentified except in those few instances where they may have left a trade label inside the case. The dialmakers (of white dials) often did leave evidence behind their dials and it is from such evidence that we can establish who each was and where he worked.

Most British dialmakers were located in Birmingham, and their name stamps or falseplates behind white dials usually include the town too. It has long been known that the 'made in Birmingham' imprint was to be seen behind clock dials, sometimes accompanied by words such as 'manufactory'. Until very recently the assumption was made that such clocks were factory-made in Birmingham and therefore in some way mass-produced. The dials of course were made in Birmingham, but the incorrect inference that such clocks as a whole were mass-produced was published in most reference books and was the major reason that clock enthusiasts had ignored painted dial clocks as being unworthy of their interest.

The subject is complicated by the fact that, although the early white dial clocks had their movements still individually made by the clockmaker himself, later on there was a degree of mass-production. We shall consider later the question of the degree of handcraftsmanship or mass-production in clock movement making. However when japanned dials first appeared, the clockmaker himself still made whatever he had made formerly, i.e. the movement.

The first makers of japanned dials (Osborne and Wilson and those who followed them) saw this very fact as a potential obstacle. They anticipated objection on the part of clockmakers who still made their own movements – which in fact meant all makers of longcase clocks (spring clocks were a rather different

FIGURE 1. *Methods of attaching painted dials to movements, with and without falseplates.*

PLATE 9. *Cast iron falseplate by Osborne (from the dial in Colour Plate 7 by Hewitt of Marlborough). The name Osborne is also punched into the rear of the calendar disc. Note click springs for moon and calendar attached to the falseplate itself.*

matter as these were often made by specialists *for* clockmakers – see page 241). They recognised that clockmakers were unlikely to be willing to change their techniques to make their movements capable of fitting the new dials, which of course had pre-fixed dial feet. They therefore devised a system whereby a clockmaker could fit the new dials to his existing movement layout, and this was achieved by means of an iron intermediate plate, fitted between dial and movement, and generally known today as a falseplate (at the time called a backplate) – see Figure 1.

The new dials were available to country clockmaker and city clockmaker alike, and instantly gave those incapable of engraving the same advantage that those who could engrave had held, in so far as each now had to buy his dial ready-made if he wanted to be in the new fashion. The country clockmaker, perhaps in an isolated rural location, was largely the one in whom true craftsmanship lingered longest, and often he was the one who continued traditional practices, doing as much as he possibly could for himself in order to keep down his prices. The falseplate fitting brought even these rural diehards within scope of the new dial.

The traditional brass dial fitted to the frontplate of the movement by means of what are called dial feet, roughly an inch long. An eight-day dial normally had four feet and a thirty-hour normally had three, but there were exceptions. Anyone trying to fit a different dial to such a movement will meet several problems (apart from the obvious one of having to position the reception holes differently), the chief one being that the dial feet may foul at some mechanically awkward point. A falseplate fitting between dial and movement frontplate removes this problem.

PLATE 10. *Late 18th century eight-day movement by Henry Ward of Blandford with its (Wilson) falseplate attached by three falseplate feet, the dial removed. The four holes in the falseplate are to receive the dial feet.*

Painted dials were supplied with their falseplates already attached, naturally on shorter (half inch or so) dial feet. Feet were then fitted to the falseplate at whatever positions would meet conveniently with the movement frontplate (Plates 9 and 10).

The use of falseplates had the added advantage that the shorter dial feet involved were less prone to flexing and straining and therefore less likely to cause chipping on the japanned surface of the dial feet ends. Such chipping was a regular problem with long dial feet, even sometimes to the point where a clockmaker might anticipate it (see Plate 228, Lister fly dial). It might even be the case that some clockmakers ordered their dials specifically with falseplates to avoid this problem, because dials seem to exist from all periods with and without them. Osborne and Wilson do stress in their advertisement, however, that the main reason for the falseplate is for ease of fitting.

Further evidence of this factor is that falseplates occur only on eight-day clocks and not on thirty-hour ones (except in special cases where a thirty-hour clock was built using an eight-day dial – see page 29), and this despite the fact that chipping was more likely to occur through lesser rigidity on the normal three feet of a thirty-hour dial than on the four feet of an eight-day one. Thirty-hour dials usually had only three feet because three feet were less of a problem to fit to the less cluttered frontplate of a thirty-hour movement than four feet were to an eight-day frontplate.

In summary, the falseplate was sold attached to the (eight-day) dial to accept more readily the movement frontplate. It was not, as was sometimes suggested in the past, sold attached to the movement in order more readily to accept any dial.

From the point of view of the owner of a painted dial clock, the fact that false-plates frequently carry the name of the dialmaker means that we have a second and most important method of establishing the age and origin of a clock. The name of the dialmaker was often placed on the falseplate in large letters of half an inch or more in height. Some were cast in when the cast-iron falseplate was made. Others were stamped into the later, thinner sheet iron plates. When the clock is dismantled such names are clearly legible (Plate 11). However even when the clock is fully assembled it is usually possible to develop the knack of reading the dialmaker's name by peering into the movement with a torch and viewing the falseplate from the side at a shallow angle. Most dialmakers are documented in this book and can be looked up very easily once the name is known.

Before we consider the dialmakers in detail, it is perhaps useful if we discuss further the question of how the dial fits the movement. The falseplate dial will not fit *any* movement. The fit depends on several factors and not only on the question of the falseplate feet avoiding fouling the movement parts. Very important are the position (on an eight-day clock) of the two winding holes relative to the hands aperture; the position of the seconds hole relative to the same; and the position of any calendar aperture relative to the same. Hands, winders, seconds (and perhaps also calendar) must all agree for position on an eight-day clock.

A thirty-hour clock generally has only the one aperture for the hands, as normal thirty-hour clocks do not have seconds dials. A thirty-hour might of course have a calendar, but calendars are not usually much of a problem in respect of lining up.

In practice a falseplate dial will fit several variations of movement. A dial without a falseplate will fit only the movement it was made for (or, of course, the move-ment made for it). The 'problem' of fitting together any dial and movement, with or without a falseplate, only exists at all if we assume the movement was made *before* the dial. If we assume the clockmaker began with the dial and made his movement to fit it, then there is no problem at all. A clockmaker starting with the movement and then hoping to get (or make or have made) a dial to fit, may have problems whether he is using a brass dial or a white dial.

In fact we now know that, as far as white dials go anyway, the clockmaker *began* with the dial. Usually he bought a selection of dials of varying sizes and types (i.e. eight-day and thirty-hour) and offered his customer a choice of dial from his available stock. This was the sensible way of going about it and we know this was the way it worked from the fact that the few inventories that survive of a clock-maker's stock in hand show that he carried a stock of dials well in excess of his stock (if any) of movements. This knowledge has only come to light in the last twenty-five years or so, when these inventories were uncovered during my own researches in preparing this book.

I suppose we should say that a sensible clockmaker began with the dial. In fact there were always a few contrary ones, or those so hidebound by tradition that they refused to bend with progress. If we look for example at those few clockmakers who persisted in using the old-fashioned birdcage construction for their thirty-hour clocks (mostly those from very traditional areas such as East Anglia), we can see what a terrible struggle they had in trying to fit white dials. By

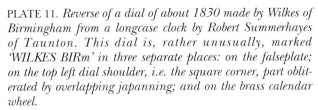

PLATE 11. *Reverse of a dial of about 1830 made by Wilkes of Birmingham from a longcase clock by Robert Summerhayes of Taunton. This dial is, rather unusually, marked 'WILKES BIRm' in three separate places: on the falseplate; on the top left dial shoulder, i.e. the square corner, part obliterated by overlapping japanning; and on the brass calendar wheel.*

PLATE 12. *Late 18th century thirty-hour posted movement, also known as a birdcage movement, seen here on a painted dial. As these dials were not designed for the (old-fashioned) birdcage movement, those clockmakers who continued to use the old system were obliged to attach fixing lugs to receive the dial feet. Here the brass lug is seen clearly attached to the lower plate to receive the dial foot. To the inexperienced such adaptation can look suspect, but it was the only way the birdcage method could be fitted to such dials. Clock by Raymond of Manningtree, Essex.*

the time white dials appeared on the scene (1770 or so) the birdcage movement was obsolete amongst all but a few diehards, and therefore white dials were not made in such a way as to fit this type of movement. Those clockmakers who insisted on trying had to alter, bend, or adapt the dial feet to achieve any sort of a fit, which was poor at the best of times (see Plates 12 and 13).

The iron dial sheet was treated on the face side with a red-lead type of paint, presumably to prevent rust. The back was often painted over in black, sometimes red, probably just for the sake of tidiness. Sometimes runs of red-lead paint can be seen spilling over on to the backs of dials. Then the face side was painted white (by which we often mean the bluish or greenish off-white shade rather than pure white), probably by being dipped into a vat of paint. The white base can often be seen to have overlapped on to the dial back through the dial apertures.

The white ground was not true enamel of course, but it was a paint of a hard and durable nature baked on by a heat process of some kind. Even after two centuries or so of wear and tear one seldom sees this ground paint wearing through, though it sometimes chips off with rough treatment or shells off through rusting.

A few early white dials, probably of an experimental nature, were made of brass,

PLATE 13. *Another late 18th century posted movement thirty-hour clock using a painted dial. Here the fixing lug is seen attached to the front left upright post to receive the dial foot. The top dial foot is seen sawn half through to produce a flat step which is then pinned down into the top plate. Note the white paint patch behind the dial on which is attached a job ticket. The dial is unmarked but is probably by James Wilson. The clock is by Thomas Barker of Framlingham. East Anglia was the main area where the now old-fashioned birdcage movement lingered.*

not iron. These sometimes have falseplates too. With such japanned brass dials the backs were usually left untreated. I do not know which concerns made these, but they were obviously specialist japanners. We have to be careful to avoid confusing a japanned dialplate using a brass dial with a brass dial clock which was japanned over at a later period to 'modernise' it (see page 63). Moon wheels and calendar wheels for japanned (iron) dials were normally made of brass, though sometimes these were of iron.

The fact that white base-paint runs can often be seen on the backs of dials indicates that these apertures such as winding holes, seconds hole, etc., were drilled *before* japanning, not after. But see page 248 regarding American dials for further discussion on this point.

The painted scenes, patterns or devices painted on to the white background appear to be in oil paints and were of a far less durable nature than the background itself, though they would not normally wear off except with abuse. The black numbering and lettering was of an even finer nature, apparently done with a very thin black paint, and often prone to wearing away, where over-zealous owners have tried to wipe the dial clean with a wet cloth.

Not all falseplates have names on them, and in some of these cases the dial-maker's name may be found stamped into the back of the dial itself, often at the top left-hand corner of the dial as seen from the back. Sometimes a mark or initials are impressed in the dial back rather than a name. These can sometimes be difficult to spot at first because of the layer of black paint or rust which may partly obscure them.

On those dials which have an aperture calendar (often known as a mouth calendar), the dialmaker's name can often be found stamped into the back of the calendar disc (see Plates 9 and 11). Sometimes, however, a dial can be found to have an unnamed falseplate, an unnamed calendar disc, and a total absence of any identification marks. Why this should be I do not know.

Not all dials had falseplates and there is a common misunderstanding about this. First of all, thirty-hour dials did not need falseplates and seldom if ever had them. I cannot bring to mind a single example, except in a particular type of instance – where an eight-day dial has been used for a thirty-hour clock, and therefore was used with the falseplate it was supplied with.

This would happen where, for example, the maker wanted to have what we usually call dummy winders, which means winding holes (sometimes even with winding squares), in order to give the clock a superficial eight-day appearance. Some makers indulged in this practice, mostly in North-west England, presumably so that the customer could purchase his cheaper thirty-hour clock at the thirty-hour price, yet the clock would appear to his neighbours to be a more costly eight-day type. Where the thirty-hour clock was also provided with a seconds dial (sometimes even a dummy seconds hand only, which did not turn), this eight-day appearance was even more convincing. It can sometimes be impossible to recognise such a thirty-hour clock for what it really is without opening the trunk door or removing the hood to look inside.

Turning to eight-day clocks, it seems to me that most of the earlier ones, by which I mean those before about 1800, were sold with falseplates. This may have been to facilitate movement fitting by the clockmakers at a time when they were still not yet fully accustomed to the new dial types. It may have been partly because during the eighteenth century there were very few dialmakers other than Osborne and Wilson who normally (though not always) used falseplates on their eight-day clocks. So perhaps what we see is the result of their regular practice rather than a more widespread tendency.

Between about 1800 and 1830 the situation seems to be that some have them and some do not, probably with a slight favour towards those that do. After about 1830 the majority of clocks seem to be without them. This may be because by now more clockmakers were buying in their clockwork with just the finishing and assembly work to do and therefore the dials were more standardised to fit the movements, thus removing the need for a falseplate fitting.

In summarising then, most early eight-day white dial clocks tend to have false-plates and most late ones do not. However, the absence of a falseplate can by no means be taken to signify that the clock was not handmade, any more than the presence of one can be assumed to be an indication that it was.

Birmingham was not the only centre of white dial making, but it was always the main centre. The other English dialmaking centres were very much lesser places of production. In Scotland Edinburgh was a strong centre of dialmaking, but not

PLATE 14. *Frontplate from a late 18th century painted dial clock by Place of Thirsk. The punched lettering 'THOMPSON DARLINGTON' indicates that though this is still a hand-made movement it was not made by the man whose name appears on the dial but by another clockmaker for him. The meaning of the large engraved letter 'E' in the lower right corner is unknown, perhaps just some sort of serial number.*

until a somewhat later period than in England, and Edinburgh only really came into its own as a regular supply base for Scottish clockmakers (hardly much at all for English clockmakers) after about 1830, by which time a regular Scottish style had emerged, which was considerably different from the English style of the day.

At one time I found it very hard to believe that clockmakers in parts of England remote from Birmingham would have sent all that way for their dials, when other sources existed closer to hand. But after years of studying white dials I was forced to the conclusion that they did. This may have been because Birmingham offered a wider choice or better quality or both. When we come to examine American clocks (Chapter 18) we will see that the Birmingham dialmakers could draw in orders not only from halfway across Britain but halfway across the world! This must be a measure of the selling techniques of the Osbornes, Wilsons and others even at this time of relatively poor communications. I wonder how many engravers or makers of brass dials could claim to have sent consignments across the Atlantic. Was there one even?

It was almost certainly on account of the centralised nature of this industry that

PLATE 15. *Rear of a thirty-hour dial of the late 18th century from a clock by Hepton of Northallerton showing two of the typical three direct-fitting dial feet. Note the dab of white paint on to which is affixed a job ticket or processing form as used in the Wilson factory. In this example the strikework is controlled by an uncommon pin-wheel form instead of the usual notched countwheel, one indication that this maker is still making his own clockwork.*

a regular and orderly progression of dial painting styles took place. If local artists here and there throughout Britain had been painting dials in a random and hotch-potch manner according to individual whims and fancies, then there would have been no orderly development of styles. It is the fact that dial styles did progress in an orderly manner that helps us understand and recognise the period of a dial simply by its appearance alone, as we shall see shortly. As it happens we also have additional aids to dating by virtue of the dialmaker's name and the name of the clockmaker too, both of which can be checked on.

We cannot be certain that all dials were supplied in a fully finished state. It is possible that some (or even all) were supplied part-finished, for example without the numbering, or without the clockmaker's name. However I feel confident from studying them that they were sold to the British clockmaker in a fully-finished state. The supply of dials to America, however, may have varied from this standard British method – see page 248.

On the back of some dials (principally if not exclusively those by James Wilson) can be seen what I take to be the dialmaker's instruction ticket, that is a job ticket which went through the workshop attached to the dial to instruct each handler/

	rais'd	moon
	gilt	common
	painted	name
	mid or arch	month
	rais'd	sil:strike
	illegible	(blank)
	gilt	(blank)
	painted	(blank)

FIGURE 2. *A dial processing job ticket as used by James Wilson of Birmingham.*

artist what design and detail was called for. These labels are interesting in their own right, but also in so far as they seem to confirm that a dial went through the workshop marked with instructions that it was to be fully finished and how.

These small job labels measure about one and a half inches wide by about half an inch tall. They are often grubby, worn and oil-stained and difficult to read, or at any rate to read fully, as often only a few of the words can be made out. Attempts at cleaning them usually result in even more of the lettering being erased. However by compiling words from several I've seen over the years, the wording generally appears to be as set out on the example in Figure 2.

The ticket was usually stuck to the dial back by means of a rough brush-stroke of white ground paint, which acted as glue (Plate 15). The labels seem to have been printed as blank forms and ruled into tiny boxes into which information was written in ink in tiny handwriting. This information appears to offer various permutations of features which the dial was to contain, yet oddly enough no ticks or check marks seem to have been put against the boxes to advise which per-mutation was needed for the particular dial in question. So exactly how this job ticket system worked we do not know, but at least we do know there was a system.

The way I imagine the dial decorating process to have worked is along the lines of a print colouring house, such as the workshops of the (American) printmakers Currier and Ives. Here prints were hand coloured by young ladies, who sat in a row along a bench in a sort of production line system. Each artist applied just one colour and the print was passed from one colourist to another, each adding her particular shade. In the centre was an example ready-coloured for them to follow as guidance. After the final colour was added a supervisor checked the quality of the finished work, adding any last-minute touches as needed. That is how I imagine the dial colourists worked, with probably someone adding numbering, lettering etc. at the later stages, but of course this is only my impression, and it may be quite erroneous. In the case of clock dials there was naturally a far greater variety than with prints, which by nature were repetitive, and so it is unlikely that a model would be set up for copying, but rather a selection of corner/arch themes from which the colourists would select. The moon discs (on those clocks which had moon dials) seem to be often of a higher calibre of artistry than the corner themes of the same dials. Perhaps moon discs were farmed out to professional artists, maybe even working in their own homes in the outwork method.

At this period clockmakers did not usually hold a stock of clocks. Clearly a city clockmaker with a retail shop would have to have something to show his customers and to offer for sale. He may well have had a clock, or several, ready-made and on display. However most clockmakers had a workshop, not a sales shop, and did not carry a stock of clocks waiting for customers; most clocks were made to order. Mr. so-and-so called to give a clockmaker a commission to make a certain kind of clock, to certain specifications and a certain size, and probably at that stage it was decided what sort of dial he wanted: one with flowers in the corners, or one with birds, or whatever.

A clockmaker with a retail shop would sell not only clocks but other associated lines. Some veered towards silversmith work and precious objects of a finer nature; others tended towards ironware along the lines of a hardware merchant. As an example of the variety of goods sold in such a 'clockmaker's' shop in the 1830s, the following are a few items taken from a clockmaker's label pasted inside the door of a longcase clock by Richard Blakeborough of Otley: hardware, jewellery, weatherglasses, bottlejacks, ear-rings, thimbles, cutlery, spoons, guns, pans, kettles, hammers and tools, *japanned* tea trays, *japanned* bread baskets, knobs, locks, keys, hinges, pencils, mouse-traps, and many other items.

PLATE 16. *Detail showing the arch of a japanned longcase dial of about 1830 from a clock by William Chapman of Lincoln (Plate 83). The dial corners are painted in the normal manner of the day but the arch is printed from a copper plate (or perhaps a transfer taken from a copper plate), and then coloured by hand. The inkwork of the printing is clearly visible. This is a most unusual method for dials. The scene shows the postman delivering a letter.*

So either the clockmaker had bought in advance a varied batch of dials so that the customer could select one, or perhaps the customer would specify the kind of painted matter he preferred and get the clockmaker to send off for it. Maybe the customer would even rely entirely on the clockmaker's own advice or recommendation and settle for one in the newest fashion or in what he considered the best style. No printed pattern books or samples in printed form appear to be known today, and it is doubtful if these ever existed.

Even the rural clockmaker who lived in a remote area would tend to operate in these same two ways. Some were also farmers, though of course in the past many country people had their own piece of subsistence land. These remote rural makers would often combine a secondary occupation with clockmaking – blacksmithing, innkeeping, boardinghouse keeping, cabinetmaking … This is the reason so many appeared in tiny out-of-the-way villages, where you might think they would never sell one clock in a year. They would of course tend to make up clocks in their quiet periods or in bad winter weather and take them to local markets to sell in the spring. So although the rural maker may have had a workshop and no sales shop, he still was able to make clocks as bespoke items or readymade to sell in local markets.

The concentration of dialmaking in Birmingham, as I have already said, means that we can recognise an orderly sequence of styles. It might be deduced that such a centralised supply would mean that dials of a particular period were the same throughout Britain (and even America too). In fact that is not the case, for there were certain regional preferences in dial tastes. Either the dialmakers were well aware of these regional tastes, or the clockmakers specified in their orders that they wanted what ultimately amounted to a regional taste. Or was it perhaps that once it had been established what preferences a particular clockmaker had expressed, the dialmakers knew the taste of that particular buyer and sent him what they knew he would find acceptable?

Such evidence as we have (and there is little of it) suggests that dial ordering was a bit of a hit-and-miss affair. The overall period style of the dial (such features as numbering pattern and style of painting, which we shall shortly examine in detail) is so distinct that we cannot fail to recognise the age of a dial by its style. Those features opted for by clockmakers as personal preferences (i.e. regional style) are such that the clockmaker could have specified them in his order.

Regional tastes include for example the presence of a pair of birds in the dial centre on some Period One and Period Two dials – such birds were more popular to a noticeable degree in North-west England than elsewhere; the use of the fully-painted dial centre scene on some Period Two dials, also more popular in North-west England and the West Midlands than elsewhere; the use of plain (i.e. un-coloured) dial corners in London and the South-east more than elsewhere; the use of smaller dials in the South in comparison with the generally larger ones in the North. These are the kind of features which fall to some degree into regional tastes whilst still within the overall style of the period in question.

Despite the strong and fairly strict development of period styles and the much weaker tendency for some regional styling, dials did not become repetitively and boringly cloned, as might perhaps have been expected. How much easier it might have been for the colouring artists to have been given a model for all to copy so that they might churn out hundreds of lookalikes, but this did not happen.

Certainly in Period One, where styles were more tightly defined than later, we do see dials which are superficially similar in terms of painting (I am not here referring to the blackwork of numbering and lettering, which can be almost identical for many clocks in a given period, but to the coloured painting in oils). Yet even though corner decoration at this time may be a single flower spray, the artists seem not to have copied one flower over and over again, but to have kept on varying such things as position, shape, size, colour, spread, etc. even in those few instances where they were repeating the same flower. By and large they varied the flower species anyway, or the combination of them.

In the pottery factories many designs were printed from transfers, often with hand painting over the black transferwork. Some clock dialmakers also used transfers, but very few (Plate 16). A dial made using transfers might have simply the black transferwork left as such (i.e. uncoloured), or might have colours applied over the transferwork. Whether dials using transfers were cheaper than others, I cannot say.

Surrounding the painted areas on most clock dials we can usually see what has been effectively described as a 'halo'. This shows as a narrow border of yellowed varnish around the edge of the painted area, exactly like the one seen at the edge of a transfer. It is most obvious on those dials which have a solid paint ground, as most do in Periods Two and Three, and is less apparent in Period One dials. The presence of this halo might seem to suggest that these were transfers, but in fact it is the yellowed coat of varnish originally applied to seal the oil paints. This is one reason the painted corners are more hard wearing than the blackwork, which was not varnished. The earliest dials, such as those by Osborne and Wilson, seem not to show this halo and probably were not varnished – hence the blackwork within the painted areas (flower stalks, etc.) often wears thin whilst the oil-painted parts do not.

CHAPTER FOUR

NAMES AND IDENTIFICATION

To be able to use the following listing it is essential to understand how it has been compiled. Most of the details come from trade directories and therefore the dates do not normally indicate the beginning or end of a man's career. The fact that, for example, Christopher Wright was listed as working in the period 1835-1845 does not mean that he could not have been working both before and after those dates. It means he is listed for the first and last times in those years, but it is quite possible that he may by mischance have been omitted from an earlier or later directory. I know of instances where clockmakers were still listed in directories two or three years after they had died! It is important therefore to appreciate that these dates are only a guide and are not definitive.

The dialmakers' listing below was compiled initially from trade directories for the following years: 1777, 1791-8, 1800, 1803, 1815, 1816-17, 1819-20, 1822, 1828, 1830, 1835-6, 1839, 1841-2, 1849-50, 1858, 1860, 1862, 1865, 1880.

Additions have been made from information supplied by Roy Gault, from information reported by correspondents and from my own personal observations and notes made since the first edition. It is as complete as I can make it.

Too much store should not be set by the terms used, which are set out here as in the directories. For example, a dial painter, dial writer and dial artist may simply be different terms for the same thing. Some made clock and/or watch dials, and where it is known which, this is specified in the right-hand column.

ENGLAND

Aaron, Solomon & Son	Birmingham 1803	watch dials
Abbott, –	not known, c 1810-c.1820	clock dials
Alldridge, Edwin	Birmingham 1860	clock dials
Allen, Joseph	Birmingham 1867-70	clock hands and bezels
Anderson & Co.	Birmingham c.1810	clock dials
Ashwin & Co.	?Birmingham c.1790	clock dials
Bagley, Samuel & Son	Birmingham 1851-61	enamellers
Baker & Son	Birmingham 1846	clock dials
Baker, Richard	Birmingham 1850-66	clock dials
Baker, Samuel	Birmingham 1823-50	clock dials
Baker, Samuel & Son (? = Richard)	Birmingham 1858	clock dials
Baker, Thomas	Birmingham 1839-50	also clockmaker
Baker, William	Birmingham 1822-31	clock dials
Baker, William II	Birmingham 1854-67	also clockmaker
Batkin, William & Son	Birmingham 1803	printed dials
Beach, Joseph (Sen.)	Birmingham 1849-63	
Beach, Joseph (Jun.)	Birmingham 1849-80	
Beilby & Hawthorn alone (partners were:	Newcastle upon Tyne c.1796-1817	clock dials

Beilby, Langlands & Robertson 1778-95
Beilby, Robertson & Hawthorn 1796-1800
Beilby & Hawthorn 1801-1817, when Beilby died)

Beilby & Hawthorn *with* William Whittaker	Newcastle upon Tyne and Halifax	clock dials
Bennett, Edward	Sheffield 1816-33	clock dial maker
Bennett, Elizabeth	Sheffield 1837-41	clock dial maker
Bingham, Charles	Birmingham 1808-18	church clocks and sundials
Bingham, Charles & Son (? = Thomas)	Birmingham 1821-25	church clocks and sundials
Bingham, Thomas, born c 1798	Birmingham 1841-61	church clocks and sundials
Blood, Richard	Birmingham 1813	dial artist
Bolton, C.	Birmingham 1866	watch dials
Boucher, Daniel	Birmingham 1808-12	clock dial painter
Brooke, Thomas	Birmingham 1812	also clock maker
Brown, William	Birmingham 1851	dial writer
Burgess, –	not known c.1810	clock dials
Byrne, F.	Birmingham c.1780-c.1810	clock dials
Carter, Joseph	Birmingham 1854	
Clarke, Henry	Birmingham 1851	
Clarke, Richard	Birmingham 1851	
Cohen, Morris	Hull 1849-58	clock dials
Cooke, James George (of Howell & Cooke?)	Birmingham 1858-88	
Cooper, William	Birmingham 1808	clock dial painter
Cox, –.	Taunton c.1810	clock dials
Crow, Edward	Birmingham 1822-39	also clock hands
Crow, Thomas	Birmingham 1841-52	also clock hands
Denniston, John	Halifax 1834	clock dials and painter
Dugmore & Foster (see Foster?)	Birmingham 1816	
Eaves, Thomas (Sen.)	Birmingham 1865-6	clock bezel maker
Eaves, Thomas Arthur	Birmingham 1865-70	clock bezel maker
Edwards, William	Birmingham 1870	engraved and silvered dials
Egginton, Thomas	Birmingham 1851	
Egginton, Thomas & James (see Wasbro/Hale)	Birmingham 1841-2	dials
Felton, Eli (see Kempson & Felton?)	Birmingham 1808-31	also button maker
Field, William	Birmingham 1854	
Finnemore, George	Birmingham 1846	clock dials
Finnemore, William I	Birmingham 1812-25	clock dials

Finnemore, William II	Birmingham 1849-52	clock dials
Finnemore, William and George	Birmingham 1839-46	clock dials
Finnemore, William (& Son)	Birmingham 1828-36	clock dials
Fletcher, John Wright	Birmingham 1841-50	
Foster, –. (see Dugmore/Foster?)	Birmingham c.1810-c.1820	clock dials
Francis, Sarah (widow of William?)	Birmingham 1835-43	clock dials
Francis, William	Birmingham c1810-31	clock & watch dials
Griffiths, Richard	Birmingham 1867-70	
Griffiths, Wm. and Richd. (succ. to Finnemores)	Birmingham 1854-66	
Guest, Joseph (or James?)	Birmingham 1864	also gun cases
H., I (i.e.I.H.)	not known c.1790	clock dials
Hand, Samuel	Birmingham 1851	clock dial writer
Harden, John	Birmingham 1816	
Hayes, Josiah	Birmingham 1800-31	
Hayes, Josiah & Son	Birmingham 1835-36	
Higgins, William	Birmingham 1839	
Hipkiss & Harrold	Birmingham 1797-1805	clock dials
Hipkiss, Richard	Birmingham 1805-1811 (? or 1816)	clock dials
Hitchens, Samuel	Birmingham 1861	clock dial worker
Hitchens, Thomas	Birmingham 1858-88	
Hobson & Hodgkins (or Hodgkinson?)	Birmingham c.1815 or later	clock dials
Hobson, L.	Birmingham c.1830	clock dials
Hobson & Todd	Birmingham 1800	clock dials
Hobson, Todd & Hodgkinson	Birmingham 1808	clock dials
Howell, Edwin & Cooke (James George?)	Birmingham 1845-67	
Hughes, William	Birmingham 1845	clock bezel maker
Hunt, S.	Liverpool early 19c.	clock dials
Jones & Carter	Birmingham c.1810	clock dials
Jukes, John	Birmingham 1839-70	clock dials
Jukes, Josiah	Birmingham 1839-42	clock dials
Keat, Edward	London c.1810-c.1820	clock dials
Keeling, Thomas	Birmingham 1800-25	
Kempson & Felton (Eli?)	Birmingham 1812-c.1815	clock dials
Landale & Todd	Birmingham c1790-c.1830-	clock dials
Leighton, Thomas	Birmingham 1870-84	clock bezel maker
Leighton Thos.& Son	Birmingham 1884	clock bezel maker
Longmore & Fairfax	Birmingham 1815-18	brass clock rings (= bezels?)

Longmore, Thos. Jun.	Birmingham 1825	brass clock bezels
McIntyre, Martin	Birmingham 1854	
Mansell & Allen (see Allen?)	Birmingham 1865	bezel makers
Meeke, Joseph	Birmingham 1864	
Minshull, John	Birmingham 1816-31	
Moon, Henry	Birmingham 1870-88	bezels & materials
Neal, Thomas	Birmingham 1785-1803	watch dials
Nicholas, William	Birmingham 1793-1825	also clock makers
Osborne & Wilson	Birmingham 1772-77	clock dials
Osborne, Thomas Hadley	Birmingham 1777-79	clock dials
Osborne, Mrs.Ann (widow of Thomas)	Birmingham 1800	clock dials
Osborne, James	Birmingham 1808-13	clock dials
Owen, Edward	Birmingham c.1795-1821	clock dials
Owen & Price (?see Price)	Birmingham 1800-01	clock dials
Parkes, S.(& Sons)	Birmingham 1861-64	sundials and toys
Porter, Nathaniel (?late Wilson)	Birmingham 1812	
Potter, John	Birmingham 1835	
Price, W.H.	Birmingham c.1790-c.1800	clock dials
Prince & Forrest	Birmingham 1870	
Prince, Henry	Birmingham 1880-88	
Pyke, T.	Bridgwater c.1820-c.1825	clock dials
Rainer, James	Birmingham 1841-51	dial painter
Reed, J.N.	Birmingham c.1850	clock dials
Riding, John	Birmingham 1816	
Roberts, –	not known, not known	clock dials
Robinson, Thomas	Birmingham 1865-67	clock bezel maker
Sandell, Isaac	Bristol not known	clock dials
Schwanfelder, James and John	Leeds c.1810-37	dial painters (? and makers)
Shreeve, William	Halifax d.1817	with Whittaker,q.v.
Shuker, Aaron	Birmingham 1870	clock bezel maker
Simpson, Edward	Birmingham 1809	japanner
Smith, Richard	Birmingham 1777-85	dialmaker
Smith, W.H.	Birmingham c.1820-30	clock dial maker
Solomon & Co.	Birmingham 1815	also materials
Solomon, Eve	Birmingham 1818-21	also materials
Stansbie, –	Birmingham c.1805-10	clock dial maker
Swinden & Sons (F.C.& Francis & Edwin Charles)	Birmingham 1851-88	also materials

Swindon, Francis Charles	Birmingham 1835-58	
Symonds, Charles	Birmingham 1851-61	dial artist with John Jukes
Todd,–	Birmingham	see Landale
Totley, Mrs.Elizabeth	Birmingham 1851	clock dial worker
Turner, I.	Birmingham c.1830-c.1840	clock dials
Tyndall Wright & Co	Birmingham c.1790-c.1800	clock dials
Vann, Joseph	Birmingham 1865-70	clock bezel maker
W., W.	monogram of William Whittaker, q.v.	
Walker & Finnemore	Birmingham 1808-11	clock dials
Walker & Hughes	Birmingham c.1811-35	clock dials
Walker, G.G.	Birmingham 1823-25	
Wasbrough, Hale & Co.	Bristol c.1830-c.1840	clock dials
Waterhouse, George	Birmingham 1818-25	also pawn broker
Westwood, Samuel	Birmingham 1880-88	also engraver
Whittaker, Sarah	Leeds 1834-37	dialpainter (and maker?)
Whittaker, William	Halifax c.1809-c.1815	clock dials
Whittaker & Shreeve	Halifax (c.1800)1815-c.1817	clock dials
Wilkes, B.& Co.	Birmingham, not known	clock dials
Wilkes & Baker	Birmingham 1815-20	
Wilkes, John & Son (Samuel?)	Birmingham 1820-31	clock dials
Wilson, James (see Osborne also)	Birmingham 1777-d.1809	clock dials
Winn, Robert	Birmingham 1815-45	all sorts!
Winn(e), –	Birmingham c.1840-50	dialmakers
Wood, –	Birmingham c.1810-20	clock dials
Wood & Cooke	Birmingham c.1810-20	clock dials
Wright, B.& Co	Birmingham c.1805-20	clock dials
Wright, Christopher	Birmingham 1835-45	clock dials
Wright, Tyndall & Co (see Tyndall)	Birmingham	

SCOTLAND

Adam, Joseph	Glasgow 1837	clock dials
Bell & Meudell	Edinburgh 1832-49	clock dials and ironmonger
Bell, P.(with 'Finest Fancy' dials)	Edinburgh 1832-52	clock dials
Burnet, J.	Edinburgh 1898	japanner
Cameron, John & Sons	Edinburgh 1898	japanner
Coats, Andrew	Glasgow 1818-20	clock dials and japanner
Craig, Peter	Glasgow 1837	clock dials
Crawford, Maurice & Co.	Edinburgh 1773	japanned ware (but probably not dials)
Dallaway, William	Edinburgh 1775-93 and later	clock dials

Dallaway & Son	Edinburgh c.1797-1812 (and later?)	clock dials
Drew, John (later Shearers)	Glasgow 1835-68	clock dials
Johnston, Alexander	Edinburgh 1898	japanner
Laing, John	Edinburgh 1848	japanner
Landale & Todd	Edinburgh c.1830 (error for Birmingham?)	
Paterson, James	Perth c.1820-d.1850	clock dials, japanner and painter
Peterkin, J.	Edinburgh 1824	japanner
Peterkin, Mrs.	Edinburgh 1832	japanner
Russell & Bell, *then:*	Edinburgh 1824	japanner
Russell & Anderson	Edinburgh 1832	ironmongers
Russell & Clark	Edinburgh c.1835-c.1840	dialmakers
Russell, Thos (alone)	Edinburgh 1848-55	ironmongers
Scott & Co.	Glasgow 1837	dialmaker
Shearer, D.L. & Co.	Glasgow 1868-88	clock dials
Sinclair, D.	Edinburgh c.1840	japanner/clock dials
Smith, T.& Stevenson	Edinburgh c.1815	clock dials
Stewart, J.	Edinburgh 1848	japanner
Todd (see Landale)		
Walker, John	Edinburgh 1824?-32	japanner and clock dials
Walker & Watson	Edinburgh 1824	japanner
Wright & Bethune	Edinburgh est. 1832-98	japanners
Wright, J. & W.	Edinburgh 1848	japanners

Some dials bear impressed marks stamped or punched or perhaps even cast into the backs. Many are self-explanatory. The initials 'W.H.' or 'W. & H.' represent Walker and Hughes, and this might be in the top left-hand corner (seen from the back) or behind the arch area. This monogram is also seen cast into clock bells and might suggest they also made these.

On some English dial backs there appears the number 14, roughly in the period 1785-1805, and the presence of the Maltese Cross symbol below some of these 14 dials suggests they are by Wilson. The number 15 appears on the back of some dials and moon discs of about 1810 and these too are thought to be by Wilson. Some which bear the number 16 are known to be by Wilson. That is not to say that all those bearing 14, 15 or 16 are by Wilson. Just what these numbers mean is not known but they do not refer to the dial width nor to the year.

Some Wilson dials have on the back what might have been some kind of checking-out mark in the form of a daub of white base-paint on to which is painted a black initial, usually 'R' or 'W'. Often too there are scratch marks cutting through this white base-paint (Plate 17). It might just be that a lost order ticket was once affixed or that this was some other sort of quality controller's pass mark system.

Some clocks reveal the words 'Ainsworth' or 'Ainsworth-Warrington' or 'G.A.' (sometimes with a crown motif), not usually on the dials but on the movements and/or bells. This was George Ainsworth of Warrington who supplied clock parts about 1790-1815. He is not known to have made dials but he is mentioned here to avoid confusion with dialmakers' marks.

Maltese cross

passing-out mark

Maltese cross mark.

PLATE 17. *Rear of a Wilson dial showing the Maltese cross identification mark and the dab of white japan paint with the crossings scratched through, thought to be a passing-out mark in the Wilson factory. Falseplate corner seen bottom right. Note the japanning ground paint spilling over the dial corner in more than one layer.*

Birmingham was the main dialmaking centre, but there were others. At Halifax, Yorkshire, the dialmakers Whittaker and Shreeve were in partnership about 1815-17. Their falseplates usually have a large serial number painted on them; its significance is not known. Whittaker was in business alone before that, roughly 1809-15. His name is sometimes written fully on his falseplates and sometimes simply as 'W.W. Halifax'. The dates when these men worked together and independently are confusing.

Shreeve was the dialpainter of the team and met an unfortunate end as an account of 1869 records: He 'was a housepainter and did business in clock faces, himself being the chief embellisher. Mr. Shreeve used to prepare his own varnish, and he was manipulating the mixture when by some accident it was thrown over him and he was burned to death.' Another account of 1875 reports that 'he was burned to death with boiling oil which he used in his trade'. Shreeve died on 15 August 1817 aged forty-three – an untimely end but a fine finish! Some movements have the name William Whittaker punched on their frontplates (probably as movement maker) but it seems unlikely this is the same man. Oddly enough a Sarah Whittaker was a clock 'dial painter, enameller and japanner' in Leeds from 1834-37, but whether she was connected to William Whittaker I cannot say.

The firm of Beilby and Hawthorn of Newcastle upon Tyne were dialmakers and they were apparently in partnership at one period with William Whittaker (about 1798-1817) and also with Whittaker and Shreeve. Ralph Beilby died in 1817, the same year as William Shreeve.

In what I call the first period (1770-1800) it is often possible to try to guess the dialmaker from the dial design and style. In this period many dials have simple corner designs of a flower spray or strawberries, often in pink, and for the sake of a term I call these 'strawberry corners' even when the objects are not strawberries. This style of dial was made by several dialmakers, but most frequently by James Wilson, so that a guess at Wilson tends to be right more often than wrong. However Wilson's dials seem to be the most numerous ones at this period anyway, so that the result is probably more to do with sheer percentages rather than identification skill.

Some strawberry corner dials by Wilson have a border of raised gesso painted gold in a sort of dot-dash pattern, as below:

Some strawberry corner dials by Osborne and other (unidentified) dialmakers can be very similar and it is doubtful if that border pattern can be relied on as a sure feature of identification. This is especially so on a restored dial, where a flourish or a brushstroke can confuse.

However, some Osborne dials have a straight-line dot-dash border, with as many as twelve dashes to the straight edge of the corner, thus:

Some dials by Beilby & Hawthorn/Whittaker seem to copy the Wilson theme, but their borders lack the sweep of Wilson's borders.

Some American-made dials of about 1790 also seem to copy the Wilson border but with a more pronounced sweep and a comma-like tail to the dashes, thus:

Another American dial I noticed has this sweeping dot-dash pattern, thus:

In any event we see few, if any, American-made dials in Britain. I do not recall ever having come across one, though one sometimes sees British clocks for sale here passed off as American when the name of the town is the same in both countries as, for example, Boston.

The recognition of dialmakers by the dot-dash border is a very hazy business and unreliable. Of course not all these strawberry corner dials do have a border. A number of Osborne's do not, and also a lesser proportion by Wilson, and no doubt others by unidentified dialmakers.

Names on falseplates are most helpful in identification and are probably the most useful of all dating/identification aids. Sometimes we are faced with the name of more than one dialmaking concern on a falseplate; for instance the well-known partnership between Beilby & Hawthorn and William Whittaker often used falseplates bearing both company names.

What is much more puzzling, however, is the situation where dual names appear on a falseplate of dialmakers who were (as far as we know) entirely unconnected. For example falseplates occur bearing the names Osborne & Wilson on one side and Wilson on the other; Wilson on one side and Walker & Hughes on the other; Wilson on one side and Francis on the other; Walker on one side and Finnemore on the other; and no doubt other combinations too. These names are often on cast-iron falseplates.

One possible explanation might be that one dialmaker bought up the old stock of another who had ceased trading, and had the plates re-stamped with his own name. The fact that the date of the successor often can be seen to follow on from the date of the succeeded party might at first seem to add strength to this possibility, were it not for one problem, namely that (I am advised that) it is not possible to 're-stamp' cast iron, which is brittle and would break in the attempt.

A more likely explanation seems to be that the foundry or foundries which cast these falseplates for, for example, Osborne & Wilson as partners (1772-1777) continued to use the same (poorly cleaned?) patterns when they later (post 1777) cast them for Wilson alone, thus these later plates carried a (sometimes faint) impression of the old partnership name.

Where dual names are found it is probably safe to say that we must use the names of the *later* of the two dialmakers as dating evidence. Sometimes there is additional evidence regarding the dialmaker to enforce that attitude. For example a dial I examined with a falseplate bearing the name Wilson and the name Walker & Hughes also had a calendar wheel stamped Walker & Hughes. The dial was clearly made by Walker & Hughes, even though the falseplate may have been made using what were formerly Wilson patterns.

The above conclusions are really no more than my own deductions made from studying the available evidence, itself often poorly documented. I know of no documented source evidence as to how these dialmakers worked in practice; no ledgers, workbooks, accounts or other written records, which might establish how the system worked.

In my opinion the falseplate was a device sold *attached to dials* purely of the japanned type. (The term white dial or painted dial is used as an alternative to the term japanned dial according to individual preference.) It follows that it was not used on brass dials. I say this even though I have come across brass dial clocks with falseplates (as no doubt have all collectors). Such clocks vary from being outright fakes to modifications, to make-do-and-mend efforts, as I will explain in detail. Some books, mostly older ones, express a contrary view, usually based on false assumptions, which cannot be substantiated by argument and which deny all the evidence we now have available.

Where dial and falseplate both bear a dialmaker's name, the two names are usually the same and are the names of known makers of japanned dials. In those few instances where two sets of names on a dial are different, both are still names of known and contemporary makers of japanned dials. I think I am correct in saying that not a single dialmaker of all those known to us (listed on pages 35-40) is known to have made a brass clock dial. These dialmakers were of course japanners, not brassfounders. Nor were they movement makers (though there were occasional exceptions who did sometimes make or sell movements, such as the Nicholas brothers of Birmingham).

Some japanned dials could not have been sold without the attached falseplate since the calendar disc is positioned between dial and falseplate and attached to each. The wording of the 1772 advertisement of Osborne & Wilson clearly implies that the falseplate was the 'method ... as will enable the Clock Maker to fix them [i.e. the dials] to the Movements'.

The view that falseplates were sold attached to the movements is expressed in some older books but is clearly inaccurate. Anyone who studies early white dial clocks can see that those clockmakers whose work betrays the idiosyncrasies and eccentricities so characteristic of individual handcraft made exactly the same type of movement for their japanned dials as they did for their contemporary brass dials.

In 1813 Samuel Harlow published in Birmingham a booklet entitled *The Clock Maker's Guide*. He explains certain benefits which might derive from standardisation of movement-making and dialmaking – from which we can gather that standardisation has not yet arrived! He refers twice to falseplates, which he calls 'backplates'. He describes 'the backplate *generally put on by* the Birmingham dial makers', and 'the backplate *commonly used by* the Birmingham dial makers, which if put on correct, might save the workman a great deal of trouble'. (The italics are mine.)

In 1951 John Daniell of Leicestershire Museum entered the old disused workshops of clockmaker Samuel Deacon of Barton-in-the-Beans. In the loft were discovered the leavings of a clockmaker which were probably undisturbed since his death in 1816. Amongst other clutter there were a dozen or so japanned dials which had never been used and were still in the same state as the day they had been delivered from the dialmakers. The falseplates, on those dials which had them, had never been drilled to take pillars to attach them to movements, and they were already attached to the dials. This confirms that the falseplates were supplied not only with, but even attached to, the dials. It also confirms the system, which we shall discuss later, whereby the clockmaker bought his dials by the batch ahead of his requirements, thus enabling the customer to pick his choice from a selection available.

Those writers of the past who assumed that 'Birmingham movements' behind japanned (Birmingham) dials were in some way mass-produced based that assumption on a half truth. Some later nineteenth century japanned dial clocks do have movements of stereotype nature, as by the 1840s or 1850s clocks could be bought by the retailer more or less in kit form, with just the finishing of the wheelwork and the assembling to do. Those in the trade who 'made' (i.e. assembled and finished) such clocks were known as clock jobbers or sometimes as clock finishers or clock dressers. James Airey of Grasmere in Westmorland was local postmaster and schoolmaster as well as a clock dresser there, dying in 1864. He is said to have dressed clocks whilst actually teaching his class in school! However, the fact that some japanned dials do have stereotyped movements behind them does not mean that they all do, and this type of clock dates almost always after about 1840.

Before that time those clockmakers who made their own movements for brass dial clocks did just the same for their painted dial ones, even though they bought their dials from specialist japanners. To the novice many movements look similar to one another, and he may be unable to recognise a standardised one from one displaying highly individual characteristics. However, a clock restorer who has handled several movements by a particular maker will be able to recognise sufficient features of his style to know that he made his own movements. If we look at makers whose style was especially unusual, then even a complete novice can see that such a maker made his own clockwork, since nothing of such an eccentric nature ever came out of a mass-production system, however prototype.

Makers with clockmaking idiosyncrasies so distinctive that their movement work can be recognised at a hundred paces include such men as Will Snow of Padside, Yorkshire, the Samuel Deacon of Barton mentioned above, Jonas Barber junior of Winster in Westmorland, and probably dozens of others whose work is less well known to me personally. The movements such makers produced for their brass dials can be seen to have continued in unbroken stylistic sequence on the clocks they made with the newer, japanned dials after about 1770, unmistakable proof of handcraftwork.

The dividing line, which varies with different makers anywhere between about 1830 and 1850, between which movements were handmade and which were bought in for assembly, is a hard one to define, and probably impossible for the beginner. Generally speaking a handmade movement will have marking out lines scratched on its plates, though these are only easily seen when the dial is removed or if the knack is developed of peering between dial and movement frontplate with a torch. Mass-produced movements did not need marking out in this way, as the plates would be drilled for positions of wheels and pinions by using a template.

Another indication towards whether such a later (mid-nineteenth century) clock might be handmade is that the presence of a falseplate on the dial would only be beneficial if it was there for its designed purpose, that is to offer a (true) maker the variety of positions he might need for the pillars to meet up conveniently with his movement frontplate. The presence of a falseplate on such a late clock is therefore a likely indication that the maker was still making his own movements. This is exactly the reverse of the conclusion drawn by some older books that a 'Birmingham' dial indicated mass-production.

We must be careful not to take the presence or absence of a falseplate as in itself being of especial significance in determining handcraftwork. Using those three basic periods into which I have broken down styles (see Chapter 6), we find that in Periods One and Two (i.e. 1770-1830) some clocks have falseplates and some do not, in an almost arbitrary way, though the majority probably do have them. In Period Three (1830-70) most clocks probably do not have falseplates and in a good many instances this is perhaps because mass-producing methods removed the need for them. There are exceptions to these very general rules and so they should not be taken rigidly.

The principles of japanned dial making as set out above are now well understood and recognised by the great majority of clock collectors, restorers and dealers, and are universally accepted with the possible exception of a few diehards of the old school, who refuse to be educated. When I first put forward these views in 1974, however, they were regarded as little short of heresy.

As with all identification hints, these must be used with care. The information we have about dialmakers can be a most helpful tool towards establishing the age of a clock, but we must take this along with other evidence and not in isolation. For example, a falseplate could be a replacement, standing in for a damaged original; it could have been fitted to marry together a dial and movement not made for each other (i.e. to assist in making a forgery); a stamped date disc could be a replacement for the same reasons.

This leads me back to the point touched upon earlier of falseplates on *brass* dials, which, if you have followed the arguments so far, you will know to be an impossible state of affairs. Yet brass dials do exist with falseplates behind them.

The very fact that a falseplate was designed as a convenient tool to fix a movement to a dial meant that it was readily seized upon by fakers and bodgers of all kinds and motivations to fit any old, spare brass dial to (almost) any old, spare movement, and thereby to make the two into an 'antique' clock. There are people who still make a good living by doing this today, selling such clocks to the unwary, uneducated or uncaring, either directly or through auctions, where responsibility for genuineness is usually denied in print in the auctioneer's catalogue.

Some 'marriages', as they are known, may themselves be of some antiquity. In the past such a marriage was sometimes performed as a cheap remedy for making a failing clock 'good' again, with no intention to deceive. Even so a fake is no less a fake for being an old fake. The least attempt at examining such brass-dial-with-falseplate clocks will probably reveal instantly the ludicrous nature of most of them, where a dial bearing the name of a maker who may have died in the eighteenth century carries a falseplate of a dialmaker not working till the second quarter of the nineteenth.

I can think of one longcase clock proudly displayed in a museum, reputedly made by a respected seventeenth century maker yet having a nineteenth century Birmingham falseplate behind its dial! However, as we know that any falseplate behind a brass dial is instant evidence that the clock is 'wrong', there is no need for anyone to take the trouble to compare the dates of a supposed maker on a brass dial with those of dialmakers named on its falseplate.

Another category of brass-dial-with-falseplate clock is that type of clock made up by clockjobbers, hobbyists and enthusiasts, often about the end of the last century. Perhaps someone wanted to make an old style brass dial clock and was faced with the problem that there was no current supply of dial parts which were a century or more obsolete – chapter rings, spandrels, etc. Such a person may have gathered together an assemblage of old fittings, fixed them on to a new dial sheet, and attached that to the movement-with-falseplate from a japanned dial clock. On examination everything will be seen to fit in a 'genuine' sort of way. However, to anyone with the slightest knowledge the brass dial fittings will be seen to be out of period with each other and/or with the movement's age, and the dial sheet will be seen to be of rolled brass not cast brass, whilst any engraving on the dial will be distinctly of late nineteenth century nature, which anyone with experience can recognise instantly from that of the late eighteenth century.

This category of clock was often made up by clock jobbers at the request of the clock owners in the late nineteenth or early twentieth century, when owners felt that a tired and worn out old japanned dial did the clock no justice and a nice shiny brass one would improve it no end. I've spoken often with people who remember father or grandfather having had this job done. So in effect these are painted dial clocks with their dials replaced by brass ones. No alterations are obvious because the dial was made to fit exactly, but a century or more later than the clock, which has of course been ruined for any serious buyer.

In America some of the clockmakers of the early nineteenth century worked in unconventional ways, may have been making brass dial clocks later than in Britain, and may conceivably have used such a thing as a falseplate on a brass dial. This suggestion has been put to me, and I can't refute it, though I've never seen such a clock myself nor ever heard of one examined by an expert and declared genuine.

I mentioned earlier that falseplates were not used for thirty-hour japanned-dial clocks with (in my experience) only one exception, and that is where an eight-day dial was used to construct a thirty-hour clock. This may need a little explanation as it must strike us initially as a very contrary way of going about things. One particular kind of thirty-hour clock was made to look like an eight-day. This type is found as brass dial clocks from about 1750 and the principle was sometimes continued into white dials. With brass dials this system was more popular in North-west England than elsewhere, and to some degree the same applies with japanned dials, though examples of the latter do crop up from all areas of England and perhaps Wales too, though not to my knowledge in Scotland.

These thirty-hours were given eight-day appearance by having winding holes and sometimes also winding squares, though of course the squares could not turn but were fixed, sometimes behind the dial and sometimes into the movement frontplates. To increase further the resemblance to an eight-day clock these thirty-hours sometimes also had a seconds dial (which most thirty-hour clocks did not). A thirty-hour clock having what we term 'dummy winders' and a seconds dial can be virtually indistinguishable from an eight-day until one looks inside the case or movement, where the single weight and movement construction will instantly reveal its true nature. With experience it is often possible to detect on sight the fact that the winding holes are positioned slightly higher on the dial than would be the case with a true eight-day.

These dummy-winder painted dials were mostly supplied purposely by the dial-makers in that form and with imitation winding squares attached behind the dial, though occasionally it can be seen that the clockmaker himself must have adapted a dial he had bought for eight-day use. Those supplied in that way by the dial-maker often have the (unwanted) seconds aperture filled in *before* japanning. When the clockmaker himself adapted an eight-day dial for thirty-hour use he would probably fill in the seconds aperture himself and paint over it to hide the infill.

Occasionally a thirty-hour clock of the dummy eight-day type did have a seconds dial. This would tend to be an example where the clock had a four-wheel train instead of the usual three-wheel train and was designed to show seconds. In those cases the seconds aperture would not need filling. A thirty-hour with a normal three-wheel train was occasionally fitted with a seconds feature, but in these examples the hand would tick anti-clockwise, which may have seemed unprofessional to most clockmakers and so was seldom done. Just occasionally a dummy seconds hand was fitted, that is one which was simply pinned to the dial and did not move at all but was there for no more than show in adding to the eight-day appearance. Why these thirty-hours were made to look like eight-days we do not know. Perhaps it was so that the neighbours or visitors would be impressed with the apparent eight-day clock, which of course was a more expensive item by far than a thirty-hour. The owner thus had the prestige of an eight-day for the price of a thirty-hour.

CHAPTER FIVE

HOW THE CLOCKMAKER GOT HIS DIALS

All clockmakers learned how to make movements and, until the arrival of the japanned dial, all learned how to make dials too. Whether an individual clockmaker did make his own dials and did carry out his own dial engraving is a different matter, but each learned how to do it, whether or not he opted to in his daily commercial life.

The clockmaker was first and foremost an engineer. He could construct a dial, but to ask him to be an expert technician as well as an artist of sufficient skills to design a beautiful dial, and then engrave that design into the brass dial sheet, was expecting rather a lot. It is likely that the majority of clockmakers did not perform their own engraved work. Those who did not had two alternatives. They could make the dial and send it to an engraver for the engraved work, or they could buy the engraved part of the dial ready-made and ready-engraved. The arrival on the scene of the japanned dial was a leveller, as all clockmakers henceforth worked on an even footing, those who could engrave having now lost the edge their skills had formerly given them over those who could not.

An example of costs of engraved work is found in the late eighteenth century advertisement of Charles Blakeway of Albrighton, Shropshire: 'Wheels cut for clockmakers at 6d [2½ new pence] per set and Dyal Plates engraved at 2s 6d [12½ new pence]'. This charge would be for him to perform the engraved work on a dial which the clockmaker had already constructed. To be able to put such prices into perspective it helps to bear in mind that a skilled clockmaker or engraver was doing quite well to earn £1 a week, so that 2s.6d. was a day's wages.

The original cost of making a brass dial is one of those facts which are very hard to obtain. When we do trace a scarce record of this nature, we seldom know what type of brass dial it was, its shape, style, size, etc. One of the very few examples I discovered in many years of searching was a dial made by Samuel Roberts, a Montgomeryshire clockmaker, working in the late eighteenth century, who made an eleven-inch (probably square) brass dial for a customer to replace a damaged original at a cost of 12s.0d. (60 new pence). It is interesting to compare that an eleven-inch square thirty-hour japanned dial cost 8s.6d. (42½ new pence) in 1820 from dialmakers Wilkes of Birmingham, but japanned dial prices had dropped considerably in the half century from 1770 to 1820. As we shall see, the prices of the earliest japanned dials were probably *higher* than those for brass ones of the same period.

The business of fitting together the dial and movement was always a difficulty and usually required forethought if the job was to be a neat one. This was especially true if the clockmaker had to send out his dial for engraving elsewhere, which needed to be done *after* he had both constructed it and ensured its neat fit to the movement, which of course would involve delay in finishing the clock.

Many clockmakers would hide potentially unsightly features, such as riveted dial feet ends, which would look unpleasant if showing on the finished dial. Common practice was to position the dial feet so that the chapter ring would cover such riveting. Some clockmakers (often rural clockmakers making lower-priced thirty-hour clocks) did not bother to hide their riveting in this way. Some clockmakers actually screwed through their dial sheets into the dial feet ends, this being common practice with even the best London clockmakers using the later single-sheet form of brass dial. I find this a surprisingly slipshod method as the sight of four screwheads can hardly have been thought of as conducive to a handsome dial, even though the screwheads may have been blued for effect or silvered over for camouflage. Yet this was done by prestigious makers on fine single-sheet brass dial clocks.

Most provincial clockmakers took the trouble to avoid screwing through the dial, though some southern makers, probably influenced by London work, did not seem to mind dial screws. Clearly this practice was thought unacceptable when white dials came into use, which is why dialmakers went to the trouble of using falseplates, though some London clockmakers still screwed on their brass dials long after white dials had arrived on the scene. Screwing through a painted dial would have chipped it.

The dial was after all that part of the clock which the customer saw. The clockmaker's mechanical skills were concealed behind it and most of those who bought a clock probably never gave the movement a second glance, any more than they do today when buying an antique clock. The dial was the thing which 'sold' the clock, and perhaps the case too, and ironically these two aspects which caught the customer's eye and on which he based his decision to buy or not were the two parts the clockmaker did not make (after the arrival of the japanned dial, that is).

So, for several reasons, dials were a headache to the clockmaker, and the arrival of the new japanned dial about 1772 took much of the worry out of the dial side of the business. For one thing there was no delay from sending work to an engraver. There was no need either to send off to the brassfounders for corner spandrels, which most clockmakers bought in rather than casting for themselves. The japanned dial was complete in itself and would fit (with the aid of the false-plate) to any permutation of movement the clockmaker made. Moreover it would do so without the problem of concealing (or screwing) dial feet ends.

If a clockmaker chose to keep in a selection of japanned dials, he could let the customer select one, and then get straight on with the job of constructing the clock without further delays or dependence on any other craftsman. He could even, as time allowed, build movements in advance of his needs and let the customer select which white dial he liked from stock, in the knowledge that it would fit any of his pre-made movements. How on earth a customer would have any say in his choice of a brass dial I do not know, unless it was a ready-made clock which he bought. But we know from such records as exist that most clocks were not pre-made in the hope that a customer would walk through the door and buy one, but rather each tended to be a bespoke item made to suit the whims and fancies of the customer.

It does not take much thought to see how the new type of painted dial was a godsend to the clockmaker, since it offered numerous advantages over the brass dial in the logistics of making a clock, apart from any considerations of style or design. It took a lot of the hassle and delay out of what was the most troublesome part of the clock to the clockmaker and the most important part for the customer – the dial. Clockmakers must have looked back ten years later and wondered how ever they managed to cope with making brass clock dials in the days before painted dials were available.

To get an idea of how the new dials were marketed we need to examine the work of clockmakers who bridge the period during which these new painted dials were first introduced to the trade. I have researched the work of one or two of these clockmakers myself and an examination of this transitional period is most informative, provided we can use the work of a clockmaker whose clocks we can date with some reliability. Without such dating we are unable to draw conclusions as to the rate of adoption of the new dials.

Very few clockmakers dated their clocks with the year of making. When this did happen, it seems to have been a chance thing with the occasional clock here and there rather than a regular practice. Fortunately, however, a mere handful of clockmakers did adopt the practice of numbering their clocks (Plates 18 and 19), often with an occasional date too. This means that we can attempt to build up some kind of a grid towards dating by numbers, and, inaccurate though this may be, it is better than having no dating grid at all or dating by mere opinion.

Samuel Deacon of Barton-in-the-Beans in Leicestershire is one of less than a handful of clockmakers worldwide who left written records of any kind. Deacon left account books and jotting books of a very disorganised nature but at least he left something to give posterity an idea of how the clock trade functioned at this vital period of change from brass to japanned dials.

Deacon was born at Ratby in Leicestershire, the son of a carpenter. After a spell as a farm worker he became apprenticed in 1762 to Joseph Donisthorpe, a clockmaker at nearby Normanton, though he had not yet learned his multi-plication tables. Even later in life he had his tables written out in full at the back of his notebook for easy reference.

According to Deacon, Donisthorpe was an odd character, an accomplished sinner who reformed later in life to become as fervent a champion of religion as he had formerly been of debauchery. After nine years with Donisthorpe Deacon moved to set up his own business in October 1771 at Barton. There his own shop clock registered time on a wooden dial overlooking the village street and was lettered 'Deacon – 1771'.

From the beginning he seems to have been keen to record his activities, though his very first account book seems to have been lost. It is clear that he set up alone in 1771 – in October 1774 his accounts begin 'the beginning of my 4th year for myself'. Yet perhaps he had been obliged to borrow money for his start, as in October 1773 he wrote in large letters across his notebook 'MY OWN MASTER', probably to indicate that he was now trading debt-free.

The series of notebooks started by Samuel Deacon was continued by his son John and his descendants and runs to the late nineteenth century, as the Deacon clockmaking family occupied the same premises till 1951. In that year John Daniell of Leicester Museum investigated and found that the Deacon workshops and forge had survived more or less intact after almost two centuries. The workshop, forge and records are now in the care of Leicester Museum.

Deacon's record books number about forty volumes; they are in a poorly preserved state, in parts difficult if not impossible to decipher. To make matters worse, Sam Deacon was not a methodical notemaker and some volumes have been opened here and there as if at random to start a new section of notes in a very disorganised way, with sometimes the back being used as the front. I've examined these books and although they may have made good sense to Sam Deacon, they are a nightmare for the modern student to attempt to analyse.

They contain all kind of day to day transactions, lists of jobs taken in, for whom, and the amount charged. Most of his time was spent on repairs and small jobs, cleaning clocks and watches and other mechanical devices. Here is an example of how he summarised his work in the year 1810:

Sold 42 clocks at	£242. 2s 6d
profit average 10%	25. 0s 0d
cleaned 438 clocks, average 1s 6d	<u>32.17s 0d</u>
	57.17s 0d
clock repairs, etc.	5. 0s 0d
	£ <u>62.17s 0d</u>

PLATE 18. *Eight-day movement frontplate seen with the dial and motion-work removed to reveal the engraved serial number 'No.637'. The clock is by Jonas Barber junior of Winster and can be dated by the number to about 1763. The upper right and lower left movement pillars are fastened by latches rather than by the taper pins used by most makers and used here in the other two pillars – this being a distinctive feature of later Barber movements. Such idiosyncrasies demonstrate how clockmakers continued with exactly the same movement-making practices after the white dial as before it.*

Incidentally the production rate of almost one clock a week is unusually high. Many makers averaged only one clock every two weeks, roughly twenty-five clocks a year, though we cannot tell how much this was due to lack of demand rather than lack of production capacity.

Samuel Deacon's records are unique in providing some insight into how the trade worked in practice at this vital time when the new japanned dial was just beginning. Within a year of Deacon's setting up in business Osborne and Wilson were advertising their new dials in Birmingham only a few miles distant.

The first example of a painted dial that I could spot in the Deacon records was this: '16 May 1774. Had an arched face japanned from Lindley for William Hall – £1.4s.0d.' Lindley may have been a wholesaler of dials but there was a Thomas

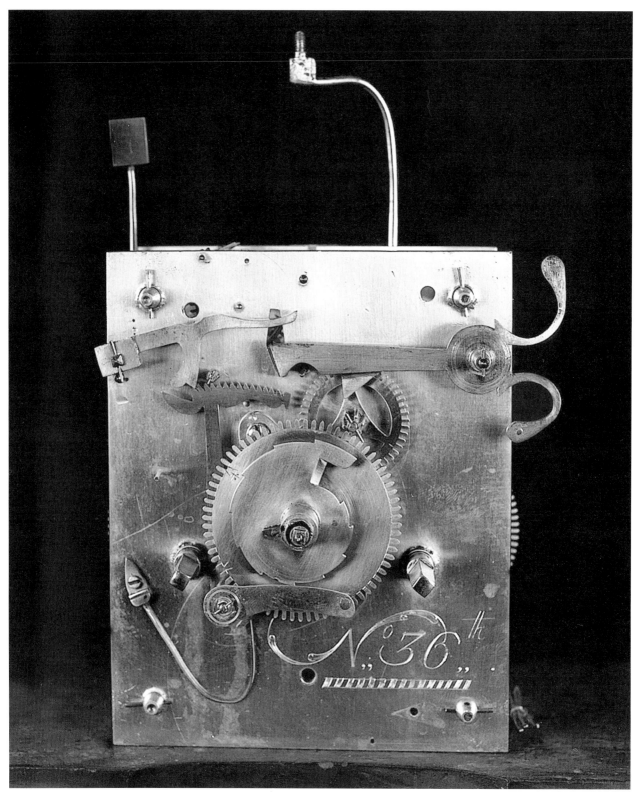

PLATE 19. *Eight-day movement of about 1780, the japanned dial removed to reveal motionwork and the serial number 'No.36', the clock being by Thomas Armstrong of Hawkshead. Serial numbering was practised by relatively few makers, but many must go unnoticed as they are often only visible when the movement is dismantled.*

PLATE 20. *Eight-day longcase dial by James Wilson of Birmingham from a clock by Samuel Deacon of Barton, the clock engraved on the frontplate with his serial number 338 and the year 1789. Original hands of blued steel in non-matching style.*

Lindley, clockmaker, working in Leicester at this time and it is possible that Deacon got his first white dial from him to try the new type. The price is *twice* that of a brass dial!

Again and again we find evidence, rare though it is, that when it was first introduced the painted dial was more costly than the brass equivalent. We shall examine later the advertisement of 1782 by John Benson, the Whitehaven clockmaker, in which he offers as a bargain clocks with the new japanned dial plates 'at the same price as those with Brass Plates, which is a great advantage to the Purchaser...' Benson takes for granted that, ten years after its introduction, the population expected to pay more for a japanned dial than for a brass one.

PLATE 21. *Movement of the Samuel Deacon clock number 338 showing distinctive Deacon features of baluster pillars and solid wheels. The Wilson job ticket can be seen on the dial back close to the bell. Such individual workmanship proves that the continuity of clockmaking practices was unchanged by the arrival of the painted dial.*

Such evidence calls for a revaluation of attitudes towards white dial clocks, for past literature has always referred to the japanned dial as being an inferior alternative, which became dominant because it was cheaper. The fact that the painted dial became the dominant type, *despite* its being a costlier form, must be an indication as to how much more it was preferred by clockmakers and the buying public to the brass dial version.

Leaving prices aside for the moment, let us look further into the Deacon papers. On 13 November 1774 is an entry:' Had faces came from Birmingham as per bill + carage [=carriage] one shilling – £4.6s8d.'. So Deacon must have been sufficiently taken by the new dial he had first tried in May to have ordered some from the suppliers later that same summer. He was an instant convert. After only two years of production the Birmingham dialmakers had converted a top craftsman to their new dials, in Deacon's case within six months of his first trying the new dial type.

One might imagine that a lesser craftsman, perhaps one who could not engrave, might be easily converted to the new form. But Deacon *could* engrave – his notebook lists several occasions when he carried out engraving of dials for others in the trade nearby who couldn't.

But how did the clockmaker select his dials? If printed patterns or printed samples ever existed, then we know of none surviving today. We can see from Deacon's notebooks how he went about it. In fact he had made a journey himself to Birmingham in 1785, perhaps to visit the new dialmakers or wholesalers. He seems to have bought mostly through wholesalers rather than direct from the makers and it may have been that this gave him a wider choice of different makers or designs or varying price/quality ranges.

Before the days of carbon paper and photocopiers business people often wrote letters in duplicate – one to send and one to keep as a file copy. Deacon sometimes wrote out his copy letters in full, and sometimes abbreviated the major points from them. On 10 December 1805 he wrote:

Ordered the following dials:
12 – 12inch square, varied, neat corners, open mouth, written figgers, 30hours, Deacon – Barton.
4 – 12inch arched 30hour, open mouth
3 – 13inch arched 30hour, two with figgers in arch, one with an urn.
1 – 13inch arched with moon.
Let some of the 12inch have a bird above the centre.

This is how it was done. The basic types were specified with a few suggestions and the supplier used his own judgement, based no doubt on his past knowledge of the customer's tastes, to send a selection. The term 'open mouth' refers to the type of curved mouth calendar. What he meant by 'neat corners' I do not know, but perhaps he was implying better quality. They were to be lettered 'Deacon – Barton'. We will see later what happened if the clockmaker did not like the range of dials when they arrived.

Samuel Deacon, and his son John after him, dealt for many years through a Mr. D. Anderson of Birmingham, presumably a dial wholesaler. We will see later that Anderson stocked dials by several different dialmakers. In 1816 Deacon wrote the following:

To Mr. Anderson, Birmingham.
Sir, I want a 13inch arch moon 8days with seconds
two 13inch 8days no moon with second

three 13inch 30hour no seconds.Good cullour & month Plates
The last 5 have sorted neat 2inch figures in arches Six 12inch 30hours, neat painting, not extra price
12 square 12inch, neat flowers in middle.
All the lot written figures.be sure to see to the cullour & the last parcel of 12inch were very bad. Some must be returned.See also to the packing, some of the last are spoiled.
18 pair of good giltt hands 12 & 13 inches, sorted, small centre holes.
24 bushes
Send the wole [= whole] soon as you can, the arches are much wanted.
Barton   Yours in haste
Jany 16 1816   S. Deacon

One or two points may need explanation. Month plates are probably calendar wheels to fit in the mouth calendars. Notice that he specifies with or without seconds dials on both eight-day and thirty-hour dials, showing that he had the option on both. The 'neat 2inch figures in arches' were probably vignette paintings, usually seen within oval shapes and often containing such a figure as a seated shepherdess, not figures in the sense of lettering.

I am not sure what he means by 'all the lot written figures', unless he had the option of having the dials without numbers, i.e. as plain sheets, which he could have numbered/lettered at his end. We shall see later that he ordered one dial to be painted elsewhere at his own arrangement. The bulk of his order is for thirty-hour dials, which probably made up most of his production. The twenty-four 'bushes' were probably what we now call hands 'collets', i.e. bevelled washers to hold the hands in place, being one for each clock dial ordered.

What he meant by a 'good colour' we may never know. Perhaps he meant strong colours. Clearly some of the previous delivery were not to his taste and some were damaged through faulty packing, something he often complained about.

Birmingham is about twenty miles from Barton, yet the consignment took seven weeks to arrive, being marked into his 'goods-in' book against Anderson's name: 'Mar 18 1816 Rec'd 24 dials 18 pair hands gilt £10.16s 2d.'

In the 1820s he wrote to Andersons complaining : 'The above dials were not Walkers and so must have more discount. NB These dials were W. Frances.' It seems Anderson charged a higher rate for Walker & Hughes dials than for those by Francis, and Deacon was content with Francis dials as long as they were at the lower price.

The names of several well-known dialmakers occur in the records, though Deacon usually bought through wholesalers rather than direct from the manufacturers. They include: Hipkiss, Wilkes & Son, Walker & Hughes, F.C. Swinden, William Finnemore & Sons and Cohen of Hull. We also know that he used dials by William Whittaker of Halifax and very many dials by James Wilson, but maybe the records for his Wilson dealings would have been in an earlier book, now lost. In fact most of the Deacon clocks I have come across seem to have Wilson dials (Colour Plate 1 and Plates 20 and 21). His dealings with Hipkiss seem not to have been very successful, for in March 1809 he writes: 'Returned 8 dials, 4 12inch & 4 13inch. Also returned the boxes they came in (that were charged 3/- to 5/6 each)'.

Ordinary thirty-hour and eight-day dials of standard size presented no problem. For a dial of special nature, such as one with three holes for a musical clock (Plate 22) or one of eccentric shape, he would have had to specify exact dimensions or send a detailed drawing. For example, on 27 May 1813 he ordered a dial for: 'chime clock for Mr.Wilson, 7 tunes on ten bells (one fiddler?), Mr.W. to find hands and painting of the dial and weights. Price £15'. So dials could be ordered

PLATE 22. *Dial of a complex musical clock made in 1787 by John Philipson of Winster, journeyman to Jonas Barber junior (whose serial number 1311 it carries on the frontplate). It plays a choice of eight tunes on thirteen bells with twenty-six hammers, the tunes being named on the dial: Lan(cs?) Hornpipe, Jockey's Horse Course, Soldier's Joy, O'er the Hills, Sailor Bold, Highland Laddie, Corn Riggs and A Gigg. Such a dial had to be purpose-made, dialmaker here unknown. Hour hand a later replacement. Case in mahogany.*

without the painting, probably just with the base layers of white japanning.

It seems that Deacon or the customer later changed the instructions for this clock, as they were amended to:

The dial to be painted by Mr.Richard Blood, No 41 Newhall St., Birmingham. Tunes:

1. Easter Hymn
2. Highland Laddie new
3. (illegible) Machree
4. Baker's Hornpipe
5. Blewbell
6. Gavott by Green(ton?)
7. Handalls march

I have come across Richard Blood's name behind two other dials. Special dials of this sort would of course need to have the tunes lettered on the dial for use with a tune-selecting lever.

Patrick Hewitt in his articles on Deacon in *Antiquarian Horology* in 1986 quotes an interesting letter concerning the dial for a special clock from the Deacon note-books written to James Wilson of Birmingham in January 1789:

Dear Sir,
I wish this face to be painted well and soon, the other side of this page shows the work in the arch (drawing of group with musical instruments who commence playing automatically when the clock has struck).
Name 'Deacon Barton' in a curve below the centre, above the centre the days of the wek as usual.
Let it be divided in 7 equal parts and a day in each.
I wish it to be returned as soon as possible. The gent is eager and I always like to strike while the iron is hot, but you will seldom let me. Oh, the money I've lost and the vexation I have had. ... Yours, etc.

Samuel Deacon numbered his clocks, usually on the movement frontplate and therefore only seen when the dial is removed or by those expert at peering obliquely behind the dial with a torch. His numbering system must have meant something to Deacon but has so far defied our attempts at understanding it. Some of his clocks bear a single number, sometimes with a year date as well and sometimes without the year. But some of his clocks bear two widely-separated numbers, again with or without a year. To complicate things even further, Deacon's cousin, also called Samuel Deacon, ran his own numbering system so that it can be difficult to distinguish between his clocks and those of the elder Deacon. Unfortunately his records have no register of numbers which can be consulted to help in understanding his system.

Patrick Hewitt has suggested that where the clock carries two numbers the higher represents his total number of clocks made to date and the lower number represents his total number of thirty-hour clocks made to date. Double numbers (when they occur) seem equally likely to appear on eight-day clocks or thirty-hours. I cannot help but note that he seems to have made far more thirty-hour clocks than eight-days. Hence a thirty-hour clock bearing such a double number as 253 and 789 (dated 1795), seems most unlikely to me to imply that he had made to date 536 eight-day clocks and 253 thirty-hours, especially as we believe his greatest output was always in thirty-hour clocks. Out of nineteen numbered examples I have come across personally, only five were eight-days. His dial ordering too seems to lean heavily towards a predominance of thirty-hour clocks.

Even though we cannot understand his numbering system, we can believe his dating and this gives us an indication of how fast and how firmly the japanned dial came to predominate in his business. We know he used his first japanned dial in

PLATE 23. *Twelve-inch thirty-hour dial made by James Wilson of Birmingham for a longcase clock by Will Snow of Padside (Yorkshire), the name barely legible above VI. The dial is in a very worn state with crude, amateurish attempts at re-numbering. Much of the fine blackwork is rubbed away, including the stalks of the flowers*

1774. Of the sixteen dated clocks I know by him post 1774 to 1800, all but one (in 1777) have white dials. One other undated (and seemingly unnumbered) clock of about 1780 also has a brass dial.

In brief we can say he very rarely went back to brass dials after 1774. Within two years of their being first produced the new painted dials were used almost to the total exclusion of brass dials.

Set out below are some of the numbered examples I know by Samuel Deacon, senior and/or junior, some carrying two numbers. From this it can be seen that such serial numbers may make little sense but do nevertheless give us some positive dates as a yardstick, and help us determine the rate of growth in popularity of the painted dial. All the following clocks are white dials (mostly by James Wilson of Birmingham) with the exceptions of numbers 2, 44, 87, and 160.

No. 2 dated 1770	No. 160 dated c.1780
No. 4 dated 1802	No. 224 dated 1783
No. 44 Dated 1773	No. 227 dated 1783
No. 67 dated 1791	No. 228 dated 1783
No. 87 dated 1777	No. 253 dated 1795 (also no. 789)
No. 101 dated 1798	No. 262 dated 1796 (also no. 826)
No. 106 dated 1794 (also no. 700)	No. 279 dated 1786
No. 127 dated 1778	No. 285 dated 1784
No. 129 dated 1791	No. 315 not dated (c.1780?)
No. 135 dated 1779	No. 338 dated 1789
No. 149 dated 1778	No. 1250 dated 1806

If it took two years for the white dial to become firmly established locally to the centre of origin (Birmingham) by a craftsman of Deacon's stature, we may assume it took a little longer further afield. As it happens the clocks of certain other provincial makers of like abilities also provide evidence of the spread of the new dial.

Jonas Barber junior of Winster in Westmorland (about 150 miles from Birmingham) was a third generation clockmaker born about 1718 and dying in 1802. Like Deacon, his major product was the simple country thirty-hour clock though he too could make superb eight-day clocks when called upon to do so (Plate 18). Barber numbered all (and dated some of) his clocks throughout this vital period of the 1770s. Before he retired in 1797 he had made over 1,421 numbered clocks, and he did not start his numbering till the early 1740s. His successor, Henry Philipson, continued his numbering system from at least no. 1427. I have studied and recorded details of Barber clocks for many years but what interests us for this present purpose is his output during the first years of the new japanned dial.

Strangely enough the first clock Barber made with a white dial was in 1774, the very same year as Sam Deacon's first. I have details of sixty longcase clocks by Barber from 1774 to 1797, though obviously there will be others still to come to light. After his 1774 white dial example he continued his brass dial production until 1777, when his next white dial example appeared, but after 1777 all but a single example had japanned dials. Of this total of sixty known clocks in that important period only nine had brass dials, and only one of these brass dials dated later than 1777.

In other words, when Barber had tried the new dials he too went over to them with barely an exception. Many of his earlier white dials are by James Wilson of Birmingham, who was probably the most important and prolific japanned dial-maker of all time and who of course also supplied Deacon and Will Snow, whose work is mentioned below. What a pity no account books seem to survive for James Wilson's amazing early business.

Incidentally, there is no question but that Deacon and Barber did make their own clocks, sometimes with the help of an apprentice or in-house workman, known as a journeyman. Anyone who has examined their work will know that their clocks have idiosyncratic features unlike those of any other maker. So distinctive is the work of makers such as these three, that if we examined one of their movements even without its dial, we could easily identify it as the work of any one of them.

Will Snow worked at Padside, a Yorkshire hamlet not two miles from my own home. He too worked during the vital period of the 1770s when the japanned dial first appeared, and oddly enough he too numbered his earlier clocks. I have records of numbered clocks by him running to over 1,200. Snow, however, adopted the unusual practice of numbering his clocks on the dials of his brass dial clocks but then, when he began using the new japanned dials (he too used Wilson dials, Plates 23 and 24), he suddenly stopped numbering.

The reason for Will Snow's sudden change of policy is obvious when we think about it. When he produced his own brass dials he could add the number immediately before selling each. Even if he had one or two dials made ahead of his needs so that his clients had a choice of design, he could run a consecutive numbering system very easily. When he began to order his japanned dials from James Wilson, however, he presumably bought in batches, as did Deacon and Barber, and at this stage he could not predetermine which dials would sell first. He could not therefore order his dials consecutively numbered from Wilson. Snow's cessation of numbering is further evidence of how the new type of dial could be, in fact probably needed to be, held in stock in sufficient numbers to offer the customer a choice.

PLATE 24. *The dial from Plate 23 seen after cleaning and restoration, and now looking more the way it was originally. The background is original – note the craze marks still showing*

John Benson was a fine clockmaker working at Whitehaven, a seaport on the Cumberland coast just up country from Jonas Barber and about two hundred miles from Birmingham. Benson was a top flight clockmaker, a man of some thirty years in the trade, whose work included some highly complex clocks and musical clocks. Within ten years of the arrival of the new type of dial, Benson was wholly won over. He advertised in the *Cumberland Pacquet* in 1782:

John Benson (who makes all sorts of plain, repeating, musical and astronomical clocks at reasonable prices) begs leave to return his most sincere thanks ... he has an assortment of the best japanned clock dial plates which he makes up to any sort of clocks, *at the same price as brass plates* [my italics], which is a great advantage to the purchaser, as they will never want silvering, but still be the same, keep as well and clean as soon as glass. Smoke, steam & damp does not affect them, which soon dissolves the best silvering and lacker that can be laid on brass;- and the expense of renewing the silver and lacker comes high or the clock looks bad and more so where they are exposed to the sea air; the japanned plates are still the same and the expense saved ... His abilities are unquestionable having carried on the clockmaking business in all its different branches during a period of thirty years in Whitehaven ...

Benson here confirms what we had already deduced: that by 1782 the brass dial was old hat; that the new dial was generally costlier than the brass one (but here can be supplied as a bargain at the same price as brass); that the dials were bought in batches and the clockmaker kept 'an assortment' in stock to give the customer a choice; and that the clockmaker made up the clock *after* the dial had been selected by the customer.

In that same year (1782), just across the Irish Sea, Belfast clockmaker James Wilson, again a man of high repute in the trade and not connected with his name-sake the Birmingham dialmaker, also advertised, in the *Belfast Newsletter:*

He also has a few clocks with white enamelled dial-plates, very strong and beautiful, that will never stain or tarnish, *being the first plates ever imported into this port ...*
[my italics]

So after ten years the white dial had just reached Belfast, though in all probability they had been imported earlier through Dublin.

In fact there is some evidence that japanned dials were actually made in Dublin, though probably few and as yet the maker seems not to have been identified. Birmingham-made painted dials were supplied to clockmakers there by such makers as Osborne and Wilson.

The new Birmingham japanned dials had also penetrated into Scotland by about 1780 to the point where by 1785 William Dallaway had set up his own japanning factory in Edinburgh, having had his son learn the trade in Birmingham. It is uncertain at what exact date the Dallaways began their own production but it was probably about 1780. The Dallaway Japan Manufactory, as it was called, is dealt with more fully in Chapter 14.

The painted dial swept the land, being readily taken to by clockmaker and customer alike. By 1790 brass dials were distinctly *passé* and few were still being made. By 1800 brass dials were obsolete, in all save a very few traditional areas, or in certain situations where a clockmaker wanted to use the brass dial for a particular purpose, such as with Regulator clocks.

The composite brass dial (with chapter rings, spandrels, etc.) is seldom found after about 1785-90, and for most areas of the country we can say that the brass dial had been totally replaced by that date by the white dial. London clockmakers never seemed to take to the japanned dial in the way provincial makers did, and amongst London makers we may find a somewhat later use of brass dials.

The single-sheet brass dial did follow on into a later period than the composite dial for those makers and regions which opted to use it. Principally it was used later in the South and especially in London and also in the West Country (i.e. South-west England). For example it would be very unusual to see a single-sheet dial from Lancashire or indeed any of the North-west English counties, where it was never a popular type.

The single-sheet brass dial lasted even into the 1840s in certain southern localities (for example in Devon), though always losing ground against the white dial. In London it was often still used for Regulator clocks almost until the end of longcase clock making.

About 1900 and for a few years thereafter there was a revival of brass dials in

PLATE 25. *Twelve-inch eight-day brass dial of about 1770, complete with separate chapter ring, japanned over about twenty years later to adapt to the new painted style. Corner spandrels removed and the holes plugged before japanning.*

longcase clocks. These were sometimes made in replica of the late eighteenth century styles, often using old dial fittings such as spandrels. Such a clock is often identifiable by its rolled brass dial sheet (instead of cast), and by its inconsistencies of dial features or engraving styles as well as by the name of its maker.

About the same time a different type of brass dial longcase was made, often manufactured in Germany but made for the English market. The style of engraving and dial design of these clocks is very different from native English brass dial clockwork, which died out in its true form in the late eighteenth century.

But what about those people who had bought a clock already just a few years earlier, perhaps a good and still serviceable clock? They must have felt rather like those who had just bought a new television set shortly before colour television arrived. Who wants to watch black and white once colour is available? These clock owners wanted the new colourful and fashionable dials too. There were several possibilities for them.

They could buy a complete new clock, with painted dial of course, but that would be a costly solution. They could buy a new dial-with-movement to put into the old case, but again a fairly costly process. They could simply have one of the new dials fitted to replace the now old-fashioned brass dial, and this was sometimes done as I have come across a few examples of this, particularly when the

PLATE 26. *An unusual black dial, being an eight-day brass dial from a longcase clock of about 1760 by John Baker of Hull, spandrels removed and then japanned over later (c.1795?) in the new style with flower corners and vignette in the arch. Note the double minute track as used pre-1770, and the 5, 10, 15 seconds numbering. Original hands throughout, non-matching in steel.*

new dials first appeared.

But there was another most interesting way in which owners had their existing brass dial clocks updated, and that was by having their brass dial japanned over its face surface. This involved removing the corner spandrels and plugging the screwholes, then japanning over the brass dial sheet itself (Plates 25 and 26). Usually any small subdial chapter rings were also removed (such as the seconds ring) but generally the main chapter ring for hours and minutes was retained and

COLOUR PLATE 1. *Eight-day longcase dial using solid ground corners, made in 1806 by James Wilson of Birmingham for a clock by Samuel Deacon of Barton, number 1250.*

that too was japanned over.

One seldom sees such clocks today with their brass dials japanned over. This is because for the past half century or more the brass dial has been more favoured by collectors and dealers than the japanned type (though there are signs that this trend is changing today). Dealers or collectors who acquired such a japanned-over brass dial clock would have been inclined to remove the later japanned surface and 'restore' the clock to its original brass dial form. I have only come across maybe half a dozen clocks with japanned-over brass dials, but I feel sure this adaptation must have been much more widespread than surviving examples suggest, and for the reasons just stated.

CHAPTER SIX

DIALS, PERIOD ONE (1770-1800)

For convenience I have divided dial styles into three broad periods. Naturally they are not definitive dates, but they do help in discussing the style and age of a japanned dial.

The dialmakers themselves called their dials 'white dials', perhaps because the first ones had an all-white background. Today the terms 'white dial' or 'japanned dial' or 'painted dial' are all used as alternatives for the same thing, that is any japanned dial of whatever period, whether or not with a white background. In fact the ground colour is seldom a true white, but more often has a tint of duck-egg green or blue, though we still refer to these as 'white'.

Period One extends from the beginnings of the white dial (about 1770 or a little earlier) to the end of the century. The fact that Osborne and Wilson were in partnership for only a five-year period (1772-1777) when they introduced this type of dial does mean that we can often recognise by the presence of their names dials of the partnership period, which I refer to as phase one (of Period One). Some recognition features of phase one were continued for a short time after 1777, when Osborne and Wilson were each working independently. But within a very few years after 1777 the 'first phase' style changed to what became the more regular style lasting more or less throughout the rest of Period One. By examining phase one in detail we shall see what distinguishes these very first dials from those of the rest of the period.

GOLD CORNERS

The very first painted dials were made to resemble contemporary brass ones, not in every respect obviously, but in one certain feature: namely the corners (and sides of the arch on an arched dial) had gold raised work not unlike the brass spandrels of a brass dial clock. Plates 7 (Osborne & Wilson) and 27 (Waren) show this kind of gold scrollwork. The raised work was built up with gesso on to the white background, then gilded on the surface.

The two dials illustrated were made by Osborne & Wilson during their partnership period and can therefore be dated accurately between 1772 and 1777. As it happens one of these clocks also has Osborne & Wilson on the dial front as retailers, a very unusual occurrence as they are not known as regular sellers of complete clocks. This might even have been some sort of demonstration clock to illustrate the new dial in practice.

Gold-corner dials of this very first phase of Period One (say the first five years or so) have a distinctive kind of raised goldwork, being raised more highly in gesso than later gold corners, with goldwork asymmetrical and more open than later.

These first white dials of the Osborne/Wilson partnership period have other features, which changed slightly soon after. Where the clock has a calendar the 'mouth' covers only a short arc, which is usually flat ended. The 'short-mouth' calendar seems to be a regular feature of Osborne & Wilson partnership dials, but was sometimes used *after* they split up too, so is not an infallible sign of phase one. In cases where the short-mouth calendar was used *after* phase one it would tend to be with gold corners of the symmetrical type described next.

Where a phase one clock has a seconds dial, the dot markings are normally *inside* the seconds numbering (10, 20,etc). Later the dots are usually *outside* the numbers. Occasional clocks will have a pointer calendar indicator, but pointer

PLATE 27. *Twelve-inch eight-day dial from a clock by William Waren of Thirsk dating from the first phase of Period One, as is recognisable by the distinctive style of heavy, asymmetrical gold corner-work, short-mouth calendar, seconds dots inside the numbers, and painted winding collet decoration. The dial was made by Osborne and Wilson of Birmingham, named on the falseplate, and dates from the partnership period (1772-1777). Original hands of non-matching pattern in blued steel with the earlier type of straight minute hand.*

calendars tend to be later in Period One and not normally in this first phase.

The winding squares on a phase one dial (only on eight-day clocks, of course) have gold-painted rims; later ones have brass winding collars known as collets. Sometimes, of course, a dial may have lost its brass collets and may have been painted round the winding holes instead, which can be misleading. The calendar mouth usually also has a gold-painted rim, but so too do mouths of some later dials.

I cannot say that all gold-corner dials of this first phase of Period One were made by Osborne & Wilson. Some such dials are unmarked by the makers and were probably by as yet unidentified dialmakers. The phase one asymmetrical gold corner style is uncommon and is probably confined to the very first few years of production.

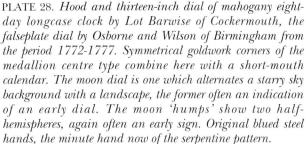

PLATE 28. *Hood and thirteen-inch dial of mahogany eight-day longcase clock by Lot Barwise of Cockermouth, the falseplate dial by Osborne and Wilson of Birmingham from the period 1772-1777. Symmetrical goldwork corners of the medallion centre type combine here with a short-mouth calendar. The moon dial is one which alternates a starry sky background with a landscape, the former often an indication of an early dial. The moon 'humps' show two half-hemispheres, again often an early sign. Original blued steel hands, the minute hand now of the serpentine pattern.*

COLOUR PLATE 2. *Twelve-inch dial from an eight-day longcase clock by Timothy Richardson of Darlington, c.1785, the dial by Francis Byrne of Birmingham. This is a variation of the symmetrical gold-corner style whereby the ground colour to the area outside the dial centre is in solid colour, here a striking, luminous blue, produced by laying silver leaf on the dial before applying the colour. The vignette painting in the arch centre is a feature often found towards the end of the century. Original blued steel hands, non-matching.*

A different kind of gold scrollwork was sometimes also used in this first phase, more often slightly later (i.e. after 1777) but still usually within the confines of what I define as Period One (i.e. 1770-1800). This type is much more common. An example is seen in Plate 28 (Barwise), which also happens to be an Osborne & Wilson dial. Both Osborne and Wilson continued to make this style independently after dissolving their partnership, and other dialmakers made this style too. This type of gold cornerwork is less highly raised and is symmetrical, quite often centring on an oval medallion or urn, cartwheel or starburst sort of effect, as here. Symmetrical gold-corner dials seem more to simulate the engraved corners of single-sheet brass dials than the cast brass corner spandrels of composite brass dials. Compare Plates 28, 29, 30 and 31 (Barwise, Rogers, Fuller and Sherwood, all of which happen to be Wilson dials) with Plate 3 (Reynolds & Earl). Note too that these later gold corner dials usually (but not always) have the extended (wider) mouth with curved ends and have their dotted seconds *outside* the seconds numbers.

Gold-corner dials of this symmetrical type were used right to the end of Period

COLOUR PLATE 3. *Twelve-inch eight-day dial of the strawberry corner type (and actually including strawberries) made about 1785 by Osborne, Birmingham, from a clock by James Anderson of West Haven, near Aberdeen. This is a handsome dial showing all the classic features of Period One. Original blued steel hands of non-matching style with serpentine minute hand. Scottish makers often used English dials at this time.*

One and perhaps even for a short time after. All gold-corner dials appear to end their goldwork without a defined border as edging.

Sometimes the gold-corner style was used on a coloured ground rather than a white ground, and an example of a coloured-ground version is seen in Colour Plate 2 (Richardson), here on a midnight blue ground colour, the dial being by Byrne. Byrne seems to have been the main dialmaker to use solid ground colours under his corner goldwork. Byrne ground colours are often of a strong nature, and I have seen them in strong red, green and blue. They can have an iridescent

PLATE 29. *Twelve-inch eight-day dial from a clock by Rogers of Leominster, made about 1790, the dial made by James Wilson of Birmingham. The gold corner decoration is symmetrical, based on a roundel centre. The calendar is now of the full-mouth type, normal hereafter. Original hands are of blued steel with the serpentine pattern minute hand.*

or luminous quality, which was achieved by laying the colour on top of a layer of silver leaf, a practice seen again much later on some Period Three Scottish-made dials (see page 202). Wilson also occasionally used solid ground corner colours under his goldwork and so probably did other dialmakers, but this was never a very commonplace style.

Gold scrollwork corner decoration on a raised gesso ground (in its two forms of asymmetrical and symmetrical decoration) was limited almost exclusively to Period One to the point where that alone can define the overall period. A different type of gold paintwork (*without* a raised gesso base and therefore painted flat on to the japanned surface) was sometimes used in Period Two.

COLOURED CORNERS

With gold corners the full potential of what an artist might achieve was limited in so far as the dial lacked colour. Coloured corner dials were apparently also used from the introduction of the japanned dial and coloured corner dials (usually of course also with colour in the arches of arched dial examples) are not necessarily later by virtue of their colour than gold-corner types.

These coloured corners on Period One dials tend to be very simple and restrained in design, often a single flower or spray of flowers, or fruit such as strawberries, and some years ago I coined the term 'strawberry corners' to describe any type of Period One floral corner, whether strawberries or not. These flowers were usually on a white ground, but occasionally a coloured ground was used, just as

PLATE 30. *Fourteen-inch dial of the rolling moon type (dial unmarked and therefore the dialmaker unknown but perhaps James Wilson) from an eight-day clock by Robert Fuller of Watton, Norfolk, c.1780-90. The dial is unusually large for this date. The gold cornerwork is of the symmetrical style. Half-hemisphere globes are typical of this early period.*

PLATE 31. *Twelve-inch dial from an eight-day clock of about 1785 by Thomas Sherwood of Yarm, North Yorkshire, the dial by James Wilson of Birmingham. Here the gold corners are of the symmetrical type centred on a medallion with the calendar of the full mouth type. Original blued steel hands, non-matching pattern with straight minute hand.*

some gold corners were also on a solid body of ground colour.

Some of the floral corners had their flower sprays unbordered, see Plates 24 and 36 and Colour Plate 4 (Snow, Morgan, and Hargraves dials), but most had a dot-dash border of gold on raised gesso. A glance at a few of these early floral corners will show the principle. It is tempting to think that those floral corners without borders might have pre-dated those with borders, but this does not seem to hold true in practice. Osborne and Wilson (and perhaps others too) used bordered and unbordered floral corners both during their partnership period (1772-1777) and after it.

COLOUR PLATE 4. *Twelve-inch thirty-hour dial of about 1790 from a clock by Thomas Hargraves of Settle, the dialmaker's name not marked but probably Osborne or Wilson, here using borderless corners. The flowers in the centre are an 'extra' not found on most dials. Original hands of blued steel in non-matching style.*

COLOUR PLATE 5. *Thirteen-inch dial by James Wilson of Birmingham from an eight-day clock of about 1790 by Benjamin Harlow of Lane End, Staffordshire. Here the dialmaker has used the rather uncommon treatment of solid ground colour for his corners (green in fact) and also solid grounds for his arch flowers. Birds to the centre were 'extras' and rather more popular in the north of England than in the south. Original hands of non-matching pattern in blued steel.*

The pattern of the gold dot-dash system of borders surrounding floral corners sometimes varies between dialmakers and may sometimes vary between different dials by the same dialmaker. Often, however, the dot-dash style is consistent and this may be a help in identifying dialmakers. For example James Wilson regularly used a particular pattern of gold dot-dash border around his flowers, so that one can often predict the dialmaker from the border pattern alone. This is however not a precise business and in general the dot-dash pattern is not a safe or reliable identification feature for a particular dialmaker, unless it can be confirmed by information elsewhere, such as on the dial back.

Towards the end of Period One some dial corners contained a solid body of paint in the form of a small complete oil painting. This was most often in the form of the Four Seasons, and represents an early use of this theme, which was far more popular in later periods. Some late eighteenth century dials by James Wilson have this theme. Occasionally other solid body corner themes appear but these are more often found in later periods.

ARCH DECORATION
An arched dial offers an additional area of decoration or other evidence which

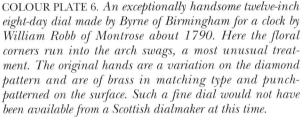

COLOUR PLATE 6. *An exceptionally handsome twelve-inch eight-day dial made by Byrne of Birmingham for a clock by William Robb of Montrose about 1790. Here the floral corners run into the arch swags, a most unusual treatment. The original hands are a variation on the diamond pattern and are of brass in matching type and punch-patterned on the surface. Such a fine dial would not have been available from a Scottish dialmaker at this time.*

COLOUR PLATE 7. *Square twelve-inch dial of 1780-90 by Osborne from a longcase clock by George Hewitt of Marlborough, showing the method of incorporating a moon on a square dial (sometimes known as a twelve o'clock moon), in this instance showing the full 29½ day lunar month. This type of moon is less common in the South than in the North of England.*

can be most helpful in dating. Moon dials which fill the arch are dealt with later, but for non-moon dials the arch might at this period contain a simple plaque of decorative work bearing the maker's name, perhaps with nothing else present or with just a couple of sprays in black, gold or colour. It might contain delicate floral work centred on a flower spray or a bird-and-flower grouping. It might contain flowing tracery of flowers or gold scrollwork.

Towards the end of Period One, and for a few years after, an oval panel often featured a vignette painted scene usually with a scroll at each side of goldwork or flowers. Sometimes the vignette painting would be in an eight-sided box, the painting itself often featuring a girl or shepherdess under a tree or a semi-classical figure perhaps representing Nature or the Harvest.

NUMBERING

The numbering pattern is a most helpful feature in identifying any dial period, and especially that of Period One, where the great majority of dials have the same, consistent style of numbering using Roman hour numerals and Arabic (otherwise known as English) numerals for minutes. Naturally the other features of the dial may be helpful too, but it is virtually possible to identify a Period One dial by its

PLATE 32. *Twelve-inch square eight-day dial (falseplate indicating the dialmaker as Wilson of Birmingham) from a clock by Henry Ward of Blandford and dating from the late 1790s. Gold corners are of the symmetrical style. The dial centre flowers are 'extras' as most dials do not have these. Matching pattern original hands of blued steel.*

PLATE 33. *Eight-day dial of the 1790s of the symmetrical gold corner style also having gold archwork, made by Byrne of Birmingham for Archibald Buchan of Perth, Scotland, an example of an English dial being used by a Scottish clockmaker. Orginal blued steel hands of matching looped diamond pattern.*

numbers alone. This is something which is especially useful when dealing with round dials, which frequently have no visible stylistic features other than numbers. Typical Period One numbering can be seen in Plates 32 and 33. For convenience I usually refer to this style as 'double numbers' since we have two complete sets, one for hours and one for minutes. The hours are marked by Roman numerals, and the minutes are noted by dots and numbered every fifth one, i.e. 5, 10, 15, 20, etc. This is what I refer to as full minute numbering with dotted minutes.

Towards the end of the eighteenth century (and therefore the end of Period One) dials occasionally omit those minutes numbers which fall between the quarters, i.e. they omit 5, 10, 20, 25, etc. numbering only at 15, 30, 45 and 60.

Very occasionally towards the end of the eighteenth century a different method was used of marking the minutes not by dots but by a single line track with bars across (see Plate 267). This is unusual and signifies that we are approaching the end of dotted minutes towards the track system used in Period Two and later. Such dials should be looked at carefully as some examples of track-and-bar numbering are really dotted minute dials which have been incorrectly restored.

Also in the last years of the eighteenth century we find a few dials which show the approaching style of Period Two in using Arabic (or English) numerals for hours while still keeping Arabics for full (dotted) minute marking. I call these dials 'double Arabics'. These double Arabics dials were principally (though perhaps not exclusively) made by James Wilson. Often they incorporate the Four

PLATE 34. *Eight-day dial of the late 1790s of the symmetrical gold corner type with rolling moon from a clock by John Simpkin of Rillington, North Yorkshire. Matching ('diamond') pattern hands in blued steel are original, including seconds hand. Here the globe transfers come fully down to the chapter ring instead of stopping short across the dial shoulder, as was the earlier style.*

PLATE 35. *Eight-day dial of the late 1780s of the symmetrical gold corner type from a clock by William Elliott of Whitby, the dial made by Osborne of Birmingham. Here the globe transfers stop short at the dial shoulder, which tends to be the earlier method. Original hands of non-matching pattern in blued steel.*

Seasons corner painting theme, which was just coming into popularity at this time. Double Arabic dials come into their own after 1800 but a few seem to date before the end of the century.

CALENDARS

Calendar dials to indicate the day of the month by number were present on most clocks during Period One, both eight-days and thirty-hours, though examples of both may sometimes be seen without calendars.

The method of showing the calendar is variable and is not in itself an indicator of period. Even so the square box type of calendar (as found on brass dials) was only occasionally used on white dials (Plate 36, Morgan) and then almost exclusively in the earliest part of Period One. The short-mouth calendar (see page 66) was also a feature used early in the period. The ordinary (full) mouth calendar occurs throughout Period One (and later of course).

The pointer system of calendar indication (using a hand to match the seconds dial and hand) occurs from the later part of Period One. This was mostly, though not entirely, confined to eight-day clocks. The reason is that this pointer type was knocked on once in twenty-four hours and required an extra intermediate wheel, known as a twenty-four-hour wheel, to drive it, making it a more costly system than

COLOUR PLATE 8. *An unusual dial, dialmaker unknown, of the late 1790s from an eight-day longcase clock by Sagar of Skipton, here having solid corner painting of the Four Seasons theme but most unusually featuring boys rather than girls. The solid-painted centre is very unusual at this early date and features an Eastern potentate and subjects. The half-globe transfers are also unusual in having degrees marked around the perimeter as done on some American-made dials.*

the mouth calendar, which needed no drive gear, but was knocked on twelve-hourly by a pin on the hour pipe.

One type of calendar, known as a centre calendar, shows indications by means of a third hand driving from the same point as the two time hands. This system was a carryover from brass dial days. It was not much used on white dials, and when it was, it was almost always during Period One. It probably fell from favour because its presence made for a more cluttered dial, thus impeding clarity of time-reading.

Yet another carryover from brass dial days was the arch calendar (Plate 223,

COLOUR PLATE 10. *Eight-day clock dating from about 1780-90 by Eli Stott of Wakefield, the dialmaker unknown. Symmetrical corners here combine with the normally earlier features of dots inside the seconds numbers, half-hemisphere globes and non-matching steel hands using the straight minute hand.*

COLOUR PLATE 9. *Eight-day white dial clock showing moon and tidal times made about 1790 by Thomas Husband of Hull, the dial by James Wilson of Birmingham. The legend above the arch reads 'Sic est vita hominis' (thus is the life of man). Original matching steel hands of curved diamond style. The mahogany case is a fine example of the East Riding pagoda type.*

Greening dial), a system seldom used at all on white dials of any period.

MOONS

A moon dial shows the lunar calendar indicating the lunar date and the moon's 'phase'. The lunar month has 29½ days in each month and is therefore a quite different feature from the normal calendar date. The phase is usually shown by a complete moon face, showing fully at full moon (the fifteenth lunar day) and as a crescent moon shape at other times. For one day of the lunar month no moon shows at all, then the new moon appears on the next day. Moon dials were used if

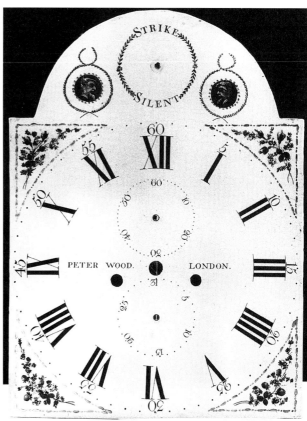

PLATE 36. *Twelve-inch dial from an eight-day clock of about 1780 by Thomas Morgan of Edinburgh, the dial made by Osborne of Birmingham. It is not uncommon at this time for a Scots maker to use an English dial. Unusual features, indicative of an early period, are: the name in the arch, the square calendar with a silvered brass calendar disc as used on brass dials, and the painted-edge winding holes instead of brass collets. Borderless corners are less common than bordered ones. Coloured corners of this nature are often termed 'strawberry corners'.*

PLATE 37. *Dial from an eight-day clock of about 1780 by Peter Wood of London, the dial made by Thomas Osborne of Birmingham, rather unusual for a London clock. The coin-like decoration in the arch is unusual as is the pointer type calendar for this early date. The minute numbers are unusually small and have the dots positioned outside rather than inside the minute numerals. Also unusual is the absence of circles inside the hours and outside the minutes, which makes this altogether a rather eccentric dial, especially for a normally conservative dialmaker such as Osborne.*

PLATE 38. *Twelve-inch eight-day dial of the strawberry corner style made about 1785 by James Wilson from a clock by William Rust of Hull, showing great similarity of overall style to the previous dial by Osborne. The pointer calendar is an insignificant difference.*

PLATE 39. *Thirteen-inch square dial of the strawberry corner style made about 1790 by James Wilson from a longcase clock by Watkin Owen of Llanrwst. The centre birds are an extra feature. Original hands in non-matching pattern in blued steel.*

PLATE 40. *Twelve-inch eight-day dial by James Wilson from a clock by Joseph Glover of Leicester about 1790. Here the ground to the corner flowers is of solid colour (grey in fact). The flowers in the centre do not appear on most dials and would have been charged as 'extras' by the dialmakers.*

for instance you were planning a night-time journey or arranging an evening social function. They were more often used on clocks from rural areas than from towns, and are uncommon on London-made clocks.

Moons sometimes occur on Period One dials, though moondial clocks were always in the minority at any period. They might be in the commonest form of a moon filling the entire arch, known usually as a 'rolling moon' (see Plates 7, 35 and 43), or they might be in the form of a cut-out moon below XII, usually called a 'twelve-o'clock moon' (see Colour Plate 7 and Plate 45). Both usually operate by knocking on one tooth twelve-hourly, by a simple pin or wedge system fixed on the hour pipe. Rolling moons may also involve an intermediate wheel or long-reach triggers, but they are generally impulsed from an hour-pipe wedge.

The moon faces of the earlier part of Period One are sometimes painted against a starry sky background, usually gold on blue – see Plate 28. From the beginning of Period One, however, the alternative form is found, which soon became standard – a background of a landscape alternating with a seascape. Two landscapes or two seascapes are not unknown, but one of each is normal – see Plates 30 and 34. Just occasionally an eccentric type of moon dial occurs – see Colour Plate 32 (Lister).

The rolling moon disc usually turns in the arch area above two 'humps'. The 'hump' traditionally carries a transfer of the two hemispheres as decoration. The transfer of each hemisphere normally runs down far enough to meet the chapter ring outer circle (see Plate 34). In Period One, however, some hemisphere

COLOUR PLATE 11. *Eight-day strawberry corners clock by Snowden of Grimsby dating from the 1790s in a very fine mahogany Hull pagoda case. Original finials. Original non-matching steel hands.*

COLOUR PLATE 12. *Thirty-hour clock of about 1790 by Richard Blakeborough of Pateley Bridge, Yorkshire, being a square japanned dial modified to an arch by the clockmaker to incorporate a rocking Father Time, locally painted so that the figure rocks alternately into Heaven then Hell. Dial-maker unknown.*

transfers are only a half transfer and finish flat at the horizontal top of the square of the dial if a sight-line is taken across from the dial shoulder (see Plate 34). In other words the spheres on these dials end at the 'equator' showing only the Northern Hemispheres (in reality many transfers are tilted and so do not end at the true equator). These 'half-transfer' moons tend to be limited to the earlier part of Period One, while the full transfers run on later and even through Periods Two and Three. More about moon dials will be found on page 94.

DIAL SIZE
Dial sizes grew gradually larger as time progressed and this can sometimes be a

PLATE 41. *Square dial showing solid ground corner treatment to the flowers (green ground) from an eight-day clock of about 1790 by Lawson of Wigan, the dialmaker probably James Wilson of Birmingham. Original blued steel hands in non-matching serpentine style. Birds to the centre were an optional extra.*

PLATE 42. *Twelve-inch eight-day dial of the 'strawberry corner' style made about 1790 by James Wilson from a longcase clock by Charles Robotham of Leicester with rolling moon feature, here having the full-depth globe transfers. The centre flowers are an extra not found on most dials. Original blued steel non-matching hands.*

PLATE 43. *Eight-day dial of the floral corner style (strawberry corners), made about 1790 for a longcase clock by Thorndike of Ipswich, the dialmaker unidentified but probably James Wilson. Here the rolling moon also incorporates high tide times, read from the inner band of Roman numerals. The seconds dots inside the numerals suggests this clock may even be a little earlier, as does the original non-matching blued steel hands style using the straight minute hand.*

PLATE 44. *Handsome eight-day dial of the 'strawberry corner' type, dialmaker unknown, from a longcase clock of about 1780 by Watkin Owen of Llanrwst, also bearing most unusually above the moondial the name of the first owner, Owen Hughes. The floral swags linking the winding collets are an unusual treatment. The calendar is of the square box type, unusual on any white dial and often an early sign. Non-matching original hands of blued steel.*

PLATE 45. *Fourteen-inch eight-day square dial of the strawberry corner style (dialmaker unknown but probably James Wilson) incorporating a twelve o'clock moon, though here showing only part of the lunar month, from a longcase clock of about 1790 by William Barlow of Ashton under Lyne. The birds to the centre are an extra, but very popular in this area. Matching brass hands look like later replacements.*

PLATE 46. *Square eight-day dial of about 1790 of the strawberry corner style but here with the unusual feature (especially for this period) of a fully-painted centre scene showing a man and wife in a formal garden, perhaps intended as the owner of the clock. Clockmaker John Tootell of Eccles, Lancashire; dial without falseplate or any identification, therefore dialmaker unknown but the style is much like James Wilson. Non-matching hands in blued steel are original.*

PLATE 47. *Fourteen-inch square eight-day dial dating from the late 1790s or even shortly after 1800, dialmaker unknown, from a longcase clock by Thomas Dean of Leigh, Lancashire. The solid-ground corners (green in fact) with a solid gold border line are unusual and reminiscent of the work of Whittaker & Shreeve of Halifax. Centre painted with a scene illustrating 'Commerce'. Centre calendar, registered by a brass arrowhead hand, whilst the main hands are of blued steel in matching looped diamond pattern.*

PLATE 48. *Eight-day dial of the strawberry corner style from a longcase clock of the 1790s by Celia Fletcher of Rotherham, using the gold dot-dash border principle yet a distinctly different border from that used by Osborne and/or Wilson. The dialmaker is Ashwin & Co. Original non-matching blued steel hands (minute hand might be a replacement); original seconds hand of brass.*

help towards overall dating of an example. Within a specific period, however, dial size is less helpful at pinning down the decade, as some variety occurred. Dials are measured by width in inches, usually also specifying square or arched. Round dials are measured by diameter. Thirty-hour dials tended often to remain smaller in size than contemporary eight-days.

In Period One thirty-hour japanned dials were sometimes ten inches wide, more often eleven or twelve, and thirteen would be possible. Eight-day dials were occasionally eleven inches wide but more often twelve and not unusually thirteen; fourteen is uncommon but does occur (see Plate 30).

An idea of the limited range of actual sizes of dials used by clockmakers of this period can be gained from those examples listed on page 120 (Chapter 9).

HANDS

The hands of a clock can serve as very helpful indicators to period provided they are original to the clock, and this is an area where experience is needed. Dials in the earlier part of Period One have hands which are identical in style to those on contemporary brass dial clocks; that is to say they have hands of blued steel in non-matching pattern, meaning that the hour and minute hands are purposely different in style from each other in order to avoid confusion between hours and minutes in a population still not entirely accustomed to clocks. Plate 31 (Sherwood) shows one version of this early style whereby the minute hand still has

PLATE 49. *Square eight-day dial of the late 1790s using the strawberry corner theme but the gold band outside the minute numerals and the multi-ringed seconds feature are unusual. The clockmaker is Bellman of Broughton (Lancashire); the dialmaker unknown. Original hands in blued steel of matching diamond pattern.*

PLATE 51. *Round dial from a thirty-hour longcase clock of about 1790 by John Holmes of Cheadle, the dialmaker unknown but possibly James Wilson. The bird to the centre is an extra not found on most dials. Blued steel hands of the non-matching type are original. Craze marks in the japanwork show clearly, and are typical of very many dials.*

PLATE 50. *Eight-day oval dial with rolling moon of the strawberry corner style (though of course there are no corners) dating from the 1790s, from a longcase clock by Lomax of Blackburn, dialmaker James Wilson. Original non-matching hands of blued steel. The globes have been re-ruled during restoration without the maps. The lower minute numbers from 20 to 40 inclusive appear to have been re-lettered upside down during restoration.*

PLATE 52. *Eight-day dial by James Wilson from a longcase clock of about 1790 by Charles Low of Arbroath, showing a fly positioned alongside the I numeral, probably for the purpose of camouflaging a flaw in the japanned surface.*

a straight pointer. Plate 29 (Rogers) shows the alternative form whereby the minute hand is serpentine in shape. Both styles of hand were used simultaneously, though the individual clockmaker would probably vary his hands somewhat, especially his hour hands. Brass hands in this non-matching style are very uncommon, and most met with are incorrect replacements.

Towards the end of Period One matching pattern hands first appear, on brass dials as well as white dials. These are of the type whereby the hour hand is of a smaller, thicker version of the same pattern as the minute hand. Matching hands appear principally in steel at this time, but by about 1790 brass hands were used, known at the time as 'gilt' hands. Some brass hands, though probably not all, were gilded. Most have had their gilding polished away long ago and now appear as polished brass.

Matching hands in Period One were often of very simple style, such as the typical 'diamond' pattern shown in Plate 34. These simple, elegant, matching patterns are very different from the much heavier and bolder style of matching brass hands used on later clocks of Period Three. They are also usually much more finely made.

At the beginning of the white dial period most clockmakers probably made their own hands. Well before the end of the century, however, hands could be bought in ready-made, perhaps with the finishing (called fettling) still to do, though gilded hands would presumably be already finished before gilding. Some clockmakers continued to make their own hands well into Period Two and even Period Three, as can be seen by the occasional appearance of some very eccentric, perhaps unique, patterns.

ROCKING FIGURES

Rocking figures, also known as automata, were not uncommon after the middle of the eighteenth century on brass dial clocks. The new japanned dials, however, seldom seem to have these features in Period One, and examples from this period are uncommon. This was perhaps because the dialmakers were loath to experiment at this early stage of their newly-developing business, and a rocking-figure dial was usually of a far more complex construction than a solid dial and even more complex than the aperture dialsheet used for a rolling moon.

FLY DIALS

Occasionally we meet with a very odd feature on some dials (mostly during Period One, but it could presumably have occurred at any time), that is the presence on a dial of a small insect in some area which would otherwise be plain ground, in other words *not* as a part of a decorative feature such as a flower spray. This insect stands isolated from other decoration. It is usually a fly, but may be any tiny, gnat-like insect, sometimes a bee, sometimes a small butterfly. Just occasionally a tiny flower may be used instead of an insect.

For convenience I refer to dials of this type as 'fly dials'. They are very unusual. Most of the ones I have come across are by dialmakers Osborne and/or Wilson, though this may simply be because these dialmakers virtually monopolised the trade in the eighteenth century, so that any dial we are likely to see of that vintage is likely to be by them.

The reason for the presence of the 'fly' is not always apparent. On some fly dials, probably the majority of them, the fly appears to be there to camouflage a blemish in the japanned surface, which would otherwise have been obvious, being on the plain white ground. Such a blemish in the painted corners would probably have gone unnoticed because of the colours catching the eye there.

It was pointed out to me by a correspondent, Douglas Stevenson, that this same practice was carried out in the manufacture of porcelain in Europe in the eighteenth century, especially at the Meissen factory, and that this was copied in the English trade. In the German porcelain trade such camouflage insects were known as flies (the German word is Fliegen) whether or not flies were actually depicted. Sometimes too the porcelain manufacturers used a flower rather than a fly, but this was still referred to as a 'fly'. In fact until the late eighteenth century the word 'fly' was used to mean any small winged insect. So, quite by chance, in calling these clock dials 'fly' dials I had hit upon the very term used in the European porcelain trade in the eighteenth century, and, as it happens, *still* used in that trade today.

As well as being used on some clock dials to camouflage surface faults, they were

PLATE 54. *Four moon discs shown removed from their dials, each disc containing two full lunations. The principle of a landscape alternating with a seascape between moon faces applied to most moon discs. The makers of the dials from which these came are unknown except for the lower right disc, which is from a dial by Walker & Hughes of Birmingham.*

sometimes used to cover a feature which otherwise might be unsightly. For example, some dials of this period employ a moon system involving a post for the moon drive which screws into the dial from behind and protrudes on the dial surface. I have seen flies used to conceal this kind of surface intrusion.

Another use of flies can be to cover the end of a dial foot (or dial feet). On a dial with moon feature from a clock by Thomas Lister junior of Halifax dating from about 1790 (Colour Plate 32 and Plate 228), the two upper dial feet carry a crossbar to which is attached the moon-drive gearing. This, it was anticipated, must have threatened more strain than normal to the dial feet, thus endangering chipping of the surface. A fly had been painted on to each of those two dial feet ends in order to camouflage this in anticipation of it happening, though as it turned out, it did not happen!

This dial is not marked with its maker's stamp, but it tells us that Lister knew when he ordered the dial that he would use the top feet as moonwork supports, suggesting a greater degree of collaboration between clockmaker and dialmaker than we might normally assume.

PLATE 55. *Eight-day clock of about 1790 by John Milsome of Newbury, the typical twelve-inch dial by James Wilson of Birmingham. The oak case (lacking finials) is of the crested dome type, a style found largely in the South. The dial bears the monogram WSS, probably being the initials of the first owners, which suggests this was a marriage clock bought as a wedding present. A lock (and escutcheon) in the hood door is a feature derived from London influence and found principally in the South. This is a fly dial, the fly just visible and covering a flaw beside the 15 numeral.*

PLATE 56. *Detail of a late 18th century dial by an unknown dialmaker from an eight-day clock by Thomas Worswick of Lancaster. The centre scrollwork decoration, though slightly worn, is evidently printed by transfer, a most unusual method seldom used. The printing is black with no added colour. Seconds hand a replacement; other hands original in non-matching steel.*

Most puzzling of all is the fact that occasionally a fly will be seen on a dial for no apparent reason. Perhaps they were specifically asked for occasionally by eccentric customers

OVERALL DIAL DEVELOPMENT

It can sometimes be difficult to position a dial within its correct place in this period, as there are some styles which can be identical whether dating from 1775 or 1795. Those factors which may help are: dial size; calendar shape/type; moon type; corner decoration, if of the asymmetrical gold type; hands pattern.

CHAPTER SEVEN
DIALS, PERIOD TWO (1800-1830)

Period Two is really a transitional phase linking the distinctly different styles of Periods One and Three. Naturally stylistic changes do not start or end at specific dates and a certain amount of overlap is to be expected. However the year 1800 is a convenient breaking point after which most dials will show certain changes from the earlier style.

It is still quite possible for a dial having double numbers in the Period One manner to appear for the next few years after 1800. For example, the dials in Plates 57 and 58 (Rutherford, Hawick and Burton, Kendal) still show clearly the double numbers system of hours and dotted minutes, yet each is clearly marked on its falseplate Walker & Finnemore, who were in business 1808-11 or possibly a year or two earlier. Most such dates are taken from trade directories, which appeared only at irregular intervals. Both these dials, however, whilst still showing Period One numbering, do have other features which indicate a change in overall style.

The Rutherford dial has its decoration based on geometrical patterns centred on a sort of starburst motif, a distinctly Period Two feature. It retains the swag effect in the arch reminiscent of Period One, yet the stylised patterns in the arch and corners and especially the Z-work bordering to the corners are of a distinctly Period Two nature. Likewise the Burton dial retains floral effects and the oval vignette arch scene reminiscent of Period One but its floral corners are also now geometrically formed in a way quite unlike Period One.

From such examples we can see that the numbering pattern alone is not the whole answer, but only one of the identification features on which to base a dating. Just as double Arabic numbering can occur late in Period One and earlier than usual, so too can double numbers using Roman hours occur in Period Two later than normal. It is the overall dial style which indicates the period, so let us consider the various stylistic aspects individually.

CORNER DECORATION

Several types of corner decoration occur. One early type is the flower spray continuing exactly as in Period One. More often, however, the flowers now fill a larger area of ground (see Plate 64, Benbow dial) with multiple flowers, in other words an extension of Period One flower corners, sometimes with a solid colour ground rather than white. Plate 62 (Fox dial) illustrates both the expanded flower theme and the coloured ground features. Increasingly, however, the flowers become a part of a geometrical pattern, perhaps its centre (Plate 65, Thompson, Darlington dial), or perhaps its framework. Fruit is sometimes mingled with flowers or shown alone – apples, pears, oranges, etc.

Seashells were now a very popular corner theme, often large conch shells or clams, possibly inspired by recent discoveries in the South Seas following the exploratory voyages of Captain Cook and others. This same obsession with shells also shows itself in clock casework at this period (and other furniture too), and many clocks with shells on their dials also have shell inlay in their cases.

Increasingly, however, patterns of geometrical nature were the fashion, whereby each corner mirrors that opposite. Often the corner itself was a fan, which could be of any colour, but green with gold was a popular choice. Flowers, fruit, shells or fans, any or all of them, may form part of a geometrical arrangement making up

PLATE 57. *Thirteen-inch eight-day dial of perhaps 1810 from a clock by William Rutherford of Hawick, Scotland, the English-made dial signed on the falseplate Walker & Finnemore, Birmingham (listed 1808-11). In this example the numbering system of Period One remains but the geometric corner and arch designs are clearly of Period Two style. Original hands of blued steel in matching diamond pattern.*

PLATE 58. *Thirteen-inch dial from an eight-day longcase clock by Burton of Kendal, the falseplate indicating dialmakers as Walker & Finnemore of Birmingham (1808-11). Again the earlier numbering system persists as does the arch vignette scene, but the flower corners are now set out geometrically. Hands in blued steel of matching type but hour and minute hand are not a true pair, so one must be a replacement.*

matching and repetitive corners.

In this period too we find the occasional tendency to paint the entire corner as a complete oil painting. The Four Seasons theme occurs, and sometimes other motifs which conveniently divide into four. Landscapes can occur too, though they came more into their own in Period Three. Often such animals as squirrels, deer or rabbits will form matching corners facing each other, perhaps with a few branches or leaf sprays.

It is difficult to specify the sequence of these corner objects, but probably flowers, fruit and shells tend to be followed by fans and pure geometrics, followed by solid-body scenes.

ARCH DECORATION

Increasingly the square dial begins to fall from fashion and is replaced by the arch form, though square dials still persist principally in cottage clocks, where the square dial enabled the clock height to be kept lower than a similar arched version. The square form was also cheaper, as we know, and hence probably more appealing to a cottager's pocket.

Moon dials fill some arches but solid arches often have flowers or fruit or birds-with-flowers-or-fruit fading into a white ground. Baskets of fruit, sprays, and swags

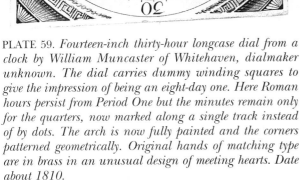

PLATE 59. *Fourteen-inch thirty-hour longcase dial from a clock by William Muncaster of Whitehaven, dialmaker unknown. The dial carries dummy winding squares to give the impression of being an eight-day one. Here Roman hours persist from Period One but the minutes remain only for the quarters, now marked along a single track instead of by dots. The arch is now fully painted and the corners patterned geometrically. Original hands of matching type are in brass in an unusual design of meeting hearts. Date about 1810.*

PLATE 60. *Eight-day dial with rolling moon and Four Seasons corner theme dating from about 1810 from a longcase clock by Samuel Pearson of Halifax, dialmaker unknown but resembles work of Whittaker and Shreeve of Halifax. Upright Arabic hours with minutes still dotted but shown only at the quarters. Most unusual place for signature below the two half-hemispheres, which are here used unusually late. Solid-painted dial centre is slightly more common at this period, but seldom includes the area within the seconds and calendar rings, as it does here.*

are often still relatively restrained and seldom fill the entire arch as a solid body of painting.

Sometimes a complete landscape scene will fill the arch. Heroes appear of naval or military fame, especially Nelson, or a naval or military battle. A whole variety of themes occur from portrayals of classical gods to romanticised rustic cottage scenes. Many of these arch themes will shortly appear in the dial corners in Period Three, but for now they are limited to the arch area. Rocking figures now become more popular than earlier.

NUMBERING

Numbering in Period Two represents a transition between Period One and Period Three by means of experimentation, and therefore is subject to constant change. Nevertheless the numbering patterns of this period are readily identifiable and are a most helpful means of dating.

As already mentioned, a few early Period Two dials have the same double numbering pattern of Roman hours with Arabic minutes as found in Period One

PLATE 61. *Eight-day dial of about 1810 from a longcase clock by Baker of Newark (or perhaps earlier as one such died in 1800?). Dialmaker unknown. Upright Arabic hours; dotted minutes marked only at the quarters. Period One style strawberry corners. Automata in the arch of Adam and Eve in the Garden of Eden, with Adam's unfortunate stance poking his fingers up the lion's nose. Matching brass hands look like later replacements.*

PLATE 62. *Twelve-inch eight-day longcase dial from a clock by Hudson Fox of Hull, the dial made by Hipkiss and Harrold of Birmingham and dating from about 1805. Arabic hours in the 'tumbling numbers' form; dotted minutes only for the quarters with asterisks taking up the missing numerals. Floral corners on to solid ground colour, but no longer 'strawberry corner' fashion. Matching main hands of blued steel in curved diamond style; seconds hand probably a replacement.*

(Plates 57 and 58). A few early ones show the continuing pattern of double Arabics, for hours and minutes. Most dials, however, show a certain progression in that within a very few years almost all dials have Arabic hour numbers but only limited minute numbering at the quarter hours. These number minutes at 15, 30, 45 and 60 units, but omit the intervening number, i.e. they leave out 5 and 10, 20 and 25, replacing the missing numerals with asterisks or similar markers. Typical examples of this are seen in Plates 62, 64 and 65, the dials by Fox, Benbow, and Thompson.

Quarter-hour minute numbering sometimes uses dots for minutes but sometimes now a single track is used instead with minute positions indicated by a cross bar, as in Plates 59, 63 and 64 (the dials by Muncaster, Evans, and Benbow). Ultimately the double track minute band becomes universal from late Period Two onwards.

The Arabic hour numerals were portrayed in two variations. One form has the numerals set radial to the dial centre, as the Roman hours numerals always were (see Plates 62 and 63, Fox and Evans dials). The problem with this style is that whilst we may be accustomed to seeing Roman numerals upside down between

PLATE 63. *Thirty-hour eleven-inch arched dial (unusually small) by an unnamed dialmaker from a longcase clock by John Evans of Newcastle Emlyn, Wales, c.1810. Tumbling Arabic hours; single-track minutes numbered only at the quarters. Original blued steel hands of matching type using the diamond form. Apples and pears to the corners; romantic scenery to the arch and dial centre. Two lower dial feet end joints show beside name.*

PLATE 64. *Twelve-inch eight-day dial with upright Arabic hours and single-track quarter-hour minutes from a longcase by Thomas Benbow of Northwood, Shropshire. Floral corners now are mirrored repeats left and right. Original brass hands in matching hearts pattern. Dial crazing shows in this lighting. Dialmakers are Walker and Hughes of Birmingham, who are not listed till 1811 but the clockmaker is believed to have died in 1809, which must put the date about 1805-09.*

the hours of IIII and VIII, Arabic hour numerals looked strange in this layout. Those which fell between 4 and 8 inclusive were therefore reversed (i.e. turned so that the numeral tops were radial to the dial centre) to make them intelligible. This form of layout is known as 'tumbling numbers'.

The alternative Arabic hour numbering was to position each number vertically, as in Plates 64 and 65 (Benbow and Thompson dials), and these are referred to as 'upright numbers'. I am not aware that either method pre-dates the other. Dialmakers in general seem to have been at a loss as to which method was preferable, and it may have been this uncertainty with Arabic numbers which caused the ultimate return to Roman hours found in Period Three.

Some Period Two dials have Roman hours whilst marking only the quarter-hours by minute numbers, whether using dots or tracks for the minutes themselves. This return to Roman hour numerals heralds the method which will shortly be in universal use in Period Three. An example is seen in Plate 59 (Muncaster dial). Some dials having Roman hours with quarter-hour minutes have their numerals radial to the dial centre, as this one does, whilst some have them as 'upright numbers'. I do not think this form of Roman-hours-with-quarter-hour-minutes dial, whether radial or upright, can necessarily be placed earlier or later in Period Two than Arabic-hour dials. They cannot be confused with Roman-hour dials from Period Three, as the latter do not number minutes at all (see page 108).

PLATE 65. *Neatly-painted twelve-inch thirty-hour dial (no maker's marking, hence unidentified) of about 1810 by James Thompson of Darlington. Upright Arabic hours; single-track minutes, numbered for the quarters only. Corner patterns mirror each other. Original matching pattern hands in brass of fine quality and unusual style.*

PLATE 66. *Thirteen-inch eight-day dial (maker not marked) from a longcase clock of about 1810-15 by George Mawman of Beverley, Yorkshire. Single-track minutes numbered at the quarters; tumbling Arabic hours. Corner patterns mirror each other. Stylised landscape to arch symbolising nature. Hands original: main hands of brass in matching pattern in a most unusual form of entwined serpents; subsidiary hands of blued steel for contrast.*

CALENDARS

Not every clock had a calendar, but most did. It might be shown by any of the methods previously described (see pages 75-76), except that the square box system no longer occurs. Of the various systems the mouth calendar was the cheapest and it follows that thirty-hour clocks will frequently have this cheaper method because of the price factor. The mouth calendar was probably the most common in this period on eight-day clocks too. Some dials, however, now have the pointer method of calendar indication (see Plate 66, Mawman), a form which grows increasingly popular as time passes, probably because it 'matches' better the layout of those dials with seconds pointers.

MOONS

Moon dials occur during Period Two at about the same overall percentage as they did in Period One, and being always in the minority. By now the old-style moon disc with the starry sky has passed from fashion and the scenes between the two moon faces often alternate a landscape with a seascape, or sometimes two landscapes. As with moon dials of all periods, the painting of the scenes on the moon disc often seems to be of higher calibre than that of the rest of the dial. Perhaps

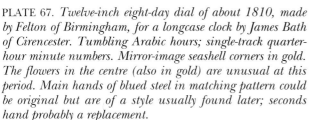

PLATE 67. *Twelve-inch eight-day dial of about 1810, made by Felton of Birmingham, for a longcase clock by James Bath of Cirencester. Tumbling Arabic hours; single-track quarter-hour minute numbers. Mirror-image seashell corners in gold. The flowers in the centre (also in gold) are unusual at this period. Main hands of blued steel in matching pattern could be original but are of a style usually found later; seconds hand probably a replacement.*

PLATE 68. *Eleven-inch dial, unmarked as to maker, from a thirty-hour longcase clock of about 1815 by John Weston of Hastings. Such small dials were still being made but became increasingly unusual. Tumbling Arabic hours now having double-track minutes numbered for the quarters only. Mirror-image flower corners here painted in gold, not in colour. Original hands of matching pattern in blued steel in an unusual design.*

different artists did the moon discs, or perhaps they were more free to give rein to their artistry than when doing the more stylised and limiting corner and arch paintings. Some moon dials incorporated times of high tide by adding an extra row of calibrated numerals usually using Romans for tide times. Moons which incorporated high water tidal times now seem to be unusual, however.

DIAL SIZE

In general, dial sizes are larger in Period Two than in Period One, though there are always exceptions. The North of England always seems to have had a preference for larger dials, so that this increase in dial size (usually referred to by width in inches) is often more pronounced in Northern England. In the North the twelve-inch dial is now less often used on eight-day clocks than the thirteen-inch (or even fourteen-inch). In the South twelve-inch dial eight-days still occur, but the growth to thirteen-inch dials and even larger still is apparent.

Thirty-hour dials often remained smaller than eight-day dials in all regions, but again Northern dials were on the whole larger than elsewhere. It is not unknown, for example, to find thirty-hour clocks still using the ten-inch size at this time in the South, though eleven or twelve inches would be more usual. In the North a ten-inch dial thirty-hour would be most unlikely, eleven inches unusual, and by now most will be thirteen and above.

With circular dials the tendency would normally be for these to be a shade smaller than with contemporary arched or square ones. Similarly, square dials would often tend to be a shade smaller than arched ones as with an arched-dial clock the greater height would keep an overall balanced proportion to the case. The generally lower height of the case of a square (or, of course, circular) dial

PLATE 69. *Twelve-inch eight-day dial with rocking ship to the arch from a longcase clock of about 1815 by John Barnsdale of Burnham (Somerset?), the dialmaker unknown. Corners are mirror-image cornucopia. Tumbling Arabic hours; double-track minutes with quarter-hour numbers. Original hands in matching pattern in brass, crescent-moon style.*

PLATE 70. *Fourteen-inch eight-day moon dial of about 1815-20 from a longcase clock by Monkhouse and Son, Carlisle, the dial signed on the falseplate by Finnemores, Birmingham. Stylised floral corners in mirrored patterns. Extra birds to the centre. Original hands in matching pattern in brass. Upright Arabic hours, double track minute band with no minute numbering.*

clock would have made too stocky an appearance if an over-wide dial were used.

For an idea of the limitations of actual dial sizes used by clockmakers of this period, see the list on page 120 (Chapter 9).

HANDS

By the start of Period Two we can be reasonably positive in saying that the non-matching style of hands as found early in Period One has passed away. Now both hour and minute hands are of the same pattern (which we refer to as 'matching'), whereby the hour hand is a shorter and stockier version of the minute hand. This 'matching' principle remains constant now throughout Periods Two and Three, though the individual hands patterns vary greatly.

Smaller hands used for seconds (and sometimes for calendars) will also tend to 'match'. Of course some clocks throughout this period use the 'mouth' form of calendar, but where seconds and calendar *both* show by hands, these two subdials will usually also have hands which 'match' each other as a pair. They may not necessarily match with the main hour and minute hands, nor are they necessarily in the same metal as the main hands.

It may seem unusual to the beginner to see a clock with both its main (matching) hands of brass and its subsidiary hands of steel, or vice versa, but this

PLATE 71. *Mahogany hood of eight-day longcase by Mortimore of Dartmouth actually dated 1817. Roman hours, Arabic minutes on the quarters. Rocking ship in the arch. Mirrored flower corners. Matching diamond pattern hands in blued steel. Despite this late date some Southern cases still have the hood pillars integral with the hood door, as here.*

was sometimes done intentionally for contrast.

Hands in this period may be of steel or of brass. Steel hands were 'blued' to give a blue-black finish for clarity of time reading; brass hands were usually polished and lacquered to keep them bright, but some brass hands were gilded. Some brass hands have a coppery colour, caused by the particular mix of components in the brass. For the most part steel hands will appear in the earlier part of this period and brass hands occur increasingly often as the period progresses, so that by the end of Period Two most are of brass, often with punchwork patterns on the surface to catch the light. Occasional makers continued to use steel hands, however, later examples of these often being of the same design as current brass

COLOUR PLATE 13. *Fourteen-inch eight-day dial with rolling moon feature from a longcase clock of about 1810 by William Johnson of Congleton, Cheshire. The 'double Arabics' dial and falseplate are by Owen of Birmingham. The Four Seasons corner theme became popular from about this time, here neatly painted. Hour hand original, one of a pair of matching pattern in brass; minute hand a near replacement.*

COLOUR PLATE 14. *Eight-day dial from a longcase clock by J.Collier of Cheadle showing twelve o'clock moon, dialmaker unknown. Full Roman hours with double track minutes numbered at the quarters. Patterned repetitive floral corners. Original hands of blued steel in matching diamond pattern. Date about 1810-20.*

ones, though steel hands lacked the surface punchwork. Brass hands were sometimes gilded, though not always, and later polishing has sometimes removed this anyway.

The designs of hands of all periods were varied and defy description. The novice will have to familiarise himself with the variety of patterns used at different times through studying actual examples on clocks or book illustrations. In very general terms the brass hands from the earlier part of this period tend to be more delicate

PLATE 72. *Twelve-inch eight-day dial bearing name of the first owner rather than the clockmaker: John Brown, Wheelwright. The hours are marked by various tools of his trade but, despite this eccentric numbering, this is still visibly a Period Two dial, recognised by double-track minute numbering on the quarters, matching mirrored corners, full arch painting, matching pattern hands in brass (though the hour hand looks like a later replacement). Date about 1820.*

than those of the later part. Steel hands seldom became really heavy, perhaps because the fashion had mostly moved over to brass by the time heavier patterns evolved.

Of those patterns most easily described the commonest are the 'diamond tip' style, found mostly in the early part of this period – see Plates 57 and 63. These occur in both brass and steel. Later on hands are based on crescent moons, acorns, thistles, as well as shapes which cannot be described.

PLATE 73. *Eight-day clock with round japanned dial by Bidlake of London dating about 1820-30. Difficult to date accurately as this has Period Three numbering (perhaps a little on the early side) and has no decoration for guidance. The original matching steel hands are of a style suggesting the earlier date.*

PLATE 74. *Dial from an eight-day longcase clock by Joshua Pannel of Northallerton. The unusual numbering pattern has upright Roman hours with dotted minutes and quarter-hour minute numbering, a mixture of Periods One and Two. A reasonable guess at date would be 1810, but in fact the maker died in 1803 which must pin this to the first year or two of the century. The battle scene with Nelson's portrait is very finely painted. Anchors in the corners echo the naval theme.*

ROCKING FIGURES

Automated figures are probably more common in this period than earlier, though only a small proportion of clocks had them. Rocking ships are probably the commonest, but swimming swans, turning windmills, hammering blacksmiths, playing fiddlers and a variety of other motions are known. Sometimes more than one automated figure appears as, for example, with a musical clock featuring a small orchestra of figures, but for most people one feature moving at a time was enough.

OVERALL DIAL DEVELOPMENT

In general Period Two dials are larger (i.e. wider) than before; contain greater amounts of colour, often symmetrically set out in geometrical patterns based on fans, circles, cartwheels, ellipses, shells, lozenges, whereby the left of the dial is a mirror image of the right; have distinctive numbering patterns usually based on Arabic hours; have matching hands. It can often be quite easy to recognise a dial by its general style as being of this period, and yet be difficult to position it clearly within the overall period. This is where biographical details of the dialmaker and clockmaker may help.

COLOUR PLATE 15. *Unusual eight-day dial from a longcase clock by Stonehouse of Leeds having the chapter ring in black and therefore with negative tumbling Arabics for hours and double track minutes numbered at the quarters. The stylised corners show Faith, Hope, Justice and Charity, known as the Four Virtues, with the Three Nuns in the arch. Original main hands of matching pattern in brass; the subsidiary hands may be replacements. Date about 1820.*

COLOUR PLATE 16. *Fifteen-inch eight-day moon dial from a longcase clock of about 1810-20 by William Nicholas of Birmingham, using the Four Seasons corner theme and with the dial centre fully painted with idyllic rusticity. The two moon 'humps' are here also painted fully, featuring Justice and Britannia. Hands of matching pattern in brass are believed original. This dial is unusually large, probably to show off better the artistry.*

CHAPTER EIGHT

DIALS, PERIOD THREE (1830-1870)

The trends in dial styles we saw developing in Period Two continue further along the same lines in this period. Small size becomes larger, delicate becomes heavier, fine becomes coarser, until finally the white dial of the 1870s is a very different product from that of the 1830s. Quality falls off drastically as this period progresses. Collectors and enthusiasts may still enjoy the dials of even the end of Period Three, but the enjoyment is that we find in jolly folk art – fairground painting, canal-boat painting, and the seaside postcard. By 1850 dial painting is almost always bright, brash, gaudy and loud, and you cannot fail to recognise it when you see it.

CORNER DECORATION

At the beginning of Period Three we find the same type of symmetrically patterned corners we saw late in Period Two, mirror-image corners based on flowers (**Plates 75** and 83, Northgraves and Chapman dials) or shells (Plates 78, 79 and 84, Miller, Braund and Richards dials), or even still on the now old-fashioned theme of fans. Such dials fall early in Period Three or even late in Period Two, and the dividing line between the 1820s and 1830s is a difficult one to pin down from style alone.

Very shortly we move into the style where the entire corner is filled with paint, whether still as mirror-image patterns (Plate 80, Wyatt dial) or as small, independent, mirror-image oil paintings (Plate 88, Crockett dial), or as small oil paintings, *not* of mirror-image nature.(Plate 76, Nicholas dial).

By about 1840 these corner paintings have increased in size relative to the dial, to the point where numbering is pushed into a white circular dial centre and the four corner paintings link together at the edges (see Plate 88, Crockett), thus forming a complete joined-up combination of paintings each running into the adjoining one. The arch too may join into the corners or may still be ruled off separately. By now these corner paintings often take the form of small landscapes, though sometimes they show figures with landscape backgrounds (as, for example, the Four Seasons, Four Continents, Four Countries – England, Scotland, Ireland and Wales).

By the time we reach the joined-up paintings stage it is usually the case that the quality of artwork has dropped considerably to a very naïve, childlike style. Now landscapes of rustic cottages or ruined abbeys and castles may look passably acceptable, but people and animals are often ill-proportioned, wooden, dwarf-like creatures. One reason the animals can look strange is that exotic creatures such as camels, elephants and lions were still little known; there were no zoos and most artists had never seen such creatures except as drawings, which themselves were often inaccurate.

Some development is apparent in this period, but there seems to be little or no progression in style after about 1850. By this time anyway longcase clock production had all but ended in most areas except for Northern England and Scotland and Wales.

ARCH DECORATION

Most dials are now of the arched form. Square dials do appear but are very much in a minority and are principally on smaller, cottage clocks. Round dials appear

PLATE 75. *Twelve-inch eight-day dial from a longcase clock by Denton Northgraves of Hull dating from about 1820-30, the dialmaker named on the falseplate as Finnemore of Birmingham. Floral corners include patterns and are mirrored. Arch landscape fades into white ground. Original matching hands of blued steel in crescent moon style. Roman hours with unnumbered double-track minutes. This dial could slightly pre-date Period Three.*

PLATE 76. *Fourteen-inch eight-day moon dial from a longcase clock by William Nicholas of Birmingham, the dialmakers also Nicholas of Birmingham as named on the falseplate, and dating from about 1820-30. Four Seasons corners are neatly painted. The moon humps also here painted with oriental pagodas instead of the usual globe transfers. Roman hours with double-track unnumbered minutes. Original matching pattern hands in brass. Note scrollwork to name, typical of this period.*

too, but mainly in Scotland or in clocks of special nature such as Regulators.

In the earlier part of this period arch paintings cover only the central portion of the arch, fading into white ground towards the border (Plates 75, 80 and 84, Northgraves, Wyatt, and Richards, dials). Later in this period the arch is completely filled with painting (Plate 88, Crockett dial). Usually a border divides the arch painting from that of the upper corners, as in Plate 88, but sometimes it runs into the upper corners without a break.

Arch paintings are usually landscapes, less often seascapes. They may depict a stylised goddess such as the goddess of the Harvest, or an idealised milkmaid or shepherdess against a landscape ground, or they may be simply rustic scenery with cottages, ruins, churches, etc. Religious paintings appear, usually after about 1840 – the Last Supper, Garden of Eden, Moses and the Tablets, Daniel in the Lion's Den, etc. However all kinds of scenes are possible, probably some done at the specific request of the customer.

It is tempting to think of such stylised scenes as being of local places. Owners

COLOUR PLATE 17. *Period Three eight-day dial of a longcase clock of about 1830 by John Ablitt of Ipswich. The theme of children playing games is most unusual. (Photograph by courtesy of Derek Roberts Antiques.)*

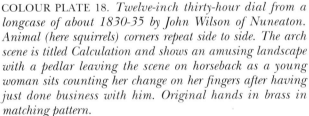

COLOUR PLATE 18. *Twelve-inch thirty-hour dial from a longcase of about 1830-35 by John Wilson of Nuneaton. Animal (here squirrels) corners repeat side to side. The arch scene is titled Calculation and shows an amusing landscape with a pedlar leaving the scene on horseback as a young woman sits counting her change on her fingers after having just done business with him. Original hands in brass in matching pattern.*

COLOUR PLATE 19. *Twelve-inch eight-day dial from a longcase clock of about 1840 by William Hewson of Lincoln, the dial impressed on the reverse with the name of the dialmaker, E. Bennett of Sheffield. Stylised rustic scene to the arch; mirrored patterns to the corners still at this late date in the manner of Period Two. Original matching pattern hands in brass.*

often think they recognise a church or castle or bridge or harbour as a certain local landmark, and explain away any differences from reality as being caused by changes over time since the painting was done. In fact the scenes are almost always invented, composed simply as pretty pictures.

When we think about it it is most unlikely that a customer would send a sketch or print or painting of his locality through the clockmaker to the dialmaker for it to be copied. There are occasions when this must have happened, and scenes that are actual representations of places are often named as such on the dial (for example, Kirkstall Abbey). When, however, we see a clock sold from a village such as Pateley Bridge, close to my own home, showing thatched cottages in a land-scape, it is very obvious that these are what the Birmingham dialpainters thought of as typical cottages, since Warwickshire cottages had thatch; cottages in this area had stone roofs, not thatched ones.

Scenes taken from literature or history sometimes appear, but this is more often a feature of Scottish dials, most of which at this time were made in Scotland, as the use of English dials on Scottish-made clocks had by now reduced considerably. See page 188 for stylistic comments on Scottish-made dials.

PLATE 79. *Twelve-inch eight-day dial with rocking Adam and Eve from a longcase clock by John Braund of Hatherleigh, Devon, dating from about 1830. The falseplate is marked with the name of the dialmaker, Finnemore of Birmingham. Note the scrollwork around the lettering, typical of the period.*

PLATE 77. *Twelve-inch eight-day moon dial from a longcase clock by William Robb of Montrose, the dialmaker unknown but certainly an English-made dial and quite probably by Finnemores of Birmingham (note strong resemblance of cornerwork to the dial by Monkhouse in Plate 70). Date 1820-30. Original hands in matching brass pattern, the main hands of a most exceptional style incorporating a bird.*

PLATE 78. *Eleven-inch thirty-hour dial from a longcase clock by Miller of Bedford, dialmaker not marked, and dating from about 1830. A difficult dial to date but the shell corners and original matching-pattern hands in blued steel suggest not later.*

NUMBERING

The numbering of Period Three dials is a very consistent one of Roman hour numerals without any minute numbering at all, though minute divisions are actually marked out on the dial as a double track. These hour numerals may look

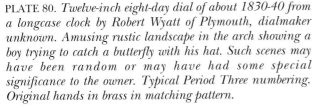

PLATE 80. *Twelve-inch eight-day dial of about 1830-40 from a longcase clock by Robert Wyatt of Plymouth, dialmaker unknown. Amusing rustic landscape in the arch showing a boy trying to catch a butterfly with his hat. Such scenes may have been random or may have had some special significance to the owner. Typical Period Three numbering. Original hands in brass in matching pattern.*

PLATE 81. *Eight-day dial from a longcase clock by John Simpkin of Rillington, North Yorkshire, dialmaker unknown, date about 1830 (the clockmaker died in 1833). Four seasons corner themes, biblical scene in the arch showing the Good Samaritan. Matching pattern hands in blued steel in perhaps unique style each showing a hand with a pointing finger.*

thin and delicate or bold and heavy, they may be long or short, and their shape and proportion seem to be very much a whim of the dialmaker, probably also depending on the dial size. This form of numbering seems to be consistent through this period.

Having said that, I should stress that, although all Period Three numerals are recognisable as being just Roman hours, not all Roman hours indicate Period Three, as there was a limited use of this numbering style towards the end of Period Two.

CALENDARS

In calendar indication we see a continuing of the trend noted in Period Two, namely that the mouth type of calendar was still used on many eight-day clocks and more often on thirty-hour clocks. However, the pointer calendar indicator, matching the seconds hand, grew increasingly popular on eight-day clocks, and towards the end of this period the great majority of eight-days have this pointer form of indicator.

Some clocks have no calendar indication at all, and this is probably more often the case with simple cottage clocks (see Plate 78, Miller dial). Occasionally a

COLOUR PLATE 20. *Detail from the arch of a longcase clock of about 1840-50 showing a scene of domestic bliss but interestingly printed in transfer and then coloured in by hand, an unusual method but perhaps preferable to the more slovenly painting of many dials of this time and allowing for finer detail.*

COLOUR PLATE 21. *Thirteen-inch eight-day dial with rocking Adam and Eve from a longcase clock of about 1840 by George Esplin of Wigan, dialmaker unknown. Typical Period Three numbering with gold band outside the numerals. Landscape corners matching side to side and incorporating pheasants at the top. Original brass hands of matching pattern.*

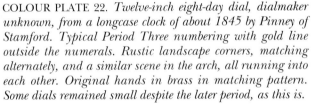

COLOUR PLATE 22. *Twelve-inch eight-day dial, dialmaker unknown, from a longcase clock of about 1845 by Pinney of Stamford. Typical Period Three numbering with gold line outside the numerals. Rustic landscape corners, matching alternately, and a similar scene in the arch, all running into each other. Original hands in brass in matching pattern. Some dials remained small despite the later period, as this is.*

COLOUR PLATE 23. *Twelve-and-a-half-inch (unusual size) eight-day dial of about 1840, dialmaker unknown but clearly English, from a longcase clock by D.W. Laird of Leith, Scotland. Typical romantic landscapes. Period Three numbering with outer gold line. Original hands in matching pattern in brass.*

calendar pointer might be simply a dummy, never having had any gearing but being there just to 'keep up appearances'. The same thing sometimes occurred with seconds hands, and occasionally dummy seconds and dummy calendar hands appear on the same dial, usually late (sometimes thirty-hour) dials of cheap quality.

The old-fashioned forms of centre calendar and arch calendar (page 75) are now long obsolete, but see Plate 223 (Greening dial) for an eccentric late instance on a special clock.

MOONS

Moon dials appear in this period in about the same proportion as in earlier periods, though the moon was possibly a little more commonplace now. There is no particularly different feature on moons of this time, except that sometimes the painting is of lower quality. Sometimes the two moon 'humps' carry painted decoration too (Plate 76, Nicholas dial) instead of the globe transfers in more general use.

Special clocks of course might vary their moon dials considerably, especially if

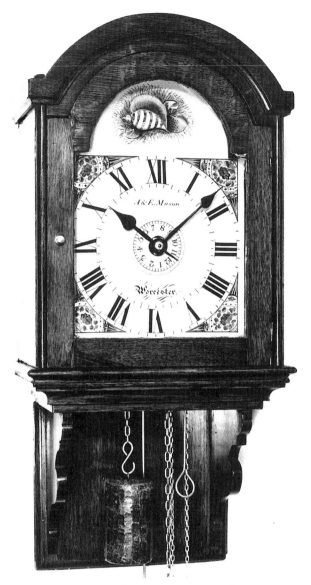

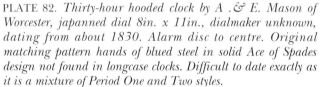

PLATE 82. *Thirty-hour hooded clock by A .& E. Mason of Worcester, japanned dial 8in. x 11in., dialmaker unknown, dating from about 1830. Alarm disc to centre. Original matching pattern hands of blued steel in solid Ace of Spades design not found in longcase clocks. Difficult to date exactly as it is a mixture of Period One and Two styles.*

PLATE 83. *Twelve-inch eight-day dial from a longcase clock of about 1840-50, no falseplate or dialmaker's mark. A restrained dial for the period in size and decoration. Arch carries a transfer-based scene of the postman delivering a letter (see Plate 16 for detail).Original matching pattern hands in brass of thistle-centre motif.*

PLATE 84. *Fourteen-inch eight-day dial of about 1835 from a longcase clock by Robert Richards of Uttoxeter. Falseplate indicates the dialmaker as Francis of Birmingham. Original hands in brass of matching pattern. Classic Period Three style.*

PLATE 85. *Eight-day dial, dialmaker unknown, of a longcase clock by James Scott of Kendal, dating from about 1840. Size unknown but unlikely to be less than thirteen inches. Original blued steel hands in matching pattern, here of the crescent moon type.*

they were to incorporate some unusual feature (see Colour Plate 39, Murray dial, for sunrise/sunset feature incorporated with a moon, and Plate 231, Henderson dial, for a special type of moon linked with tidal rise). The high water tidal features sometimes found on earlier moon dials seem now to have fallen from fashion or at least to be very uncommon.

DIAL SIZE
Dials continue to grow larger, the thirty-hour clock, as always, tending to remain one stage smaller, though sometimes large thirty-hour dials occur. Many dials now reach fourteen inches in width, though certain areas (Scotland for instance) seldom exceed thirteen. Fifteen inches wide was about the limit for even the boldest styles, but in special clocks (such as some musical or astronomical clocks) even wider dials are known.

When John Manby of Skipton bought his clock dials from three different suppliers in the 1830s, he bought nothing other than fourteen-inch dials (see page 122).

HANDS
Period Three hands are normally of matching pattern in brass (Colour Plate 18 and Plates 80 and 84, Wilson, Wyatt and Richards dials). Occasional clockmakers

PLATE 86. *Eight-day longcase dial of about 1840 from a clock by Stokes of Knutsford, Cheshire, the dial made by Wrights of Birmingham. Size uncertain but believed thirteen or fourteen inches. Continued use of the twelve o'clock moon, which is by now uncommon. Original matching pattern hands in brass, here unpolished as dial and hands are unrestored.*

PLATE 87. *Fourteen-inch eight-day moon dial of about 1840 from a longcase clock by Hallam of Nottingham, the falseplate carrying the name of the dialmaker Walker & Hughes of Birmingham. Four Seasons corners. Typical Period Three numbering layout. Original hands in brass in matching pattern.*

PLATE 88. *Thirteen-inch eight-day dial from a longcase clock of about 1850 or perhaps even later, the dialmaker unnamed, clockmaker John Crockett of Pontypridd, Wales. Animal corners match side to side. A gold circle surrounds the minute track, often a late feature. Little Bo Peep in the arch. Original matching pattern hands in brass of the crescent moon style. The four corner paintings link together by continuous painted ground, a late sign. Dial centre is convex.*

still sometimes used matching pattern hands in steel (Plate 75, Northgraves dial), and steel might well be used for special clocks, where the hands were far from conventional (Plate 223, Greening dial).

Usually hands are of well recognised and popular styles. Colour Plate 18 and

PLATE 89. *Eight-day dial of about 1850 or later by John Catchside Elliott of Leeds, dialmaker unknown. Exotic dial with camels in the arch, the corners and arch all linking together in background paint. Gold line outside the minute track. A large dial, perhaps fifteen inches, producing elongated hour numerals. Brass hands of matching type, though they do not match, suggesting one is replaced.*

PLATE 90. *Eight-day dial of late and cheap type (dialmaker unknown), dating from about 1845, from a longcase clock by Richard Blakeborough of Otley, Yorkshire, a maker who numbered his clocks, this being No.2343. Four Continents corner theme; religious scene in the arch of an angel's visitation. Gold line outside the minute track.*

PLATE 91. *Longcase regulator dial from a clock by Harrison & Sons of Darlington, with single winding hole (being a timepiece only) set eccentrically. Hours are shown on the lower dial, minutes from the centre. Such dials would be made specially to order and would not have the coloured decoration normal on an ordinary domestic clock. Dialmaker unknown. Hands of blued steel are of a one-off style to suit the occasion.*

Plates 80 and 84 (Wilson, Wyatt and Richards dials) show styles often met with, though there are many more patterns. An occasional maker might decide to make (or buy?) hands of a more interesting and distinctive style, whether in steel or brass. The finger-pointing hands of Plate 81 (Simpkin dial) and eagle hands of Plate 77 (Robb dial) are examples of this nonconformity, which can make a pleasing change.

ROCKING FIGURES

Examples of rocking figures still occur in this period, but this is now mostly confined to the rocking ship theme. The Adam and Eve rocking figures (Plate 79, Braund dial) are a variant sometimes seen now, but this was never a commonplace form.

OVERALL DIAL DEVELOPMENT

Painting styles progress in this period from acceptable to very heavy, from artistic to crude, from charming to downright gaudy as quality increasingly deteriorated. Poor quality dials can be found at any time in this period, but towards its later stages this is often more apparent.

It may be that quality fell as a result of cut-throat price competition as clock-

PLATE 92. *Eight-day dial of about 1850-60 from a longcase clock by John Waite of Bradford, dialmaker unknown. The Four Continents fill the corners with the Garden of Eden in the arch, all crudely painted. Gold line outside the minute track and the corner paintings join together in background, both late features.*

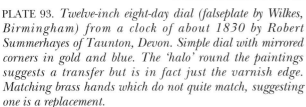

PLATE 93. *Twelve-inch eight-day dial (falseplate by Wilkes, Birmingham) from a clock of about 1830 by Robert Summerhayes of Taunton, Devon. Simple dial with mirrored corners in gold and blue. The 'halo' round the paintings suggests a transfer but is in fact just the varnish edge. Matching brass hands which do not quite match, suggesting one is a replacement.*

PLATE 94. *Thirteen-inch dial, maker unnamed, from an eight-day clock of about 1850 by Robert Marshall of Shotley Bridge, County Durham. This 'Little Bo Peep' style was popular and often, as here, had an all-gold background to the paintings. Matching brass hands, though the calendar is a dummy, never having had any gearwork – probably for cheapness.*

makers struggled increasingly to compete with cheap imported clocks. Certainly a dial could be bought in the 1840s for one third of the price of a 'similar' dial of the 1780s, though of course the quality was probably much lower. It seems that in the later stages of the longcase clock the clockmaker was seeking a more down-market customer and he probably cheapened his product to this end.

Iorwerth C. Peate quotes in his book *Clock and Watch Makers in Wales* a letter from the son of clockmaker William Williams of Dolgellau, who was working in the 1870s:

> When I was a lad my father had in his shop nothing but large eight-day clocks with William Williams on the dials. They were not made in Wales. When a young couple were married, in particular a farmer's son or labourer, his ambition was to buy one of these clocks as the principal piece of furniture for the house and scores of these are to be found up and down the countryside.

This type of customer could not have afforded such a clock in earlier periods, when the price would have kept it above the purchasing power of a labourer. It was perhaps in an attempt to sell to this kind of market that quality was reduced after the mid-nineteenth century.

CHAPTER NINE

ORIGINAL PRICES OF DIALS AND CLOCKS

Original prices of dials, clocks-with-dials, and complete clocks with cases are very difficult to uncover, yet when we can trace examples these are most illuminating as offering an indication of the status of the object relative to earnings of the day. The source records for these facts can also in themselves illustrate trade practices: what did the clockmaker make and when? what did he buy and when? did he opt to buy or was he obliged to buy? what did he charge for his product? and so on.

Some years ago my attention was drawn by the then county archivist for Westmorland, Miss S.J. MacPherson, to a document then unpublished relating to the transfer of stock of a retiring clockmaker to his successor in the year 1800. The clockmaker was the Jonas Barber (junior) of Winster mentioned on page 60. His successor was his former apprentice and journeyman, Henry Phillipson.

Many aspects of this stock are of interest to us. The clocks, as yet unfinished, were all of the japanned dial type, as brass dials were by this time long obsolete. We can suppose that the stock was being passed on at cost, or maybe a slightly discounted price below cost. Barber was holding a stock of sixteen dials, four eight-day movements and seven thirty-hour movements.

This is exactly the sort of information we need to illustrate how the white dial clock trade worked, and as it happens it confirms the view I have already suggested. We must bear in mind that this particular clockmaker was about eighty years old and might have been holding a lesser stock than a younger man pursuing his trade more vigorously.

He held sixteen dials but only eleven movements, which supports my view that a stock of dials was held ahead of orders to enable the customer to select from stock. When time allowed (as here) movements would be made up ready to fit the dials. A stock of ready-made movements of both thirty-hour and eight-day type meant that any customer's order could be assembled without delay, provided of course the movements were made to a standard fitting system (whether with or without falseplates). In fact we know that Barber generally used dials at this time from James Wilson of Birmingham, with falseplate fittings on his eight-day clocks, none of course on his thirty-hours. We cannot be certain that his stock of dials was from Wilson, but this is quite likely.

The dial price structure was as follows (my words in brackets):

Double Moon Clock Faces, 13in (arched moon dials)	£1. 2s 0d
Land Skip 13in (landscape painted in arch)	16s 0d
30 hours, 13in with arches (arched dial)	14s 0d
13in square	12s 0d
12in with arches	14s 0d
12in square	10s 0d
11in square	8s 0d

The 'double moon' type was his description of an ordinary rolling moon dial and cost three times as much as the simple eleven-inch square dial. Also in the document was listed 'seven pair of Pointers (i.e. hands) at 7d per pair'.

This was the first price list of japanned dials ever published (in my 1974 book). However, a few years later Alan Treherne was researching amongst the business archives of the company of Peter Stubs, the Warrington toolmakers, when he came across the following printed and dated price list from dialmakers Wilkes & Son of Birmingham:

Birmingham, January 1820
Prices
of
JAPANNED CLOCK DIALS
manufactured
by
WILKES & SON
Whittall-street, Birmingham.

Fourteen inch Arch Moon dial	£1 4s 0d
Thirteen inch ditto ditto	£1 2s 0d
Twelve inch ditto ditto	£1 0s 0d
Fourteen inch square ditto	£1 2s 0d
Thirteen inch ditto	£1 0s 0d
Twelve inch ditto ditto	18s 0d
Fourteen inch Solid Arch Eight Day	16s 0d
Thirteen inch ditto ditto	14s 0d
Twelve inch ditto ditto	12s 0d
Fourteen inch Square ditto	14s 0d
Thirteen inch ditto ditto	12s 0d
Twelve inch ditto ditto	11s 0d
Fourteen inch round ditto	13s 0d
Thirteen inch ditto ditto	11s 0d
Twelve inch ditto ditto	10s 0d
Thirteen inch Arched Thirty-hour	13s 0d
Twelve inch ditto ditto	11s 0d
Eleven inch ditto ditto	10s 0d
Fourteen inch Square ditto	13s 0d
Thirteen inch ditto ditto	12s 0d
Twelve inch ditto ditto	10s 0d
Eleven inch ditto ditto	8s 6d
Ten inch ditto ditto	7s 0d
Fourteen inch Round ditto	12s 0d
Thirteen inch ditto ditto	10s 0d
Twelve inch ditto ditto	9s 0d
Six inch Round Spring Dial	7s 0d
Eight inch ditto ditto	8s 0d
Six inch Arch ditto	8s 6d
Eight inch ditto ditto	10s 0d

Oval and Round Dials of all Sizes

Additional Paintings and Movements charged as follows:

Seasons, Quarters, Virtues, Elements, Etc	8s 0d
Landscapes or Figure Pieces in Arch	4s 0d
Single Figures painted in Arch	2s 0d
Adam and Eve to move	7s 6d
Ditto if Serpent to move	10s 0d
Ship to move, Old Time,Etc	6s 0d
Swan's Neck to move	6s 0d
Boy and Girl swinging, Harlequin & Columbine,Etc	7s 0d
Shuttlecock and Battledore to move	7s 0d

Movements and Paintings of every Description.
Printed by R.Peart, Bull-street, Birmingham.

Wilkes called them japanned dials, which was probably the most widely-used term. All manner of permutations were available and the price structure is not dissimilar to that of Jonas Barber's stocklist.

Dials with a fixed arch (called here a solid arch) were cheaper than those with a moon or moving figure; square were cheaper than arched; round were cheaper than square – smaller dials needed less metal and less artwork than larger ones. Thirty-hours were cheaper than eight-day, as they would involve less artwork, having no seconds dial lettering. 'Spring dials' were dials for bracket clocks. Small arched dials (six inch and eight inch) were for bracket clocks too, or perhaps also for hooded clocks, though hooded clocks were old-fashioned by this time. Oval dials were available, though not priced.

The optional extras may need explanation. Seasons were the Four Seasons corner patterns; quarters were the four Continents, i.e. the four quarters of the world; virtues were the four virtues or four graces (faith, hope, charity and justice); elements were the four elements (earth, air, fire, water). All these are corner motifs popular at this period. They were extra in price because they involved more artwork than a simple flower spray or pattern.

'Single figures' in arch means the vignette type of painting as in Plate 58 (Burton, Kendal). Adam and Eve dials are self-explanatory, though some more complex versions had the serpent moving as well. 'Old Time' means a rocking Father Time. 'Shuttlecock and battledore' was the old term for what we now call badminton. By 'movements', of course, they mean moving figures, not clock movements. Rocking figures could be made to any design of the customer's inclination apart from the ones on regular offer.

An example of this was drawn to my attention by Canon Miles-Brown, author of *Cornish Clocks & Clockmakers*. This is the clock formerly in the Levant Mine count-house, which has a Walker & Hughes falseplate dial with a scene in the arch showing a mine (engine house, cables, shaft, etc.) entitled 'Levant Mine, St. Just'. Interestingly it is not a true representation of the Levant Mine, which stands on a clifftop, nor is the winding engine remotely like any used in the region. The artist had apparently only a vague idea of what a mine looked like. Nevertheless the dial must have been specially ordered – 'One arched dial please, the arch to show the Levant Mine'. One wonders what the reaction was when the clock was delivered.

Occasionally one sees a dial made in a particular personalised way and using the name of the owner for numbers, a system occasionally used on brass dial clocks too. The dial lettered 'John Brown, wheelwright' in Plate 72 is a similar principle but uses tools for numbers.

Customer-requested scenes I have come across include a dial showing and lettered as the Leeds Cloth Hall, and one showing and lettered as Carisbrooke Castle (in the Isle of Wight), though this too bears no resemblance to the real Carisbrooke Castle. This lack of resemblance to the real scene arose from the centralisation of dialmaking in Birmingham, where the artist might be willing but ignorant of the realities of the building called for.

On later Scottish-made dials it is not uncommon for the arch scene, maybe one from history or literature, to be titled: for example, Lady of the Lake, Escape of Mary Queen of Scots, etc. This is relatively uncommon in English-made dials, however. For further information on Scottish-made dials see Chapter 14.

Some interesting business records are preserved concerning the clockmaker John Manby, who set up shop in Skipton, Yorkshire, about 1815. Many invoices are preserved concerning the goods he bought, with sales ledgers of those he sold, and these go back to about 1822. The family business still continues today as iron-mongers, and I am obliged to them for allowing me to examine some of these accounts, extracts from which appear below.

John Manby was typical of thousands of country clockmakers and hardwaremen of this period. He bought his clock dials from Birmingham from at least 1832 from Joseph May of St. Paul's Square, from 1833 from Messrs. Mabson, Labron & Mabson, 'gunmakers', and from 1837 from John Balleny of 50, St.Paul's Square, and no doubt from others too. These were merchants who supplied the hardware and clock trades with all kinds of wares. The dials from Mays seem to have been almost half the usual price, but perhaps of poorer quality, as Manby bought from two other suppliers at the same time despite having to pay the full price there. It is interesting to compare these prices with those we have already seen dating from as much as thirty years earlier. Mabsons charged for '14inch arch 30 hour dials, assorted pattern, no seconds, open month (or mouth?) and named (i.e. with seller's name painted on) ...' 15s.0d. each. This was in 1833 and 1835.

Balleny charged in 1837 (the bracketed words are mine):

14inch arch 8day dials, solid months & seconds	16s 0d
14inch ditto, 30 hour	15s 0d
14inch ditto with convex* centres	16s 0d
[*see Plate 88 dial by Crockett]	

However in 1832 and 1835 May's dials were much cheaper:

14inch arch 30 hour	7s 6d
14inch 8day	8s 0d
14inch 30hour single figures	7s 0d (hour numbers only?)
14inch 30hour ship to move	12s 6d (rocking ship in arch)
14inch 30hour Adam & Eve	14s 6d (automata in arch)

It is interesting that Manby bought nothing less than fourteen inches in width – a measure of the fashionable dial size of the day.

Manby bought other clock fittings from these suppliers, some of the prices being (descriptions as in the accounts, my words in brackets):

spire clock balls, set of three	1s 5d (spire finials)
eagle clock balls, set of three	1s 7d (eagle finials)
clock hands, per pair	8d
seconds hands, each	2d
clock case hinges, each	4d
2inch clock roses (paterae), approx. each	½d

We must bear in mind that these seemingly trivial prices were measured at the time against a weekly wage of £1 a week for a first-class craftsman, such as a clockmaker. An extra four shillings for a landscape in the arch represented more or less an extra day's wages into the cost of the item. With the later, half-price dials no doubt the quality was much lower. John Manby bought his movements from Greaves & Newton, 'knifemakers', Portobello Works, Sheffield, not as complete ones but in ready-to-assemble form. Movements seem to have been bought by weight of worked materials at so much per pound weight:

3 sets of 8d(ay) clock, brass at 1s lb
3 sets of forg'd work & pinions at 1s2d.

There are a number of such entries, some more explicit, costing the brass parts and steel parts separately. Jonas Barber too had sold his (?already assembled) movements by the pound weight:

Seven 30 hours movements 39½ pound @ 1s 4d lb = £2 12s 8d

This system of selling worked materials by weight may have been the standard method used in the trade, though I know no other reference book which mentions the practice.

Manby sold 'a new clock & balls' to a Mr Lister of Grassington, a joiner, for £4.2s.0d. We can assume that this was without a case, which Lister would presumably have made himself. Manby's charge for cleaning a clock was a very reasonable 1s.6d. Gillows, the Lancaster cabinetmakers, sometimes sold cases complete with clocks, the clock part supplied by a clockmaker, of course. One such clock they sold in 1771 was charged out at £4.4s.0d, plus a case for £3.13s.6d, presumably a brass dial eight-day clock. In 1799 Gillows paid £2.11s.0d for a thirty-hour clock with 'china' dial from Newbys of Kendal. This would be a japanned dial, which Newbys would have got from Birmingham for a movement they had made themselves. This was to be sold by Gillows in a case of their own making. Depending on materials and quality a case from Gillows in 1771 would have cost as little as £2.5s.0d to as much as £10.0s.0d, the lower extreme in pine, the upper in mahogany.

Seldom is the original bill of sale preserved with a clock. One brought to my attention recently was an eight-day solid arch white dial clock by Benjamin Cope of Franch(e), near Kidderminster, It reads:

clock	£4 10s 00d
case	£4 0s 00d
glass	4s 2d
	£8 14s 2d

On 4 March 1795 a group of twenty or so local clockmakers met at the Admiral Rodney Inn in Leicester to set up a price-fixing ring, which they called the Society of Watch and Clock Makers in Leicestershire. John Deacon, son of the Samuel Deacon mentioned earlier, was secretary and treasurer. They resolved to set a minimum price list below which no member would sell his clocks (or watches). If anyone broke the agreement and undercut his 'competitors' in price, then the others agreed to subsidise work in order to underprice the offender and run him out of business. The only loser was the customer! These were the agreed minimum prices *without* cases:

30 hours		
square or round dial	12 inch	£3 0s 0d
ditto ditto	13 inch	£3 3s 0d
arch ditto	12 inch	£3 7s 0d
ditto ditto	13 inch	£3 10s 0d
8day (with or without seconds)		
square or round	12 inch	£4 12s 0d
ditto ditto	13 inch	£4 14s 6d
solid arch	12 inch	£4 17s 0d
ditto	13 inch	£5 0s 0d
landscape or figure	12 inch	£5 0s 0d
ditto	13 inch	£5 5s 0d
	14 inch	£5 10s 0d

PLATE 95. *Square dial oak case with pitched (and pierced, which is unusual) pediment, crossbanded in mahogany for a thirty-hour clock by Samuel Deacon of Barton, Leicestershire made in 1803. Shell inlay to door typical of the period. Simple style yet with a few refinements. Dial by James Wilson, Birmingham, described in the original receipt as 'best face'. The case probably cost under £1. A casemaker's printed label inside the door reads: 'J.Hopson, cabinet manufacturer, 33 Church St., Shoreditch – Thomas Clark', indicating that Hopson made it for Clark, who supplied it to Deacon.*

Moon		12 inch	£5 10s 0d
	ditto	13 inch	£5 15s 6d
	ditto	14 inch	£6 0s 0d

NB the above with common steel hands. If gilt ones they must be charged extra.

For extra painting	25% on the Birmingham prices.
Cases oak/deal plain	10% on joiner's wholesale
ornamented ditto	15% ditto
plain mahogany ditto	20% ditto
ornamental mahogany ditto	25% ditto

It is interesting to note the availability of 'gilt hands' as early as this, and this is the oldest evidence I know to prove their use. They would of, course, be in matching pattern in brass, then gilded.

Round dials were popular in this area, and though they were a little cheaper from the dialmakers (about a shilling each) this list of prices makes no allowance for that fact. So the clockmaker had an extra shilling profit when he sold any round dial clock.

Round dials were not popular in all areas, though an occasional example can crop up almost anywhere. The area of their greatest popularity was in the Northern Midlands – Derbyshire, Nottingham-shire, Leicestershire and South Yorkshire. Some clockmakers seem to have almost specialised in round dials, as this form is seen regularly in the work of certain clockmakers.

Oval dials seem to have been available from very early white dial times, perhaps the late 1770s or 1780s. These were seldom used and are uncommon today, probably because they were never very popular. This may have been because of the difficulty of fitting an oval dial into a conventional hood shape of the day. Round dials could impose some awkwardness of design into a clock hood, and each enthusiast must decide for himself the degree to which the casemaker succeeded or failed when housing any individual round dial example. This problem was greatly increased with an oval dial, and it is probable that such dials were only ever supplied by special order.

A very interesting account of the problems with oval dials is recounted by Patrick Hewitt in his article on the Deacon family in *Antiquarian Horology* for December 1986, and this explains why we see few of them. Samuel Deacon (of Barton) had made a clock with an oval white dial for a Colonel Wolaston, who had later changed his mind and cancelled, leaving Deacon with a clock which was very difficult to sell. Deacon asked him to consider taking the clock anyway, even if only to put in the kitchen, since nobody wanted to

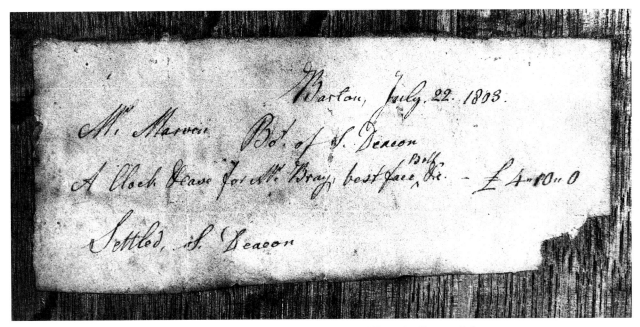

PLATE 96. *Original receipt pasted inside the door of the case of Plate 95 reads: 'Barton July 22 1803. Mr.Marven Bot. of S.Deacon A Clock & case for Mr.Bray, best face, bell, etc. £4.10.0. Settled S.Deacon.' The clock cost was about £3.10s.0d. of this. Such a receipt is a very rare survival and adds greatly to the interest of a clock, though not necessarily to its value.*

buy oval dial clocks and he expected it might take him up to eighteen months to find another buyer for it.

Over the years I suppose I have come across less than twenty clocks with oval-shaped dials. I have never yet owned one as I have not found the style attractive. However some enthusiasts do find these clocks highly desirable because of their uncommonness.

There is no reason a dial could not have been made to any shape at all. I saw one once with a rectangular dial about half as tall again as it was wide (12 inches), but it struck me as very unappealing in appearance, rare though it undoubtedly was. I also saw one once with a pointed arch to the dial, a most eccentric shape echoed in the case hood, and probably made specially for a customer who wanted to be different (see Plate 232, rosewood clock).

An interesting example of a square dial thirty-hour clock by Samuel Deacon of Barton in its original case and with its original receipt is seen in Plates 95 and 96. This has a twelve-inch Wilson dial with double Arabic numbering and cost £4.10s.0d in 1803. It is described as 'best face' indicating that Deacon regarded Wilson's as being the best quality dials. Judging by the agreed price list, this puts the case at £1.10s.0d.

An eight-day rocking ship arched dial clock by Robert Mortimore of Dartmouth in its original mahogany case (Plate 155) has the original price chalked inside the door, with the date October 13 1817 – £9.0s.0d. with a further 3s.0d., probably being the glass price. When clocks were being shipped to some distance by the clockmaker, he often gave the option of having the clock with or without glass, probably on account of the risk of its breaking in transit.

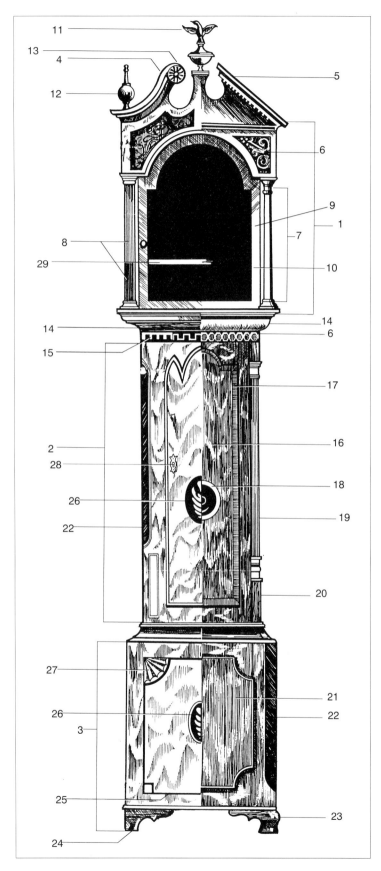

FIGURE 3. *Terms used in describing casework.*
1. *Hood*
2. *Trunk or body*
3. *Base*
4. *Swan-neck pediment*
5. *Architectural pediment*
6. *Blind fretting*
7. *Pillar caps and bases*
8. *Fluted pillar with double-reeded base*
9. *Plain pillar*
10. *Hood door*
11. *Eagle finial*
12. *Spire finial*
13. *Patera (plural paterae)*
14. *Top of trunk moulding*
15. *Dentil moulding (simple left, key pattern centre)*
16. *Trunk door*
17. *Crossbanding*
18. *Lenticle glass*
19. *Fluted quarter columns*
20. *Pedestal for quarter column*
21. *Base panel*
22. *Canted corner*
23. *Ogee bracket foot*
24. *Plain bracket foot*
25. *Stringing line*
26. *Shell inlay*
27. *Fan inlay*
28. *Escutcheon plate*
29. *Seatboard*

CHAPTER TEN

Long Cases: General Considerations

The subject of clock casework is a massively complicated one even when we select a relatively short period such as that of painted dial clocks, covering as it does approximately a century. There are several reasons for this, principal amongst them being that a clock was frequently a custom-made item and might reflect in its style not only the whims or fancies and preferred dimensions of the *owner* but also those of the *cabinetmaker*, those of the *period*, those of the *region*, and those determined by the *cost* and by the size of the *dial*. Given that every owner might have different tastes, the wonder is not so much that styles are so very varied but that there is any regular stylistic sequence at all.

The drawing in Figure 3 shows a hybrid clock case, which never existed in reality, combining many of the features we shall need to examine, and detailing the terminology of casework. A longcase is essentially only a box, its purpose being to hold the clock at an adequate height from the floor to give it the required duration of run via the weight drop and to keep it reasonably free from dust and from tampering fingers. A tall apple box with a hole for the dial would do the job, and some ancient cases do exist which are little more than that. By the time of the painted dial clock, however, we have passed on a bit from apple boxes. But where did all the complicated features in this drawing originate? How do we make any sense of the vast variety of shapes sizes and styles? Is there in fact any sense in them, or are they no more than a hotchpotch of fancy features showing off the cabinetmaker's skills? Let us first examine some basic aspects.

DIAL SIZE

The case has to fit the dial, so everything begins with the dial size (and shape), which will probably vary between eight-day and thirty-hour examples. At the start of the painted dial period thirty-hour dials might be as small as eleven inches, eight-days as small as twelve. Exceptions are known, such as ten-inch thirty-hour and eleven-inch eight-day, but these are very unusual. Each type grew rapidly in size as the dial, which was after all the most important part of any clock, grew more important and usually more colourful.

In general the thirty-hour clock was a cheaper type, made for a less well-to-do customer who lived in a smaller house with lower ceilings and therefore had considerable height limitation on his case size. Thirty-hour dials were simpler, cheaper (less artwork on the dial) and usually smaller (less material in the making). Because of the smaller dial size the thirty-hour clock was capable of being built to smaller overall dimensions than the eight-day, and usually was. It follows that in all periods thirty-hour clock cases were usually smaller, simpler, and cheaper than eight-day ones, and we must separate the two categories when making observations on quality and style.

PROPORTIONS

The more slender the clock, the more unstable it is likely to be, not so much in terms of its being likely to be knocked over as in its easily tilting out of vertical and thereby being thrown out of beat so that it stops. Increasingly cases grew wider, and a wider stance gave the clock greater stability. By 1870 longcase clock dials had reached a width of fourteen inches or more, with the cases having widened to suit. From being a slender, narrow-waisted item the clock case had grown to a

PLATE 97. *A group of three longcases showing the three stages of case development. Right: an oak and mahogany eight-day of about 1790 by Kelvey of Gainsborough showing typical long door. Centre: a mahogany eight-day of about 1820 by Stonehouse of Leeds with short door. Left: a mahogany eight-day of about 1850 by Elliott of Leeds showing short door, short trunk, very high base and broad proportions.*

heavy, often waistless shape, and this change from slim to wide is one marker of the change of style during this century of longcase clockmaking. From what I have already said it will be obvious that the thirty-hour clock, by virtue of its smaller dial, will be less subject to this broadening of style or more slowly subject to it.

In 1770 cases had a long slender trunk with what we call a 'long door', which filled almost all of it (see Plate 98). By 1870 the trunk of a longcase was much shorter, as the base rose higher, and the door was now a 'short door' in a short

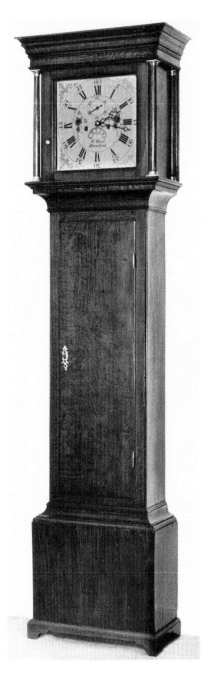

PLATE 98. *Very simple oak-cased cottage clock of the late 1790s housing a twelve-inch eight-day painted dial clock by Henry Ward of Blandford, Dorset, typical of the long door style. Such a case could equally well house a brass dial clock of this time, and is little changed from a cottage case of half a century earlier. Height 6ft 8in.*

trunk (see Plate 185). These two extremes summarise in oversimplified manner the development of longcases over that period. Around the 1810-1840 period there is an in-between style, referred to as a three-quarter length door, whereby the trunk is still relatively long but the door has shortened, leaving a space below the door which is often filled with a panel for decoration (see Plate 178). Clearly there is much more to it than this, but the door style, shape and proportion will alone give a very broad indication of period, especially when we combine this with the factor of overall width originating from dial size.

WOODS
The choice of timber may have a bearing on the period of the clock but certainly will have a bearing on its calibre and therefore its style. It would generally be safe to assume that the thirty-hour cottage clock, made down to a price, would hardly be in the rarest and costliest woods embellished with inlays, frettings and carvings; a grand, gentleman's clock would not be in cheap wood and is unlikely to have been plain. Those master cabinetmakers keen to show off their skills and knowledge of architectural concepts and furniture design were unlikely to be making thirty-hour clocks in pine.

By 1770 it is safe to say that only three timbers were in use for (longcase) clock casemaking – pine, oak and mahogany. Other fancier woods (rosewood, satinwood, etc.) were used in inlay work, bandings, etc. but not in the main construction. Humbler woods (such as elm, solid walnut and fruitwoods) had run their course by 1770, had been tried and found wanting. The cheapest serviceable timber regularly available was pine (deal is the same thing), despite the fact that it was often imported from Norway as well as, of course, from Scotland. A simple clock case of pine could cost under ten shillings (50p), a more complex one £1. Oak was next in the hierarchy and a simple oak case could be bought for about fifteen shillings (75p), a more complex one for £1.5s.0d. (£1.25p). Mahogany, the King of Woods, was hauled halfway across the world from the Americas and West Indies before being selectively sawn, and its best cuts made into fine veneers. Its principal ports of entry were London and the ports of the Atlantic seaboard – Bristol, Liverpool, Lancaster and Glasgow. A very modest mahogany clock case could cost anywhere from about £4 upwards and a fancy one £10. It is immediately obvious that mahogany is in a world of its own and that we are likely to see very few thirty-hour clocks in mahogany. American walnut (known here as red walnut and looking a little like plain-grain mahogany) also came into the west coast ports, but its use in longcase work had largely passed by 1770.

Pine was originally sold with a painted surface, black or green or whatever colour you painted the house woodwork. Today we mostly see it as stripped pine, with all the knots, nailheads and filler showing, which is the current fashion but quite contrary to what was intended originally. When stripped down to bare wood it is often found that a pine case is a mixture of all manner of oddments of varying

woods, perhaps including sections of oak or beech, as such a mixture would have been concealed by the painted surface. Pine has a rather miserable figuring, at least one not thought worthy of showing in the past, though today's pine devotees may throw their hands up in horror. Pine was a relatively soft wood, very prone to woodworm, and would not lend itself to much finely detailed work in the way that oak or mahogany would. Pine clocks are therefore likely to be of the cheaper type (at original cost, that is), simple in style, and probably of small height to suit cottage ceilings. Pitch pine was stronger but was also painted.

Mahogany was a densely-grained and very hard wood, so hard that workmen complained about it at first for spoiling the sharpness of their tools, so hard it was immune to woodworm. Its choice parts showed the most amazing fiery figuring. It was capable of being minutely worked and shaped by carving, fretting, piercing, moulding, reeding, turning – in fact it was so versatile you could do with it anything of which any wood was capable. It follows that mahogany was used for cases on clocks for those customers who could afford the best, cases which were the grandest, fanciest, most ornate and lavish ever made, and which would probably also be amongst the tallest, since their wealthy purchasers owned grand houses with very tall ceilings. By and large the person who bought a fine mahogany clock did not live in a cottage, so a small (cottage sized) mahogany clock, other than perhaps a very plain one, is a most unusual exception.

Mahogany might be used in solid or veneer form. Most all-mahogany cases were constructed of solid, straight-sawn mahogany (sometimes called slash-sawn) of quite plain, figureless appearance in all but the front, which was usually veneered with the best-figured pieces, either used to form patterns (for example by bookmatching) or as single flame sheets. Bookmatching describes the method of applying two consecutive slices of veneer side by side, the second slice reversed as, for example, on the door of a clock, to produce a mirror image side to side, like the pages of an open book. This highly-figured mahogany is sometimes called flame mahogany or crotch mahogany, being cut from the crotch of a tree, which is the part where a large branch joined the main trunk. Any tree, therefore, had a very limited amount of crotch wood, which was highly sought after and was used exclusively as veneer. This was partly because it was too costly to use as solid and partly because the stresses and tensions in such complex

PLATE 99. *Pine-cased thirty-hour cottage clock made about 1840 by Webber of Ilfracombe,Devon. In this example the case style has changed very little in half a century apart from the somewhat broader proportions, because of the larger dial. Height 6ft 2in.*

PLATE 100. *Hood of oak-cased eight-day clock of about 1790 by Eli Stott of Wakefield in its original, highly-typical Leeds-made case with mahogany trim. Note the mahogany crossbanding is set in from the edge of the hood door and trunk door in a distinctive way. This is a common style of case in the area at this time, but this one, quite exceptionally, is punch-stamped with the cabinetmaker's mark – W. Westmoreland, Leeds'.*

PLATE 101. *Rear of upper door on the Eli Stott case (Plate 100) showing the punch-lettered stamp of cabinetmaker William Westmoreland of Leeds. He is known to have been in business in 1786, when he advertised for more workmen, including a clock casemaker, which implies this was a specialist branch within the trade.*

wood would have led to movement such as warping and splitting. Crotch mahogany is unlikely to be seen on cottage cases.

Mahogany could also be quarter-sawn, a treatment more often associated with oak and described below. Quarter-cut mahogany was used in solid form to produce a more interesting figuring than straight-sawn, though nothing so wild as crotch mahogany.

Oak was somewhere in between. Oak cases could be simple, cottage clocks made of the one timber only with little in the way of fancywork or embellishments, or they could be lavish and ornate, akin to mahogany ones. Oak could be quarter-sawn for greater strength and fancy figuring, a more wasteful method of cutting done by sawing wedge-shaped pieces; or it could be straight-sawn, done by slicing planks along the trunk length, which was a cheaper method with less waste but with hardly any figuring. In practice oak was mostly used in quarter-cut form for the frontal area of the case, which was the part that showed most and had larger panels needing greater strength and resistance to warping, and was used in straight-sawn form for the sides and other less visible areas. The door and base panels were the largest individual areas of the clock, thus needing greatest strength against warping or splitting.

Other than in the simplest cottage clocks oak was very often mixed with mahogany, the latter used for crossbanding, veneered sections, applied frets, and so on. By 1770 oak alone (i.e. used as a single timber) was falling from fashion and increasingly was mixed with mahogany trim. By the second quarter of the nineteenth century mahogany increasingly took over and by mid-century oak (especially oak used as the sole timber) was becoming unusual in longcase work.

Oak cases were sometimes busily carved, especially on the frontal areas. Most were stained to a near black colour after carving. Almost without exception such carving was done at a later date, often around the end of the nineteenth century, and so is not original to the clock. Most clocks with carved cases are of a slightly earlier period than that which concerns us here (i.e. pre-1770), but an occasional painted dial clock is seen in a carved case (see Plate 138, Pattison case).

In understanding the styles of clocks we have to recognise that case features will usually differ between thirty-hour and eight-day clocks, between cottage style and grander styles, and between the varying timbers used. They will differ too in the varying periods, which will affect overall width and proportion and the long-door/short-door factor. All these aspects will guide us towards the period in question.

REGIONAL FEATURES
There are no books dealing with regional styles of clock casework, other than my own *Grandfather Clocks & their Cases*, which makes a start. However, there are features available to offer us understanding as to the region, though this is a much more complex and imprecise subject than periods. Regional aspects will be pointed out where possible in each illustrated example as we run through them. The grand stylistic division is between North-west England (including Wales) and South-east England, best thought of as splitting the country by a diagonal line, with the extreme centres of influence being London on the one hand and Lancashire on the other. Scotland is a special case dealt with on page 208.

PEDIMENTS
The pediment, being that part of the case closest to and enclosing the dial, so to speak, is the part which most catches the eye, the part which is dominant and from which is formed an immediate impression, favourable or otherwise. This must have been so in the past just as much as it is today, in that from the hood of a

clock we receive an instant signal transmitted by its style. Such a variety of hood and pediment styles exist that with some of the more distinctive types it is possible to recognise immediately the locality of origin.

As an indication of the most obvious sort of stylistic variation by region, let us consider the swan-neck pediment, the style of hood which terminates in two curving 'horns'. The swan-neck was the most popular and most widely-used of all hood pediments throughout the period in question. It had established its popularity well before 1770, and the great majority of all white dial clocks met with will have this pediment, certainly the majority of arched dial clocks (though with square dials flat-topped cases sometimes persisted, mostly for cottage use, and the swan-neck was not popular with London clockmakers, who seem not to have been keen on the painted dial longcase clock anyway).

If we examine a few swan-necks it soon becomes obvious that there are very many variations in the shape, height, boldness and balance, in other words in the interpretation of a swan-neck pediment. So much is this the case that we can often attribute an area style to that feature alone. A typical small and neat 'Edinburgh' style of swan-neck (Plate 200, Morgan clock) is quite different from a North-western swan-neck with infilled centre as used in Lancashire (Plate 140, Scholfield clock). The two are like chalk and cheese. Many other versions exist and we cannot always be sure when the interpretation is a general regional feature or whether it is merely a whim of the particular cabinetmaker.

Many swan-necks are what we might term 'neutral' in that they are moderately well balanced and give no strong indication as to area of origin. Even some which are of strong regional styling may show that style in an extremely obvious or in an understated manner. Sometimes a very strong regional hood style such as that of south Lancashire can be played down by the individual cabinetmaker to the point where it is recognisable only as being a slight variant from 'neutral'.

Other types of hood pediment are met with. The domed top, sometimes called an arch top or break-arch top or broken-arch top (indicating a shouldered arch) was common in earlier periods (i.e. before 1770), but had faded in popularity by the time of the white dial. It is not uncommon for what we today see as a domed top to be in fact a cut-down version of some other pediment such as, for instance, a pagoda or a swan-neck with their upper sections removed. The true domed top is more a Southern than Northern style.

BASES

The base of the clock too varies with certain regional influences. In very general terms a Southern clock (based ultimately on London influence) will tend to have a base which is square or wider than square, i.e. wider than it is tall. A Northern base will often be square or taller than square. Plates 116 and 125 show the two obvious extremes. It follows that where a solid timber is used for the base the grain will normally run horizontally in a Southern clock and vertically in a Northern one, just for strength of construction. With a veneered base in mahogany, for example, the grain of the veneer will normally be vertical even on a Southern clock, just so that it follows the direction of the veneer grain on the door, etc.

Base shape (with consequent grain direction) is such a generalisation that there will be many exceptions, and these will vary with differing periods too, but never-theless it is a useful clue to bear in mind. In fact this principle tends to apply more strongly as time progresses. Some cases will have been shortened later in the base, either to reduce height or remove rot or both, and we need to be careful when considering this aspect to watch for cut-down examples. One guide to a shortened

base is that crossbanding (when present) will usually run round all four sides of a base, and the absence of the lower banding can indicate a shortened base, though there are exceptions to this.

Many clocks have a flush-fronted base, which was normal in most regions. A raised panel in the base, often with clipped corners, as in Plate 117, was sometimes used, especially in Periods One and Two, and this too was primarily a North-western feature. A different type of raised panel was sometimes used in London and environs, having a separate edge beading to it (Plate 125). In London work a beading sometimes formed an apparent panel, giving the same effect. In South-west England, centred on Bristol, a raised base panel was sometimes used having wavy edges, this being a style mostly confined to that region.

DOORS

The trunk door of a clock can be a guide to region too in a very general sense, and therefore also with exceptions. A Southern clock will often have a door top which is flat across the top or of arched shape (Plates 111 and 125); far less often will it have a shaped door top. A Northern clock will sometimes have an arched door top but far more often will have a shaped top, frequently of a combination of curves (Plates 112, 116 and 140). There is of course more likelihood that a simple, cottage-style clock of whatever region will have a flat door top, especially if this is a square dial example with a flat-topped hood, so that for this category the Northern shaped-top rule will apply less strongly.

MOULDINGS

Mouldings can sometimes indicate area, though their style is less reliable when viewed in isolation, and moulding shapes are a greater help when taken in conjunction with other features such

PLATE 103. *Casemaker's chiselled 'signature' on the case of the Rutherford clock (Plate 102) on the lower door frame lip, reading 'W.Hogg, Hawick No.133', which presumably indicates the number of his case. A casemaker's imprint can very easily be overlooked, as this one was for some long time until a certain trick of light revealed it.*

PLATE 102. *Oak case with mahogany trim made about 1810 to house an eight-day clock by William Rutherford of Hawick, showing the neat and relatively neutral style of many cases from East Scotland, based on English styles. Note the neat swan neck and sound-fret in the hood sides. Height 6ft.9in.*

PLATE 104. *Cabinetmaker's label of William Cock of Bristol, hidden well up inside the trunk of a mahogany longcase clock of about 1830 by Thorpe of Bath, probably hidden purposely to avoid owners being tempted to scrape it off, as they often did. Base of the going weight visible on the right; strike weight removed for the photograph.*

as those just described above. The top-of-trunk moulding (the one attached to the upper case body and on to which the hood slides) is generally convex on very early clocks (roughly before 1730) and concave thereafter, so that by virtue of the period white dial clocks normally have a very simple concave mould there (see Plates 111, 113 and 122). Some clocks, however, have what we call an ogee mould there, being part concave and part convex (Plates 112, 114 and 137) and this is usually a feature of some North-western cases, especially from the Lake District and Lancashire. Not all cases from that region have ogee moulds, but cases which do are usually North-western.

Trunk-to-base moulds on clocks from many regions tend also to be very simple concave moulds (see Plates 111, 125 and 141). However a far more complicated and detailed mould was sometimes used again almost exclusively in the North and West of England, and primarily in the North-west but over a much wider area stretching from the Lake District down as far as the Midlands, its highest popularity being again Lancashire, Cheshire and the Lakes. Plates 112, 114, 116

and 140 show this type of complex mould which quite often accompanies canted corners to the base, as in Plates 114, 116 and 117.

Some clocks have a base with square corners to the sides (Plates 111, 112 and 115). The canted corner base (Plate 116) was a feature more often found in the North-west, far less in the South-east. This might be joined to the trunk by a single, square-jointed mould (i.e. two pieces forming the corner), or a canted mould (three pieces forming the corner). Canted base corners, especially with canted trunk-to-base moulds, are a strong North-western feature.

Often a combination will occur of complex trunk-to-base mould, canted base corners and raised base panel, especially in Period One, and the combination of such features is an even stronger regional indication than one feature used in isolation.

CAPITALS

Many clocks from all regions have brass capitals and bases to the hood pillars. Often too in those clocks with swan-neck pediments the cases will have brass paterae terminals on the ends of the swan-necks and often brass finials. The general exceptions to this are very simple country cases, where the joiner has used wood for cheapness, sometimes gilding the turned wooden caps and bases to look like brass. However in North-western England, principally Lancashire and the Lake District, casemakers often avoided this brassware, using wood instead, even on grander mahogany cases, where hood pillar capitals and bases may be in mahogany (sometimes ebony or black wood) and paterae may be carved or turned wooden terminals, any finials often also being of wood. Naturally the greater the number of regional features present together on the one case, the greater the likelihood that they are a regional indicator. Brass reed-like inserts into the lower sections of fluted hood pillars (and/or to the quarter trunk pillars) are a feature of some London work.

FINIALS

Finials themselves are worth a mention. The two types generally met with are of brass and represent a ball surmounted by an eagle with spread wings, or a ball surmounted by a spire. Both are regularly seen and may be found singly or as a set of three, all of the same pattern or mixed in any combination of spires or eagles. A third uncommon pattern is a flaming torch, known as a 'flambeau', which is found on some London clocks and those imitating them.

PLATE 105. *Typical oak and mahogany case of an eight-day clock of about 1840 by William Chapman of Lincoln. The door-centre diamond panel appears on many such cases, as does the yellow stringing in the canted corners and the hood door. Often, as here, the oak is pale in colour to show a strong contrast of the mahogany trim. Height about 6ft.6in. Case made by Henry Blow of Lincoln.*

Many clocks had their finials removed in the past. Some were thought too fussy by past owners. Some (being hollow) were polished till they wore thin from the outside, corroded from the inside and finally collapsed. Many eagle finials were purposely removed during the First War because of the association of the German eagle. For those who wish to replace missing ones, modern reproductions can be bought today, but you'll have to guess which type would be most appropriate.

Some clocks (often country ones) had turned finials made of softwood gilded over. Those mahogany clocks mentioned earlier which shunned brass fittings would have their finials made in mahogany too and usually not gilded, though occasionally carved mahogany paterae were gilded.

FEET

Many clocks have lost their feet or had replacements fitted over the years. With cases which still have original feet, the tendency for ogee bracket feet was stronger in North-west England and even in Western England generally than in the East or South-east, where plain bracket feet would be more usual. This applies most strongly to Period One and increasingly less so as time passed and the bracket-foot fashion changed. London clocks and those of immediate London influence often had a double plinth, one above the other, the lower one shaped into tiny feet at the sides (Plates 125 and 141, Thorndike and Milsome clocks).

By 1800 French feet were becoming fashionable, both in the outward splayed form of the true French foot, and the vertical 'semi-French' foot, whereby the foot itself is simply a downward continuation of the base (see Plates 171 and 109).

Most clocks had four feet but some had front feet only and therefore had to lean against the wall. The tendency towards two feet rather than four was strongest in the North.

FRETS AND INLAYS

In Western England in Period One (decreasing thereafter) there was a taste, especially in mahogany casework, for fretwork and other applied decoration in the form of blind frets in the Chippendale manner, and it is not unusual for a case to be described as 'Lancashire Chippendale' (whether from Lancashire or not), indicating that it has this type of decoration, even though it may not be a Lancashire clock. In Eastern England the taste at this time, again principally in mahogany casework, was often more towards the inlay decoration of Sheraton in stringing panels and sometimes inlays of shells, swags, urns, etc.

For a few years either side of 1800 oak and mahogany cases often had a central inlay in the door and often another in the base

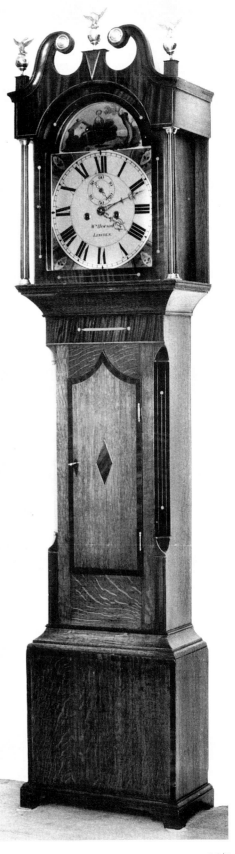

PLATE 106. *Another highly-typical Lincolnshire case of about 1840 in oak with strongly contrasting mahogany trim, diamond to door centre and yellow stringing to canted corners and hood door. The clock is by William Hewson of Lincoln. Height 6ft.8in. Case made by James Usher of Lincoln.*

PLATE 107. *Casemaker's card of Henry Blow of Lincoln, tacked to the back of the William Chapman longcase in Plate 105. Handwritten in ink. Actual size 3½in. x 2½in. Henry Blow regularly left his cards in his cases.*

in the form of a seashell, or urn, or cartwheel, sometimes also having similar inlays of fans in the corners of the door and/or base. This fashion coincides roughly with a similar use of shells on clock dials and may perhaps be the result of voyages to the South Seas which returned home with exotic seashells capturing the public imagination.

Before we can make any attempt at studying this subject, we need to be sure we are considering clocks in their original cases, something we will discuss later. If casemakers had obligingly signed their work it would serve as a considerable aid to recognising that clock and case had been together since new.

CASEMAKERS' LABELS

As a general rule the clock casemaker did not leave any evidence as to who he was, and therefore remains to this day unknown. There are exceptions to this, but they are so unusual as to be noteworthy. The clockmaker was, after all, the man who designed, planned and sold the entire clock complete with its case, and generally he did not want to advertise anyone's skills but his own.

What we shall never know, of course, is just how many casemakers' labels once left inside clock cases have later been removed by owners, who perhaps didn't want the neighbours to know who supplied it, or how much it cost. Over the years I have come across clocks still bearing the label of the casemaker, but not often. Some were general cabinetmakers who included clock cases in their output. Others were makers of clock cases only. Those cases which were the product of a country joiner or carpenter are unlikely to have ever been labelled in this way, so

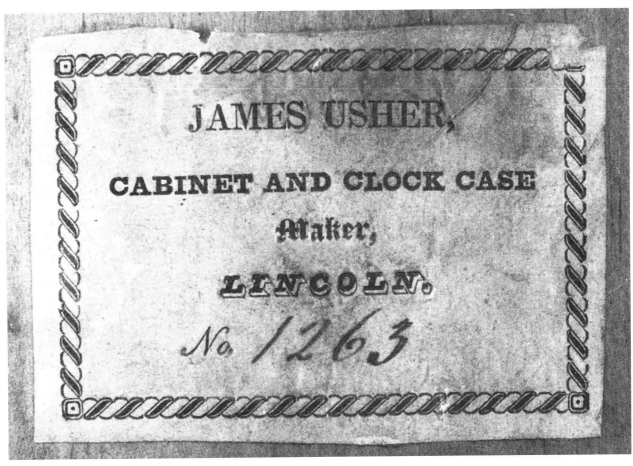

PLATE 108. *Casemaker's printed label inside the William Hewson case (Plate 106) showing the maker as James Usher of Lincoln, actual size about 3in. x 2in. Usher numbered his clock cases, the number of this one is hand-written in ink as 1263. It is unknown whether the number relates to clock cases alone or to cabinets of all types.*

that those we do meet bearing such a label are inclined to be the more sophisticated work of true cabinetmakers. Not many of them labelled their clock cases, but those who did so probably did it on a regular basis and we can assume they did it with the clockmaker's full consent.

An example of a general cabinetmaker who included clock cases in his work was William Cock of Bristol. One mahogany clock case I came across bearing his label (hidden away well up inside the left flank) dated from about 1830 and housed a clock by Thorpe of Bath. The label, only noticed when the case was laid on its back in the cabinetmaker's workshop for repair, read:

> William Cock, camp writing desk inventor and manufacturer, makes every description of clock and spring cases, medecine chests, etc. Cock's Buildings, Hillgrove St., Bristol. Merchants and captains supplied, beer engine cases, bagatelle tables, wholesale & for exportation.

This label probably only survived because it was hidden from obvious view.

Another label by the same man was seen inside a mahogany longcase clock of about 1790 by Eggert of Temple Cloud, Somerset, and read:

> William Cock, clock case manufacturer, Hillgrove Street, Bristol. Camp writing desks made in the neatest manner on moderate terms.

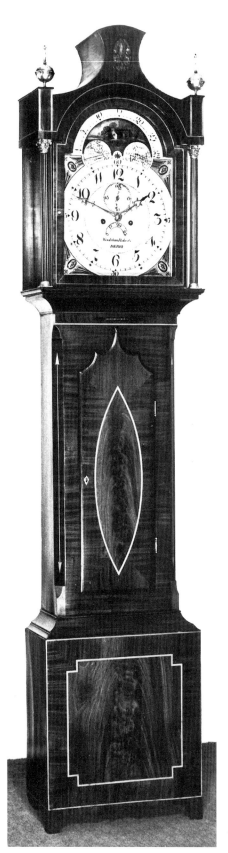

William Cock is mentioned purely as an example of this type of cabinetmaker, in this instance one who seems to have been very proud of his 'camp writing desks', which were portable desks of the type we usually call campaign chests.

Lincolnshire was a county where several casemakers took up the idea of labelling their cases, usually by means of a printed label pasted inside the case on the backboard. Perhaps they copied each other. J. Summerscales of Lincoln, clock casemaker, left such labels in cases in the early nineteenth century, each one numbered in sequence. Charles Oliver of Spalding, Lincolnshire, also left such labels between about 1810 and 1830, and so did John Wilcox of Dyke, near Bourne, in the 1840s and 1850s. Henry Blow of Lincoln left stiff card labels written out in ink in longhand between about 1800 and about 1830 (Plate 107). James Usher, the Lincoln clock case maker, left numbered labels inside the back of his cases in the 1820s and 1830s (Plate 108). Stuart Walker, whose book on Lincolnshire clockmakers is going to press as I write this, has recorded several numbered examples by Usher running from No.573 to 1918, quite a prolific maker. I've seen a number of labels by each of these casemakers over the years, but just why there should be such a concentration in Lincolnshire and an absence elsewhere I have no idea.

CASEMAKERS' PUNCH MARKS

Sometimes a casemaker's mark may go unnoticed, as it may be small and insignificant. Illustrated in Plate 101 is a punchmark made by a cabinetmaker's metal hammer punch and reading 'W. WESTMORELAND, LEEDS'. This was found on the inside of the trunk door of a longcase clock of about 1790 by Eli Stott of Wakefield (Plate 100). This man proved to be a known cabinetmaker who advertised in the *Leeds Mercury* in 1786. This particular case is in a very distinctive Leeds style of the period, probably all made in the same workshop. I have examined many Leeds cases but only on this one did I ever find the punchmark. Punchmarks by other cabinetmakers are occasionally found but may be overlooked or forgotten, especially if the owner does not know where to attempt to look up details of the maker.

Another interesting type of label occasionally found on clock cases is the delivery label or instructions from the casemaker to the clockmaker. These are very uncommon and often infuriatingly fail to specify the casemaker's name and address. They can however be illuminating in showing from just what distances cases were sometimes sent. An example of one is given here in Plate 110, on the case of the clock by Roberts of Derby (Plate 109). See also Plate 96 for an original receipt pasted inside the case of a clock by Samuel Deacon of Barton.

Apart from interest for its own sake, the value of a casemaker's label or even a delivery label is that it can give confirmatory evidence that

PLATE 109. *Mahogany eight-day clock of about 1810-20 by Woolston Roberts of Derby in its original case, which is clearly of the highly distinctive Hull pagoda style. The case was made in Hull and then shipped to Derby. Height 7ft.2in.*

PLATE 110. *The original delivery instructions are still pasted on the backboard of the Woolston Roberts case (Plate 109), written in rather erratic spelling: 'Mr. Wolster Roberts Watch & Clock maker, Derby, 2 Clock Cases to be forwarded Direct with A Derby Boat With great Care and kept Dry By the Nottingam Steem Packet to Gainsbro'. The steam packet was the delivery boat. The casemaker is unfortunately not named.*

the case is original to the clock, as for instance when we have a Lincoln clock in a Lincoln case. But what about the vast majority which have no such labels? Can we tell if the clock is in its original case, and, if so, how?

CHAPTER ELEVEN

CASES, PERIOD ONE (1770-1800)

Clock casemaking continued in exactly the same way when the new japanned dial arrived as it had previously. The earliest white dial cases would therefore have been very similar if they had been made to house brass dial clocks. In fact cabinetmakers and clock casemakers during the overlap period of about 1770 to 1790 must have supplied cases which could house either type. Amongst the earliest are those very simple country longcases, such as those shown in Plates 111, 112 and 122 (Rogers, Hargraves and Bullock clocks), often of oak but sometimes of pine or fruitwood, and even conceivably in plainer mahogany.

Square dials were probably the simplest to house and such clocks in oak or pine would be amongst the cheapest – cheap because the square dial was one of the cheapest forms of dial, and because the square-dial case was also easier to make than a similar arched or round dial as it involved less work in the hood. These cases are usually small in height (often between 6ft.6in. and 7ft.), as an arched dial would have added a few inches in the dial plus some shaped pediment to the case. Such very simple painted-dial cottage clocks of the last quarter of the eighteenth century often looked little different from their brass-dial equivalents of even fifty years earlier. The long door shape and long trunk is obvious. Although some such clocks have considerable crossbanding in mahogany and even fluted quarter-columns to the trunk (Plate 112, Hargraves), they are still simple cottage clocks. Occasional examples were a little grander by virtue of such things as a pediment, finials, raised base panel, etc. (see Plate 114). After the end of the century, however, this simple type begins to disappear in favour of more complex versions.

It can be very obvious when contrasting North-western with South-eastern 'country' case styles that the former are made far more strongly in the quality and thickness of timbers used, and more ornately and expensively in the cross-bandings and/or fluted columns and complex mouldings. A North-western cottage case can often be much sturdier, stronger, heavier and showier than, for example, its East Anglian counterpart. Compare the Owen and Russell cases in Plates 114 and 115. The Russell case with its light pine backboard can literally be carried (empty) under one arm; two men would struggle to carry the body of the Owen clock with its ¾in. heavy oak backboard. Whether you prefer one or the other aesthetically is a very different and much more personal matter. I am here referring to cottage style casework and not to high-blown London or London-quality cases.

The several features which together may indicate a general or even precise region may individually be little more than clues, but the combined effect of a number of such features on a single case is often very helpful, and the more so as experience adds to the enthusiast's overall view of style. But none of the individual features can be relied on entirely as an unfailing guide.

The square dial was also made in grander form in mahogany, and North-west England probably excelled at this form. Plates 116, 117, 118 and 119 show how the form is now much more ornate with book-matched veneers, fluting, inlays, dentil moulds and swan-neck pediments making these clocks far more imposing. They tend to have larger dials, are taller in height (between 7ft. and 7ft.6in. or taller), and are usually of stockier proportion. The trunk is still a long one with a long door but bands of decoration are beginning to appear above the door, and

PLATE 111. *Simple cottage case standing 6ft.9in., housing an eight-day clock by Rogers of Leominster, here unusually in fruitwood with a mahogany fret to the hood. Date about 1790 but such a simple style continues a tradition almost unchanged from half a century earlier. Separate hood pillars now are normal instead of pillars integral with the hood door which were used earlier. Simple moulds above and below the trunk are Southern features, as is the flat-topped door. An interesting comparison with Plate 112.*

PLATE 112. *Simple cottage case in quarter-sawn oak, about 7ft., housing a thirty-hour clock of about 1790 by Hargraves of Settle, Yorkshire. Crossbanded in mahogany to the door, hood door and base and with a mahogany band below the hood topmould. Mahogany is used too for the fluted hood pillars and trunk quarter-pilasters. Key pattern dentil mould to hood top. The highly-complex trunk-to-base mould is a strong North-western feature, as is the ogee mould to the top of the trunk and also the shaped door top.*

PLATE 113. *Eight-day clock of about 1790 by Evans of Shrewsbury, in finely-figured quarter-sawn oak and having mahogany in the form of crossbanding, hood fret and fluted pillars and quarter pilasters to the hood and trunk; a highly typical mixture of the two woods. Complex trunk-to-base mouldings, shaped door top, and raised base panel are all regional features indicative of Western styling, even North-western. Height 6ft.10in. Cottage height and style, but with quality.*

PLATE 114. *Eight-day oak-cased cottage clock of about 1790 by Watkin Owen of Llanrwst, North Wales, standing 6ft.10in. Of better quality cottage style but with the architectural pediment which was not universally popular but occasionally used in North-western areas. Shaped (Northern) door top echoed in shaped top to base panel. No mahogany – even the fret and fluted quarter columns are in oak, which is a little unusual. Complex canted trunk-to-base mouldings, ogee top-of-trunk moulds, and square-to-high base are all distinctly North-western.*

PLATE 115. *Eight-day cottage clock in straight-sawn, figureless oak of about 1790 by Edward Russell of Catton, Norfolk. No trim woods used. Simple, square-trunk style and arch-top door contrasts with busier Northern look. Southern features are: pillars integral to hood door (a feature by now passed from fashion elsewhere); horizontal timbers to base which is wider than high; simple moulds above and below trunk. Pillar caps/bases and finials are in softwood and gilded – cheaper than brass fittings. Hood top style is very East Anglian, being a sort of crested, mouldless finish to a flat-top hood with a pagoda shape to the centre, which is only of single timber thickness, its purpose to link together three finial stands. These East Anglian crests often look like (but are not) an afterthought to the design. About 6ft.8in.*

PLATE 116. *Eight-day clock of about 1790 by Barlow of Ashton under Lyne in its high quality mahogany case, the door and bookmatched base in finest crotch-figured veneers. Distinctive North-western features are: combination of shaped door top; complex canted trunk-to-base mouldings and highly-detailed moulds elsewhere; higher than square base; relatively tiny original ogee feet; ample proportions. Much use of brass fittings to trunk and hood. Height 7ft.5in.*

PLATE 117. *High-quality all-mahogany case of about 1790 housing an eight-day clock by Wignall of Ormskirk, Lancashire, having finest crotch mahogany to the bookmatched door and bookmatched raised base panel. Lancashire styling obvious in: combination of shaped door top; cushion mould in top-of-trunk mouldings; complex canted trunk-to-base mouldings; canted base with shaped raised panel; 'box' top projecting above swan-neck corners as finial stands. Mahogany finials (centre brass one replaced?) and mahogany pillar caps and bases also tend to be Northern. Height about 7ft.7in.*

PLATE 118. *Eight-day mahogany clock of about 1795 by J. & R. Coats of Wigan, much inlaid with pale stringing lines and using finest crotch mahogany veneers to the bookmatched door and base. Obviously North-western in the shaped door top, canted square-to-high base with tiny ogee bracket feet, complex and canted trunk-to-base moulds, mahogany caps and bases to pillars and mahogany finials (here of the distinctive Lancashire 'flying saucer' type). Height about 7ft.8in.*

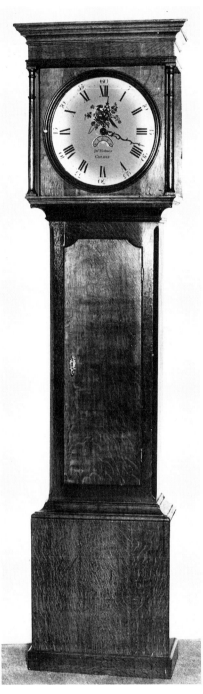

PLATE 119. *Eight-day mahogany clock c.1800 by Thomas Dean of Leigh, Lancashire, showing many typical Lancashire features: shaped door top; complex canted trunk-to-base moulds; canted base; tiny ogee feet; bookmatched veneers to door and base; mahogany fitments to the hood instead of brass, etc. Now, however, a new feature appears in that the trunk 'quarter-columns' are of square section and are reeded rather than fluted, a style confined more or less to the North-west and to the early 19th century. Height about 7ft.6in.*

PLATE 120. *Round dial thirty-hour cottage clock of 1780-90 by John Holmes of Cheadle, Cheshire, a relatively simple style of case entirely in quarter-cut oak but for the mahogany 'bezel' surround to the hood door – the medullary fleckings show well on the base. A relatively neutral case with little in the way of strong regional styling, except that the round dial itself is at this period predominantly a North Midlands style and the kink-cornered door hints towards the North as does the higher than wide base. Narrow canted corners to the trunk are a period feature rather than regional. Height about 6ft.6in.*

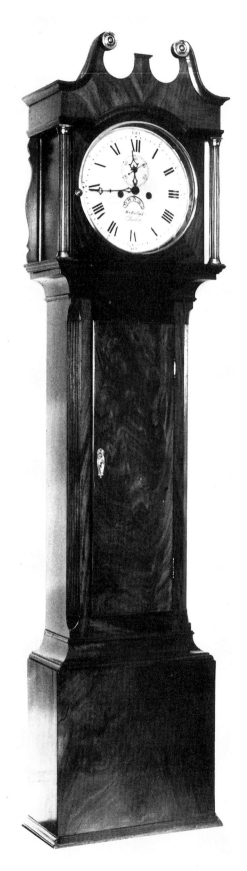

PLATE 121. *Slightly more sophisticated round dial eight-day clock of about 1785-90 by Richard Boyfield of Melton Mowbray, Leicestershire, dial by James Wilson of Birmingham. Oak with mahogany trim in the pillars, trunk quarter columns, bookmatched veneers and crossbanding to hood door, crossbanding to main door, and dentil mouldings across the hood and along the pitched pediment, sometimes known as an architectural pediment. Indicators towards the North (Midlands) are the pediment, the round dial style itself at this period, and the inner-curving pointed door top. Height about 6ft.8in.*

PLATE 122. *All-mahogany round dial eight-day clock of about 1785 by William Bullock of Bath (believed died 1790), the dial by Osborne, Birmingham. The pillars have been kept lower than dial height to help proportion and lower the swan-neck, which can be ungainly on a round dial. Little regional detail except the flat door top often favoured in the South, the wavy hood back splats more Southern than Northern, and the lack of decoration such as stringing or panelling which a Northern clock may well have had to the rather large area of door and base. Fluted canted trunk corners are period rather than regional features. Height 6ft.9in.*

the trunk is not quite so long and slender as Southern counterparts. These cases were obviously much more costly than the oak examples.

The oak-cased round dial longcase could appear in similar cottage form to its square dial equivalent (Plate 120, Holmes). It could be aggrandised somewhat by crossbanding, pediments and dentil mouldings (Plate 121, Boyfield hood). It could appear in mahogany in relatively simple form (Plate 122, Bullock). Or it could appear in mahogany in much grander style such as a taller gentleman's clock (Plate 123, Worswick), or as a fine quality London example (Plate 147, Handley & Moore, of slightly later date). A grand mahogany version with an unusual oval dial is illustrated in Plate 124 (Lomax).

The arched dial case often attempted to be a cut above the square form in being more ornate, obviously taller and almost always with some form of shaped pediment to complement the arch of the dial, usually by following the shape of the arch. An arched dial case with a flat top is not always the most graceful form, and was not common, those we some-times see today often having had a pediment removed later. Seldom was the oak arched dial case without crossbanding or fluted quarter-columns or inlay of some kind to give it that bit more status.

The swan-neck pediment was the most popular pediment on arched dial clocks, but was never popular in London. Some other pediment styles were often more of a regional nature. London cases (Plate 125, Thorndike) usually had a pagoda top, as here. In the South of England a good many London cases were bought originally to house provincial clocks. In all parts of the land this could also apply and a London-made case can often be quite original to the clock even though the clock was not made in London, as is the case with this particular clock.

Another hood style found in London and in London-influenced areas (principally of course the South-east of England) was the crested top as in Plate 141 (Milsome). This can be seen as a dome-top hood sur-mounted by two side and one central finial supports, each linked together by a crested section, sometimes with similar crestpieces along the top of the hood sides. Sometimes the cresting pieces are pierced, as in Plate 130. In fact occasionally these cases have lost their crests and stand now as dome-tops, but they look ridiculously nipped in the hood as a true dome-top has a heavier topmould. The dome-top style was little used in London anyway.

London and London-influenced cases, whatever their hood style, may be used in the provinces, and usually have features not found on regional style cases: namely locks and escutcheons to the hood door, otherwise simply a friction fit; double plinths, either as one solid plinth

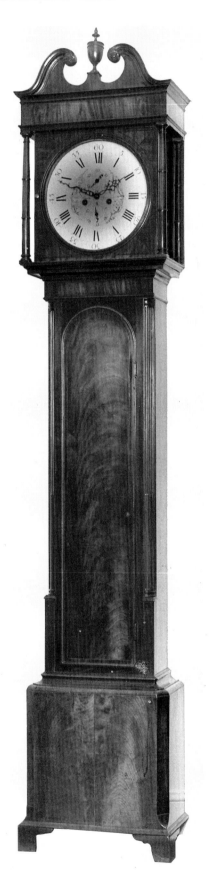

PLATE 123. *Northern round dial eight-day clock of about 1780, perhaps earlier, by Thomas Worswick of Lancaster showing numerous Northern features even though the round dial was not popular in the area. The maker married into the Gillow cabinetmaking family, and the case is almost certainly Gillow work (they did not sign clock cases). Complex canted trunk-to-base moulds, canted-cornered bookmatched base, simulated bamboo effect hood pillars, all-mahogany hood fitments rather than brass, are all Northern features. A regular Gillow feature is the rounded door top (though others did it too) and the mahogany urn finial. Height about 8ft.*

PLATE 124. *Eight-day mahogany clock of about 1790 by Lomax of Blackburn with unusual oval dial by Wilson. To accommodate this unusual shape hoods often have a strange proportion which upsets our regional recognition points, but Northern pointers are still there: pitched pediment; shaped door top (here unusual, perhaps to echo the oval dial); complex canted trunk-to-base mould; canted-corner base; tiny ogee bracket feet. Bookmatched flame veneers to door and base. Overall very fine quality. Height 7ft.8in.*

PLATE 125. *Eight-day clock of about 1790 by Thorndike of Ipswich in its original all-mahogany pagoda-style case of London origin. This is the square-cornered typical London case, easily identified by its combination of double plinth to base wider than high, thumbnail-moulded edge to base panel and arched door, brass reeding to lower section of hood pillars, hood side windows, distinctive shape of pagoda with brass fret to front. Centre finial missing. Height about 7ft.8in.*

PLATE 126. *Eight-day clock of about 1780-90 by Richard Kirkland of Port Glasgow in its original London-made mahogany case, demonstrating that London cases were sometimes supplied even at this great distance. Shallow base and simple mouldings are general Southern features. London features are: combination of arched door top; simulated bead-edged base panel; double plinth; brass piping to lower hood pillars; brass fret to pagoda front. Height about 7ft.8in. Three finials missing.*

PLATE 127. *Eight-day mahogany clock of about 1785 by William Rust of Hull, the provincial equivalent of the London pagoda case, a style made only in East Yorkshire/North Lincolnshire. Main differences are, generally: no brass piping to hood pillars; square-to-high base; no hood side windows; side finial supports stand proud of pagoda sweep; wooden fret (sometimes inlay) to pagoda front; use of crossbandings. Height about 7ft.7in, though many are taller.*

PLATE 128. *Another even finer example of a 1790s 'Hull pagoda' style of clock in mahogany, the clock by Snowden of Grimsby. Here the canted corners are inlaid with flowers and the base is quite exceptional in design and execution. Original finials. Height 7ft.8in.*

PLATE 129. *Oak-cased clock of about 1780-90 by Robert Fuller of Watton, Norfolk. Simple moulds and shallow base suggest Southern, as do wavy hood backsplats. Hood is a variant of the crested top, three finial supports here being joined by a pierced mouldless fret somewhere in style between a swan-neck and a 'whale's-tail' crest; these fret shapes vary considerably in this style of case. Diamond-shaped inlays of alternate light and dark woods below the crest are an East Anglian feature. Fan inlay to door top is a whim of the casemaker and not a regular feature. Two side finials missing. Height 7ft.10in.*

PLATE 130. *Hood of about 1785 showing another version of the East Anglian crested top style often loosely classed as a whale's tail crest. Here a pierced crest links the three finial supports. Makers Lumley and Gudgeon of Bury St. Edmunds. Wavy back splats match the wavy side crests. Side windows echo the London theme. Inlaid diamond pieces are distinctively East Anglian. Original gilded wooden finials of the flame (or flambeau) type.*

below another or as a shaped bracket-footed plinth beneath a solid one; hood side windows (though these were used occasionally on non-London examples too); on some examples only, brass piping along the lower one third of fluted hood pillars and/or trunk pilasters. A combination of these features, or even any one of them in isolation, would be very uncommon at this period on cases other than those of London origin or influence (but see page 211 concerning hood side windows on some Scottish cases, which copied this London idea).

A different form of pagoda hood pediment was used in East Yorkshire and Northern Lincolnshire and seldom elsewhere, though an example of this type is seen most unusually housing its original clock by Woolston Roberts of Derby in Plate 109. Many of these cases were made in Hull and I usually call them Hull

PLATE 131. *Oak hood of an eight-day clock of about 1785 showing another form of East Anglian mouldless whale's tail crest, the clock by Forster of Norwich. Such frets usually lack any moulded edge, as here, therefore appearing two-dimensional and looking almost like an afterthought.*

pagodas to distinguish them from London pagodas. The Hull version has its finial supports standing proud of the pagoda curve, lacks the double plinth of the London form, lacks the brass piping sometimes found in the pillars of the London form, usually lacks hood side windows, and generally has more ornate inlays and crossbandings about it, so that the two can easily be distinguished. London pagoda examples at this period would be only in mahogany (walnut examples in this style from earlier periods having finished by this time); provincial ones might be in mahogany or oak.

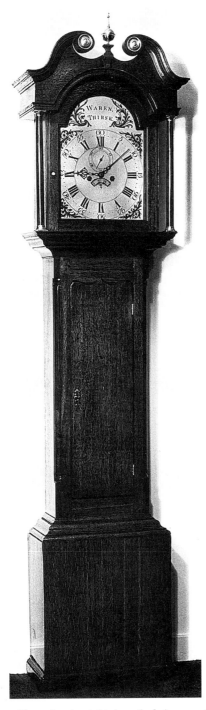

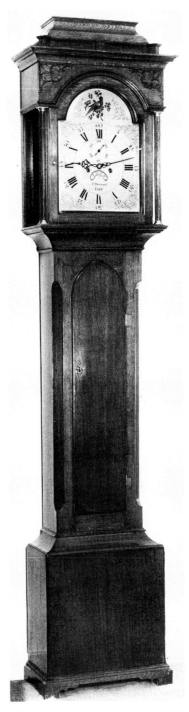

PLATE 132. *Very simple eight-day clock in quarter-cut oak made about 1775 by William Waren of Thirsk, Yorkshire, about 7ft. Northern features are: moulds more complex than a Southern clock; base higher than wide; shaped door top. Otherwise the style is not strongly regional and the modest swan-neck is of neutral style.*

PLATE 133. *Eight-day clock of about 1785 by Thomas Sherwood of Yarm, North Yorkshire, in straight-sawn oak. Unusual hood style of a caddy on a flat top. Three finial supports across the flat here have their finials missing. Northern styling evident in the square-to-high base and the caddy itself. Fluted canted corners to the trunk could be from anywhere but are more often Northern. Otherwise a relatively neutral style with simple moulds. The arch to the door top is a one-off whim rather than a regional feature. About 7ft.5in.*

PLATE 134. *Eight-day clock in quarter-cut oak with mahogany crossbandings and trim, dating from about 1790 by Benjamin Harlow of Lane End, Staffordshire. Relatively neutral in style but certain features suggest Western/ Northern trends, namely: canted trunk-to-base moulds; canted base; square to high base with raised, clip-cornered base panel; shaped door top; well-made and detailed mouldings. Inset gold scrollwork panels below swan-necks on a green ground are a North-western alternative to frets. Height 7ft.2in.*

PLATE 135. *Mahogany clock of about 1790 by Richard Johnson of Ripon, Yorkshire, the dial of the gold corner type on a solid ground colour. Restrained styling with just a hint of Northern features: shaped door top; square to high base with raised panel; well-detailed moulds (though not complex). The shaped section between the swans is distinctive to a number of cases from the Leeds area, and may be a localised styling. Height about 7ft.8in.*

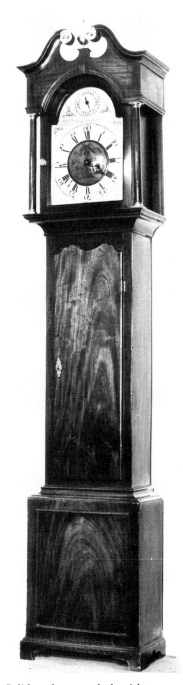

PLATE 136. *Solid mahogany clock with true enamel dial of about 1790 by W. & C. Nicholas of Birmingham. Northern features: high base; shaped door top; complex trunk-to-base moulds. Otherwise a relatively neutral style with little in the way of regionalism. The base has a bead simulating a panel effect, not a real panel – notice the grain of the base continues under the beading. Height about 7ft.7in.*

PLATE 137. *Mahogany eight-day clock standing 6ft.11in. made about 1805 by Burton of Kendal. The curved door top is reminiscent of Gillows of Lancaster but inside the base during restoration was found the stencilled name of the casemaker, 'Stuart, cabinetmaker, Kendal'. Northern features are: ogee top-of-trunk moulding; complex canted trunk-to-base mould to canted, bookmatched base; base higher than wide; canted trunk edges with stringing; mahogany caps and bases to hood pillars. The marquetry inlay below the canted trunk corners and similar flower inlays in the swan-necks are unusual and a whim of the maker.*

PLATE 138. *Thirty-hour oak clock of about 1790 with rolling moon by Pattison of Halifax. Northern features are: high base; shaped door top; cushion mould below top-of-trunk moulding; ogee top-of-trunk moulding. The carving is well done but probably performed at a much later date, at which time too the clock was stained black. The barleytwist hood pillars are unknown on plain examples of this period and were probably replaced during carving. About 7ft.6in.*

PLATE 139. *Fine mahogany clock of heavy and unmistakably Lancashire style made about 1790 by Probert of Wigan and standing about 7ft.10in. Fourteen inch dial. Northern features: box top above swans;* verre eglomisé *panels below swans, here on tin; wavy door top; complex moulds, especially canted trunk-to-base mould; canted base; square-section reeded and inlaid quarter columns to trunk; short door (for this period) with decorative panel below it; hardly any 'waist'. Shell inlays to quarter-column supports and above door are unusual for this area, as are fan corner inlays to base.*

PLATE 140. *Mahogany clock of about 1785 by Major Scholfield of Manchester standing about 7ft.10in. Northern features: infill centre to swan-necks; mahogany rather than brass fittings to hood; 'Gothic' triple-point door top to bookmatched door; square-to-high bookmatched base with canted sides; complex canted trunk-to-base moulds; tiny feet. The trunk quarter-columns are here of the triple-cluster type in simulated bamboo pattern, often known as 'Chippendale sticks', and are uncommon but principally occur in Lancashire. The three frets in the hood are unusual for this region, being more often of the* verre eglomisé *type.*

PLATE 141. *Eight-day oak-cased clock of about 1790 by John Milsome of Newbury standing 7ft.2in., the case of the crested top style based on London taste. Southern features: crested top itself (three finial supports linked by wavy infills, finials here missing); lock and escutcheon to hood door; glass hood side windows; simple moulds; arched door top; double plinth. Altogether plainer and simpler styling with square-cornered trunk and base.*

The clock by Fuller of Watton (Plate 129) has a type of pediment seldom found outside Norfolk and Suffolk (an area often referred to as East Anglia), being a sort of variation on the crested top theme. This particular crest is pierced through, though some are solid, and this is a version of what is sometimes called a whale's tail fret, some being shaped a little like the flukes of a fishtail.

The caddy top (Plate 133, Sherwood clock) is unusual with an arched dial and tends to suggest a Northern or North-western influence. This particular example is from Yarm in North Yorkshire.

The strength of influence of Lancashire in casework is apparent from the very beginning of the white dial. Cases here were usually exceptionally well made using very heavy timber frameworks and oak backboards. London cases also had oak backboards as normal but in most parts of Britain pine was used for backboards, so that Lancashire (and sometimes its immediate counties of influence, i.e. Cheshire and Cumberland) was unusual and generally consistent in this. Craftsmanship in Lancashire was often of an exceptionally high standard. Design, however, was very much heavier than in the London-influenced areas.

Some cases are met with which are busily carved and usually also stained to almost black. These cases more often house brass dial clocks, but they do occur sometimes on painted dial clocks. It is generally believed that such cases were originally plain and were carved and blackened much later (even as much as a century later). This is sometimes very obvious, but at other times it can be hard to decide how old the carving is. Carved cases can occur at random throughout the land, but the heaviest concentration of them is in Northern central England along the Yorkshire/Lancashire border in the Pennines. Why this should be I do not know.

Lancashire cases were often ahead of their time; earlier than elsewhere the base and hood both begin to enlarge, leaving a trunk somewhat shorter than in most areas, and this despite the taller height of many of these clocks. This is the beginning of the trend towards a shorter door, and it often combines with a fashion for the trunk not to come in so far as a waist, in other words a stockier and shorter trunk. This stocky appearance, exaggerated further by larger dial size than was universally popular (and sometimes further exaggerated by an infilled swan-neck), meant that Lancashire clocks were often decried in the past by writers whose experience was based on London and London-influenced work. Lancashire-style clocks may not be to everyone's taste today but they often represent magnificent workmanship of an avant-garde nature in their day.

The 'Gothic' door top, so often thought of as 'Victorian' in style, was in use in Lancashire clocks in the 1780s-90s. Fluted square-section quarter pillars to the trunk and sometimes the same type of square fluted pillars to the hood were a Lancashire innovation beginning towards the end of the eighteenth century and occasionally copied elsewhere, though these were never universally popular.

The section below the swan-neck upper mould on these clocks was often either fretted or carried a glass insert having a blue or green painted back side and gold scrollwork on the front. These are sometimes known as *verre eglomisé* panels. A clock with this feature would therefore have two such panels, one each side, but some had a third panel in the central infill area between the swan-necks. Sometimes these panels were of painted tin or wood instead of glass. The *verre eglomisé* panel instead of a fret was sometimes used on square dial clocks too. These panels were a Lancashire innovation, sometimes imitated in adjacent counties. So far was Lancashire ahead of other areas in these stylistic trends that it is very easy to assume a later date by a generation or so on such clocks. It is therefore important to study them carefully and to have regard especially to the dial style, which is more consistent with the national trend.

CHAPTER TWELVE

CASES, PERIOD TWO (1800-1830)

My division of styles into periods is done purely to break up what would otherwise be a long and perhaps complicated sequence of stylistic development. Naturally there is no real division of styles, no break in continuity. Casemakers continued exactly as before, varying their styles according to the quality and nature of the case required, the specific instructions of their clients, their own personal whims and the general stylistic taste of the particular region.

The desire to experiment with new styles and tastes was strongest in the towns, weakest in rural areas where traditional ways lingered longest. Oddly enough London itself, by far the largest city, was conservative in its tastes except at the very top of the market, where occasional avant-garde casework might be adorned with gilded brass caryatids, sphinx heads and the like, presumably influenced by the recent Egyptian campaigns.

We can expect cases from rural areas, especially those remote from larger towns, to be highly traditional. It is therefore no surprise to find that cases from rural East Anglia (principally Norfolk and Suffolk) and from the West Country (Somerset, Devon and Gloucestershire) tend to retain longer their earlier stylistic features such as the long door, and pillars attached to hood door (known as integral pillars). It is in the towns that stylistic progress will usually be first apparent, as case styles move towards those of the ultimately short door in Period Three.

The North/South divide persists and the difference becomes increasingly apparent, splitting the country diagonally in the sense that Northern and Western England were foremost in the advance of case styles towards the short door form, and especially the newly-prospering larger towns of the North and West such as Bristol, Birmingham, Manchester, and Liverpool. The dividing line is difficult to define but can be thought of roughly as running between Bristol and Hull, which towns were in the Northern/Western sector. The larger towns would tend to house the more prosperous, even newly-rich, merchant classes, who could afford the costlier, showier, new styles.

In the towns too there would tend to be a concentration of higher quality eight-day clocks, as had always been the case to date, and it is in those types of clocks where the newest fashions occurred first. Rural makers of thirty-hour clocks changed more slowly, partly from tradition but partly also as thirty-hour casework was often built down to a price, and this would not allow costly decorative treatment.

When the shortening door did begin to appear, initially as the 'three-quarter door' style, it was the trunk areas above and below the door which were the 'newly available' spaces used chiefly for decorative work such as stringing, crossbanding, panelling, book-matching, etc., as well of course as the traditional areas of door and base. Thirty-hour casework for the most part would not allow this costly treatment by virtue of its price, nor even would more modest eight-day work. By the time we reach Period Three that situation was to change, but through most of Period Two, and especially in the earlier part of it, this consideration still applied.

PLATE 142. *Simple thirty-hour arched dial cottage clock of about 1810 by John Evans of Newcastle Emlyn, Wales. Traditional long door giving slender proportions, the more so by virtue of the small (eleven-inch) dial. Moulds and shaped door top incline towards the Western/Northern taste. Neat, 'neutral' swan-neck. Little regional styling but for the unusually thick timbers used, typical of some Welsh oak clocks. Height 7ft.*

PLATE 143. *Cottage thirty-hour clock of about 1815 by John Weston of Hastings, here unusually in mahogany, which was not often used for thirty-hour clocks at this period. Such very simple cottage clocks tend to show little in the way of regional styling, except that a Northern one would probably have been less simple. The flat-top door and shallow base are typically Southern. Height 6ft.1in.*

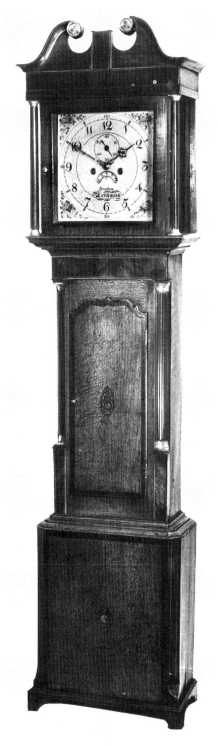

PLATE 144. *Eight-day cottage clock in pine dating from about 1810 and standing 6ft.4in., made by James Bath of Cirencester. Pine was more usually found in thirty-hour examples. Wavy back splat to the hood and simple mouldings are both more Southern than Northern. Shaped door top and reeded trunk corners are not typical of the South.*

PLATE 145. *Eight-day cottage-sized (though far from simple) clock of about 1805-10 by Thomas Benbow of Northwood, Shropshire. The oak case has much mahogany trim. High base, shaped door top, canted complex trunk-to-base moulding and canted corner base are all Northern features. Shorter trunk develops sooner in the North. Shell type inlays to door centre and base centre are typical of the period rather than regional. Height 6ft.7in.*

PLATE 146. *Thirty-hour cottage-size clock in plain mahogany by Bulgin of Marshfield, Gloucestershire, dating from about 1820. Mahogany is unusual on thirty-hour examples. Height about 6ft.7in. Swan-neck is integral with hood pediment (rather than separate), a method more often of the South than North. Other Southern features are wavy back splats to hood and flat door top. The base is unusually high for the area, perhaps because this would otherwise stand too low to give a full thirty-hour run, and perhaps also indicative of the gradual shortening of the trunk at this period.*

PLATE 147. *Crotch mahogany eight-day clock of about 1820 by Handley & Moore of London, standing 7ft.2in. including finial. The London case retains the long door look and slender lines. London features include: double-reeding to canted trunk and hood corners; beading on base to give a panel effect; lock to hood door; glass hood side windows; double plinth; arched door top. The unusual hood pediment has no particular name and is a feature seldom found on any but dome-top London cases.*

PLATE 148. *Simple oak cased eight-day clock of about 1805 by Symonds of Reepham, Norfolk, standing 6ft.11in. The long door style often persists longer in rural areas. Shallow base and simple mouldings are Southern. Hood side windows are Southern/East Anglian. The hood pediment is a sort of mouldless swan-neck but verging on a whale's tail crest and is typically East Anglian. These cases are often of very thin timbers and light construction.*

PLATE 149. *Square dial version eight-day of about 1805, also by Symonds of Reepham, Norfolk. Many features are similar to the previous clock. Here the swan-neck is of the same nature and typical of the region, having no moulded edge. Original gilded wooden finials. Height about 6ft.8in.*

PLATE 150. *Detail of the hood of Plate 148 by Symonds of Reepham showing the mouldless swan-neck. The two box-top like corners would probably also each have originally carried a finial. Unmistakably East Anglian.*

PLATE 151. *Oak hood of a thirty-hour clock of about 1810 by John Spendlove of Thetford, Norfolk. The swan-neck is of the East Anglian mouldless type, here positioned between three finial supports in the way that a crest would have been. Finials now lost. A Western or Northern swan-neck would have had the moulded edge and would probably have been much bolder anyway.*

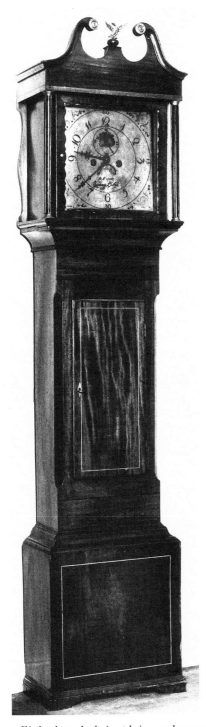

PLATE 152. *Eight-day clock in plain mahogany of about 1805 by D. Eggert of Temple Cloud, Somerset. The door is shorter now as a three-quarter door with space above and below it on the retained long trunk. Southern indicators are: flat top door; simple moulds; wavy backsplats to hood; and the swan-neck running integral with the pediment front. Height about 7ft.*

PLATE 153. *Eight-day clock of about 1800-1810 by Baker of Newark, in oak with mahogany trim and much use of cartwheel and fan inlays, a popular feature at this period. The break-arch pediment has inlay along its length, matching that on the top-of-trunk moulding, done to resemble dentil moulding. Shaped door top hints at Northern styling, and this hood pediment is a style more favoured in the North than South. Height about 7ft.6in. Note pale sapwood streaks in the base.*

167

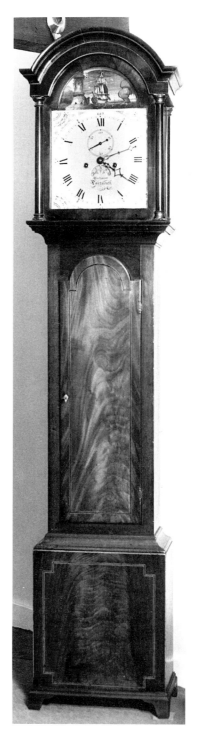

PLATE 154. *Pine thirty-hour clock of about 1810 by James Thompson of Darlington with the break-arch hood style, a hood variation found mostly in the North. Height 7ft.2in. Still a long door but the high base means the trunk has not quite the pencil-slim lines of earlier periods. Clip-cornered door top is a hint of Northern styling on an otherwise stylistically 'neutral' case.*

PLATE 155. *Eight-day clock in mahogany, actually dated 1817, made by Mortimore of Dartmouth, Devon. The wood is well figured and the style very traditional retaining certain features of an earlier period (such as pillars attached to hood door, dome top to hood and arched door top). It is only in the South that such old-fashioned features would linger this late. The long door persists too, which at this date could apply more generally, but is gradually being replaced by the three-quarter length door. About 7ft.2in.*

PLATE 157. *Mahogany eight-day clock by Woolston Roberts of Derby made about 1810 and standing about 7ft.6in. The case is of the Hull pagoda type, yet original to the clock, having been shipped from Hull. Corinthian brass capitals are unusual on this case style. Centre finial now lost.*

PLATE 156. *Oak cased eight-day clock of about 1805 by Hudson Fox of Hull, East Yorkshire, in a typical and unmistakable Hull pagoda style case, cross-banded in mahogany. Still of the long door proportions, with a shaped door top characteristic of many Hull cases. Moulding on this case style are simple but this form of pagoda occurs only in East Yorkshire and North Lincolnshire. Height 6ft.11in. Finials lost.*

PLATE 158. *Eight-day mahogany clock of about 1815 by Mawman of Beverley, East Yorkshire, in the unmistakable Hull pagoda style of case. Here the original centre finial support survives (many have been removed to reduce height), as do the original finials throughout. The stepped door top is sometimes found on the second generation of these cases, as here. Otherwise little change in overall style from Period One examples of this type. Height 8ft.*

PLATE 159. *Mahogany thirty-hour clock of unusually high quality (for a thirty hour) dating from about 1810 by William Muncaster of Whitehaven, Cumberland. The clock has dummy winders to simulate eight-day work. The long door now shortens slightly to use the space below the hood for inlay. Very Northern in:* verre eglomisé *panels below the swan-necks; simulated bamboo pillars; square reeded trunk quarter columns inlaid across, and the same in the base; ogee top-of-trunk mould and complex trunk-to-base mould; shaped door top. The circle inlay within a square base is a period feature found principally in the North. Height 7ft.5in. Inlays of shells (upper trunk) and fans (base corners) are a period feature.*

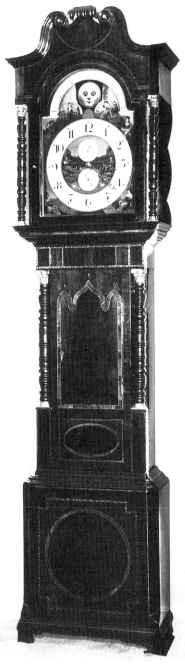

PLATE 160. *Ornate mahogany eight-day clock by William Nicholas of Birmingham showing very advanced stylistic trends for the date (1810-20). Height 7ft.9in. Western (and North-western) features are: heavy swan-neck with infill and overhang top-piece; short door still using long trunk with decoration above and below door; shaped door top, here Gothic triple pointed; complex moulding, the lower ones canted; canted base corners; busily-turned pillars to hood and now also to trunk, each having Corinthian brass caps. Shaped hood back splats are probably more to match the style than a regional factor here. Circular inlay to base (and again below door) is a period feature.*

PLATE 161. *Exceptionally ornate mahogany eight-day clock of about 1810-20 by Stones of Blackburn, Lancashire. Unmistakable Lancashire styling, very advanced for its day. Northern in every aspect: heavy swan-neck with infill and overhang and box top (i.e. squared box sections above the base of the swan-necks); full pillars to base and trunk as well as hood, each on high squared supports; short triple-point Gothic door with decorated trunk space above and below. Inlays of circles within squares theme indicate period and point Northwards. The extraordinary amount of inlay work is a whim of this casemaker rather than a regional feature. Height 8ft.*

171

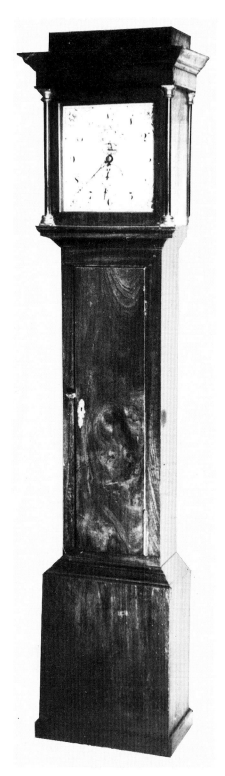

PLATE 162. *Thirty-hour clock dated 1825 made by Joseph Keys of Exeter, Devon, in mahogany case, unusual for a thirty-hour clock, and standing 6ft.3in. Very old-fashioned in style using pillars integral to hood door and long door style. Clearly Southern by its simplicity and flat top door, though with a base slightly higher than some.*

PLATE 163. *Thirty-hour clock in oak with mahogany trim made about 1815 by Richard Snow of Pateley Bridge, Yorkshire, standing about 7ft. Very different in proportion from the Keys clock with higher base, shortening door (not now filling all the trunk), and much heavier overall appearance.*

PLATE 164. *Thirty-hour clock in oak with mahogany trim actually dated 1817 and made by John Palliser of Thirsk, Yorkshire. High base and shaped door top are typical Northern features, but the door no longer fills the still long trunk. Height about 7ft.*

PLATE 165. *Thirty-hour oak clock with mahogany trim made about 1820 by Thomas Place of Bedale, Yorkshire. The higher base and shortening trunk are a Northern feature of the day. The mahogany trim now forms an entire border outside the base panel, covers the entire door frame and all the hood door and hood front, as well as the pillars and quarter trunk columns. Front feet only. Height about 7ft.*

PLATE 166. *Eight-day clock in oak made about 1800-1810 by Thomas Howse of Tetbury, Gloucestershire. Shell and cartwheel inlays to door and base are period features. Unusual form of pitched hood pediment. The door is still in the long door style, with unusual matching curved ends top and bottom. The distinctive feature of some West Country clocks is the wavy inner edge to the hood door, a feature more or less confined to this region. Height about 7ft.6in.*

PLATE 167. *Mahogany eight-day clock of about 1815 by Monkhouse of Carlisle, Cumberland, standing about 7ft.8in. Three-quarter length door now not entirely filling the long trunk, the space above and below used for decorative stringing. Circles within squares are a period feature, especially in the North. Northern complex trunk-to-base moulds in canted form. Tiny original ogee feet.*

CHAPTER THIRTEEN

CASES – PERIOD THREE (1830-1870)

Period Three takes us through a sequence of styles which initially may be unchanged from Period Two to those of the extreme and latest case styles. Some clocks of the 1830s are very difficult to distinguish from similar ones of the 1820s, but by 1840 the new style is usually very apparent. The development increasingly takes place in those features we have already considered – mouldings, door shape and length, trunk shape and length, hood pediment styles, and base shapes. The changes we saw beginning, if at times hesitantly, in Period Two now take on a more obvious character and by the end of the period we can clearly see a difference in most of these respects.

In the South this development is less pronounced than in the North, though it is still there. At the beginning of this period in the South we may have to consider individual case features one by one to form an overall opinion of period. By the end of the period the change has usually been such that an overall glance will be adequate to assess the age.

There are certain considerations applying to Southern work, however, which do not apply in the North. First of all the longcase clock seems to have fallen from popularity in London before it did elsewhere. After 1830 we see far fewer London-made longcase clocks other than those made for special purposes such as Regulators. As the South in general often took influence from London, this applies too to some degree in those counties closest to, and most strongly influenced by, London. Further away from London (still within the South in general) longcase production continued quite strongly after 1830. Even so by the 1850s longcase clock production in the South in general was nearly over. Presumably the increasing availability of cheap, imported clocks such as American wall clocks provided the householder with a timekeeper which would fill his requirements conveniently cheaply. In the North/West and Wales production of longcase clocks continued longer, and particularly in the northern part of those regions it is not uncommon to find longcase clocks still being made into the 1870s, which means that the recognition of period becomes easier by virtue of the longer duration of style development in the North. Post-1850 production continued in Scotland too, though here the styles developed little after that date.

Furthermore, the differentiation of styles between North/West and South/East increases quite rapidly after about 1835. This means that in Northern clocks we often have an extra dimension of recognition. Southern styles develop distinctly, but Northern English styles (and for this purpose we include all of Wales in that category) develop in a much more marked fashion within their own territory. This makes the recognition of period increasingly more obvious in Northern clocks as time passes, and the difference between Northern and Southern ones increasingly easy to recognise. Scotland, of course, is a different story.

In the last chapter we saw how the distinction between town clocks and rural clocks (and cases in particular) was still quite strong, a tradition carried over from earlier times. This is soon to change in this present period, as rural customers increasingly sought what they thought of as the sophistication of the town styles. To provide the newest and most fashionable cases rural clockmakers must have dealt with town casemakers or had their local cabinetmakers produce work in the town styles. An example of this is the clock by John Crockett of Pontypridd, South

Wales (Plate 179) in a case from (or based on those from) the city of Bristol, and the Richard Snow of Pateley Bridge clock (Plate 182) in a case little different from those made in the city of Leeds.

Of course we have seen that it was always possible for a clockmaker to order a case from even as far as London, but formerly these had usually been exceptions for special customers of town and city clockmakers. The difference is that now even the rural cottage customer wanted the city (his nearest city) style. We are reminded of the story of William Williams of Dolgellau, Wales, who was working in the 1870s and 1880s selling these massive late clocks, when every labourer and farmer's son had as 'his ambition ... to buy one of these clocks as the *principal* piece of furniture for the house'. The clockmaker himself may have been partly responsible for this trend, in that, as cheap imported wall clocks increasingly took over his traditional market, one response was for him to offer extra opulence in the case by making it into an ornately large piece of furniture – something which the imported clocks could not rival.

As an example of how far styles have progressed by the 1840s from the first painted dial cases of the 1780s, we can often recognise an early Victorian case from an isolated part of it – for example, the hood alone, or the trunk alone, or the base alone. We could seldom have done this fifty years earlier. An illustration of the hood of many of the clocks in this chapter would probably be adequate for us to be able to pin down both period and region without knowing the name of the clockmaker and without seeing any other part of the case.

Dealers who make their living buying and selling such clocks, as I do, can often reach the point where they can virtually buy a clock on the telephone (subject obviously to eventual examination of it) just from an accurate description given by another experienced dealer. They can probably even do this without any dimensions other than the dial width, though the total case height is a great help, and in any event other dimensions are normally available too. Assuming the clock is in its original case, then verbal details of the dial too will readily mean the clock's period can be recognised. They can thus form unseen an adequate impression from an accurate description of the *important* stylistic features indicative of period and region, together with a description of condition and the more difficult factors of colour and patina. If nothing else, they can very easily form a picture adequate enough to be able to dismiss those they do not want to buy.

The beginner cannot expect to do this, but the very fact that it can be done shows that this variety of styling does conform to an understandable and mostly logical sequence.

PLATE 168. *Simple oak cottage-style thirty-hour clock of about 1830 by Miller of Bedford retaining the traditional long-door look with a combination of Northern and Southern features. High base and wavy doortop suggest Northern influence; integral swan-neck and simple moulds suggest Southern influence. Simplicity of style (and therefore low cost) outweighs other factors. Height 6ft.6in.*

PLATE 169. *Eight-day clock in oak with mahogany trim by John Bishop of Sherborne, Dorset, dating from about 1830 or perhaps a little earlier. Still very conservative in the long door style. Shell inlay to door is a little old-fashioned by now. Flat door top and wavy back splats to hood are Southern features. Height 7ft.2in.*

PLATE 170. *Eight-day clock in oak with mahogany trim in the Hull pagoda style made about 1820-30 by Denton Northgraves of Hull. Distinctive case style little changed from twenty years earlier, and still retaining the long door, though these pagoda cases never develop into the true short door. The three original finials survive, the centre one on its original support block. Height 7ft.7in.*

PLATE 171. *Eight-day mahogany clock in the Hull pagoda style dating from about 1820-30 by Tate of Winterton, Lincolnshire. This mahogany pagoda style has changed little since Period One, becoming perhaps a little simpler and a little lower in quality. The 'Zulu shield' door centre is one variation of several. Semi-French feet are a continuation of the base and at the front only. Original finials preserved, including the centre support. Height about 7ft.10in.*

PLATE 172. *Eight-day round dial clock in mahogany by Bidlake of London dating from about 1820-30. Classic London style of the day, being more formal. Hood has the crested finish, here with a pierced crest, and its original finials. Glass hood side windows are typical, as is the beading to the base to give a panel effect, the arch-top door, and the key-locking hood door. Bracket foot probably original – double plinth not used in this example, perhaps because it would be too heavy for this more delicate style. Height about 7ft.2in.*

PLATE 173. *Mahogany eight-day clock of about 1830 by Robert Wyatt of Plymouth, Devon, standing 7ft.1in. Still in the conservative long door style, but the broader crossbanding to base, door and hood hint at a later period, as do the rope-twist pillars to hood and trunk. Unusually high swan-neck is probably just a whim of the casemaker.*

PLATE 174. *Oak-cased eight-day clock with rocking Adam and Eve made about 1830 by John Braund of Hatherleigh, Devon. Height 6ft.9in. The dome top is uncommon this late, here finished by a box-top. Other traditional features are long door, integral pillars to the hood door, starburst inlays to door and base, all by now a little old-fashioned. However the black stringing line to base, door and hood door is a very up-to-date feature. Slender and very obviously Southern.*

PLATE 175. *Thirty-hour clock in oak with mahogany trim dating from about 1830 by Fothergill of Knaresborough, Yorkshire, and standing about 7ft.4in. The door is now very short (in this instance flat-topped, which is uncommon in the North), the trunk areas above and below used for decoration. Front feet only, not uncommon in the North. The case is of relatively neutral design, but the short door this early is a Northern indicator.*

PLATE 176. *Eight-day clock in oak with mahogany trim made about 1830 by William Nicholas of Birmingham and standing 7ft.3in. Turned hood pillars, here as it happens having Corinthian brass caps and reeded centres, are an indicator of the later style, and similar pillars to the trunk are an even stronger period pointer, as is the three-quarter length door with decorative panel beneath. Features showing Northern/Western styling are: wavy door top; box top to hood; complex mouldings including canted trunk-to-base mouldings; canted base.*

PLATE 177. *Mahogany eight-day clock of about 1830-40 by Hallam of Nottingham standing 7ft.4in. Period pointers are: shorter door with decorative panel above and below; full pillars to trunk matching those to hood. Indicators of Northern/Western style: shaped door top, here triple-point Gothic; infill between swan-necks; higher than square base; complex mouldings including canted trunk-to-base mould; canted base.*

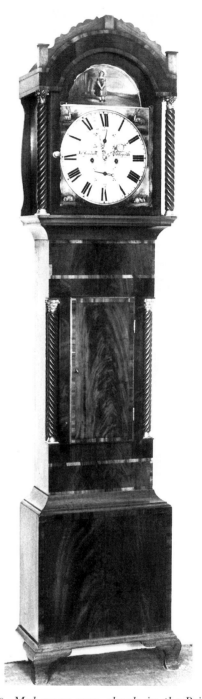

PLATE 178. *Mahogany eight-day clock of the 1830s by Thorpe of Bath, the case by William Cock of Bristol. Flat-topped, three-quarter length door using space above and below for decorative effect. Rope-twist pillars to hood and similar full pillars to trunk, the latter a period indicator. Serpentine inner edge to hood door is a regional feature. Height about 7ft.4in.*

PLATE 179. *Mahogany case, clearly in the Bristol style, housing an eight-day clock of about 1850 by John Crockett of Pontypridd, South Wales. Crested top with serpentine infill between the finial stands (finials removed) matches the serpentine inner edge of the hood door, a distinctive regional feature. Front feet only. Rope-twist pillars to hood and matching full pillars to trunk, all with Corinthian brass caps. Flat-topped, three-quarter door, the trunk space above and below used for decorative bandings. Wavy backsplats to hood. Almost all of these are regional features at this period. Height 7ft.3in.*

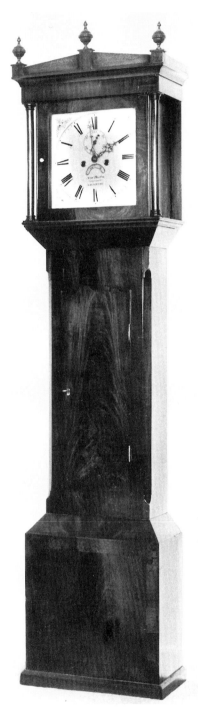 

PLATE 180. *Mahogany eight-day clock of about 1840-50 by Samuel Burton of Salisbury, Wiltshire, standing about 6ft.6in. The flat-surface mouldings are veneered (shaped mouldings were normally solid) and can occur in any region at this period but are uncommon. Altogether a very angular style of case probably owing more to the whim of the case-maker than regional styling. Three-quarter length door, here with a wavy top, which is unusual for the South. The dial has gold flower corners as transfers, barely showing in the photograph.*

PLATE 181. *Eight-day mahogany longcase clock of about 1850 by Paul Ganter of Huddersfield, Yorkshire, standing about 8ft. Very heavy style with wavy-topped short door, short and thick trunk, high base with 'dartboard' centre (here as a raised panel though some are recessed), heavy broad door hood, and fancy-turned hood pillars. All are features found only at this period in the North of England. Shorter, busily-turned quarter trunk pilasters now accentuate the short trunk and wavy backplates to the hood sometimes echo the busy style. Semi-French feet at the front only.*

PLATE 182. *Heavy mahogany eight-day clock of about 1840-50 by Richard Snow of Pateley Bridge, Yorkshire, showing all the classic period features of the area – busily-turned pillars, wide hood door, short trunk door with short quarter pilasters (here rope-twisted), high base. Nothing of this nature ever appeared in the South or in Scotland. Height about 8ft.*

PLATE 183. *Two clocks seen together for contrast. On the left a mahogany clock of about 1850-60 by J.C. Elliott of Leeds, Yorkshire, of the typically heavy late Northern English style. On the right a clock of about 1800 by Richard Morland of Kirkby Malzeard, Yorkshire, in oak and in the more restrained and relatively neutral style of the day.*

PLATE 184. *Detail of the J.C. Elliott clock in mahogany and rosewood in very fussy style matching that of the dial. The band of marquetry inlay is unusual. Note the flat-surface, top-of-trunk moulding, veneered on its surface. Note also absence of brass fittings for hood capitals, etc., as they could not be obtained on this massive scale. Full pillars to the trunk. The wide hood now incorporates a door framework outside the hood door itself, a feature not found earlier.*

PLATE 185. *Eight-day mahogany clock of about 1870 by Owen Roberts of Caernarvon, North Wales, in very fussy and heavy late style, a last fling at exotic casemaking as an attempt at competing with cheaper, imported clocks. Height about 8ft. The applied roundels are a whim of the casemaker rather than typical, but are just an extension of the fussy taste of the day. Full trunk pillars (turned, fluted and carved) match those of the hood and extend to just the height of the short door. Dartboard base here takes the form of yet another gadrooned roundel. Lion's paw feet are cut short in the photograph.*

PLATE 186. *Detail of the Roberts clock, which is a late example of a rocking ship dial. Extreme late features include: flat surface mouldings to swan-neck and below hood in pale (African?) mahogany; unmoulded edge to main door; side frame-pieces to hood door, in this instance carrying bobbin-turned half sections; lack of brass hood fittings (at this period).*

PLATE 187. *Trunk section of a mahogany longcase of about 1840 of the wide-bodied style with short, wavy-topped door having stringing-framed veneered sections above and below, canted corners and complex mouldings. Instantly recognisable as to period and region, without even seeing the rest of the case. The clock was made by William Moorehouse of Wetherby, Yorkshire.*

PLATE 188. *Mahogany clock standing 6ft.9in. dating about 1830 by Robert Summerhayes of Taunton, Somerset. Many typical Southern features including simple moulds, three-quarter length door with flat top, wavy backsplats to hood. Corinthian brass capitals are unusual, as are the swan-necks in being mouldless on the face rims.*

CHAPTER FOURTEEN

DIALS IN SCOTLAND

USE OF ENGLISH DIALS

Within a very few years of its introduction by the Birmingham dialmakers, the painted dial was in use in Scotland, supplied to the clockmaking trade there from England in just the same way as it was supplied to their English, Welsh and Irish (and even American) counterparts. I cannot personally recall having seen a Scottish-made clock with a dial by the first partners (Osborne & Wilson, 1772-77), but certainly English japanned dials were in use by Scottish clockmakers within a very few years after 1777 and quite possibly before.

There is nothing very different about English-made dials of Period One as used in Scotland. They are of the same nature, style and combinations of features as those same dials were when supplied to English makers. In other words, nothing on the face side of an English-made dial identifies a white dial clock as being Scottish other than the maker's name. The dialmaker's name will often be found behind the dial, exactly as with English clocks, sometimes with and sometimes without a falseplate fitting. The movements may have distinguishing features, which we come to recognise as being different from their English equivalent, but not the dials.

Indeed it is largely true that throughout the entire period of white dial clock-making, the work of those Scots makers who decided to use English dials can be recognised only by the name on the dial face. Those stylistic features we recognise on a dial as being distinctly Scottish are found only on those clocks having dials which were themselves made in Scotland.

Scots-made movements often have rather differently-shaped pillars from English ones in that they frequently taper towards the centre knop, thickening in the middle and narrowing towards the plate ends. Not all Scottish clockmakers did this, but many did, to the point where it is thought of as a typically Scottish feature, though of course occasional English clockmakers did it too. Otherwise I am aware of no other recognisably Scots feature of clock movements, though an oddity of the country seems to be that thirty-hour clocks are virtually unknown in Scotland. When a Scot wanted a longcase clock, it seems he wanted an eight-day. So for stylistic features on Scottish clocks with English-made dials, the reader needs to refer to the earlier chapters on the japanned dial in England.

DIALMAKING IN SCOTLAND

The first maker of japanned dials in Scotland, or at least the first one we know about, was William Dallaway of Edinburgh, who was working there about 1775. When he made his first white dials is not known but it was probably in the 1780s. At that time he worked at 'the foot of Tollbooth Wynd, Canongate'.

Dallaway made japanned goods of varying kinds and not just dials for clocks. In 1793 he advertised in the Edinburgh *Evening Courant* that:

> He has taken in partnership his son, who has been in London and Birmingham for the improvement of that art [i.e. japanning] and has procured the secret of inlaying stove fronts, dressing cases, candlesticks, etc, which is a thing never attempted here before…

We can probably deduce that his son had learnt the process in Birmingham. The advertisement adds that Dallaway 'still continues to teach drawing in all its

PLATE 189. *Twelve-inch eight-day dial of about 1790-1800 from a longcase clock by John Barron of Aberdeen. Believed to be a Scottish-made dial, though unmarked as to dialmaker. Dial sheet thinner and more flexible than English ones, with floral corners unbordered and not quite English in style. Name lettering not evenly spaced, yet original. Original hands in blued steel in matching style of diamond pattern.*

branches as usual'. This suggests that Dallaway himself was an artist, and he may well have done artwork on the dials he manufactured. William Dallaway is believed to have died shortly after 1793 and the business was continued by his son, H(enry?) Dallaway. The Dallaways also supplied special strong varnishes (for chairs, tea trays and mahogany tables) 'that will not fly although ever so hardly handled'.

In 1797 another Dallaway advertisement reads:

H.Dallaway & Son, Japan Manufactory, North Back of Canongate, Edinburgh.
H.D.& Son return their grateful acknowledgements for past favours. They beg leave to inform their friends and the public that they have on hand a complete assortment of the following articles, which they continue to sell Wholesale, Retail, and for

PLATE 190. *Eight-day dial of about 1790 with rocking ship made for a clock by Colin Salmon of Dundee, the dialmaker unknown. This could perhaps be an English-made dial; rocking figures seem not to have been a common feature on Scottish-made dials. Matching hands in blued steel, though the minute hand appears to be a replacement and does not quite match the hour hand.*

Exportation:-

Japanned Fire Screens of black iron, a capital invention, and for elegance and neatness nothing can excel them: *Clock dials a fine collection*; Tea Trays, Waiters, Candlesticks, Snuffer Stands, Knife Slips, Bread Baskets.

H.D. & Son cannot let slip this opportunity of particularly recommending their Tea Trays, Waiters, etc. as they have now brought them to that perfection as would do honour to an English Manufactory. They flatter themselves that from their perseverance and attention they still will merit a continuance of past favours. Commissions from the country in the Japanning line or for any of the above articles will be carefully attended to.

So Dallaways made and held stocks of white dials for the trade, for private purchasers (though I can't imagine there were many of those), and for export, by which they presumably mean to America, not England. Most interestingly they

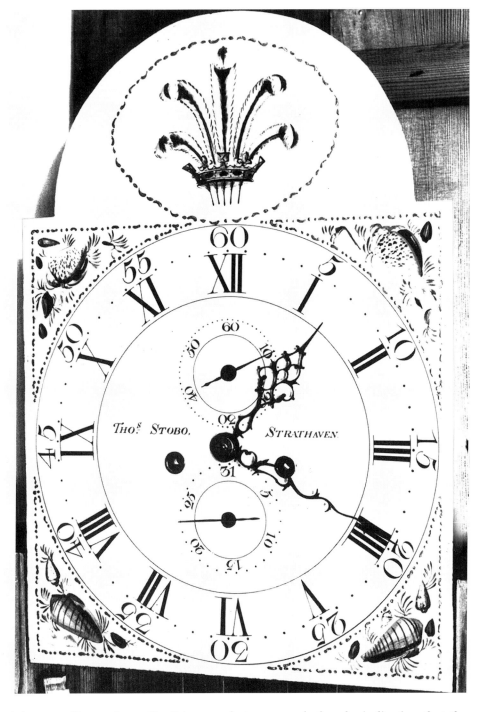

PLATE 191. *Thirteen-inch eight-day dial from a longcase clock of about 1790-1800 by Thomas Stobo of Strathaven, the dial unmarked but believed to be of Scottish make. The dial is of thinner and more flexible iron than English ones and the corners and their dot-dash borders, though of the Wilson concept, seem less well done than in England. Original blued steel hands in non-matching pattern.*

claim a quality to do an English manufactory proud, thereby indicating that the Scots japanners themselves still regarded English dials as the best and as a quality target they should aim for.

Patrick Dallaway, believed to be another son of the late William, was in dispute in 1809 with the local guild, known as the Incorporation of Hammermen, for allegedly infringing their rights by trading when not a member. He was principally an ironmonger but did some trade with the company of William Dallaway & Son, presumably including clock dials. The point of interest to us in this dispute is that the Hammermen mentioned in one letter that: 'as the father of Mr.Dallaway *had introduced the Art of Japanning into this quarter,* which had turned out to be

PLATE 192. *Thirteen-inch eight-day dial of about 1790-1800 from a longcase clock by Dallaway and Son of Edinburgh, the dial also marked by Dallaways on its falseplate. The crazing shows clearly. Note the 60, 20, 40 seconds numbering and the 10, 20, 30 of the minutes, both very un-English. Matching main hands in steel of thistle pattern may be later replacements; smaller hands in brass appear original. The goldwork of the arch and corners is especially delicate and neat. The legend 'Venit Summa Dies' means 'the high-point of the day approaches', referring to time and Judgement Day.*

beneficial to the whole of the country, they therefore recommended that out of respect to his memory his son should be allowed to carry on the tinsmith trade within the city (for the sum of forty pounds, etc) ....'

It is not clear from this whether William Dallaway was the first in Scotland or just in Edinburgh, but it is believed that he was the first in Scotland to make japanned dials.

In 1811 Patrick Dallaway wrote: ' from the death of my father I find that I cannot carry on the ironmongery business and follow the japanning also; therefore I must relinquish one of them. I have now come to the resolution of giving up the said ironmongery and mean to devote my attention to my (japan) manufactory'. However, Patrick is known to have gone back to tinsmith work in 1812, but whether he continued dial production is uncertain.

PLATE 193. *Circular eight-day dial dating from about 1820-30 from a longcase clock by Peter Keir of Dalkeith. The dialmaker is unknown and could be English or Scottish as there seem to be no distinguishing features. The minute hand appears to be a replacement in brass; the hour hand original in a matching pattern in blued steel.*

DIAL TYPES

A few aspects of painted dial clocks in Scotland are distinctly different from the English counterparts. I have already mentioned the lack of thirty-hour clocks of Scottish origin. It also seems true that at all periods in Scottish-made white dials, moon dials are far less numerous than in England, and when a moon does occur it is often on a clock which also shows tidal times as a moon-with-tides feature. As with English moon-dial clocks, the quality of painting of the moon disc often seems to be consistently higher than that on the rest of the dial. Why it may have been felt that the moon was more important than the rest of the dial is hard to imagine, but it seems to be the case that moon discs were often painted by a different (and often more skilled) hand from the rest of the dial.

There is also a very strange (when seen with English eyes) dearth of square dial clocks there. Most Scottish-made longcase clocks have arched dials, the square dial being little used, except that after about 1840 clocks of the more formal (semi-Regulator) type sometimes had a plain square dial or a plain round one.

These square dials (and round ones too) were more along the lines of a Regulator dial and were used for Regulators, though they were often used on non-Regulators too. Such clocks were perhaps made for a gentleman's library or study, or for public institutions, offices, banks, being generally of a more austere nature than a household clock, and usually lacking any decoration to the dial. Such dials were either plain white, or plain gold, or sometimes plain silver in colour, but

COLOUR PLATE 24. *Thirteen-inch dial from an eight-day longcase clock of about 1790 by Walter Scott of Lauder, the dialmaker indicated on the falseplate as Dallaway of Edinburgh. The floral corners are in the English manner but executed rather differently with solid black-line borders. Note the crazing in the ground. Original matching pattern hands in brass in a most unusual style. This clock has a deadbeat escapement, though this is not apparent from the dial.*

over the years the varnish on once-silver dials has often yellowed and makes these look like gold ones. Round dials were available throughout but were less common before about 1830. Some round dials had the gold or silver just on the chapter ring area, and all these gold-banded types, round or square, date from Period Three, i.e. after 1830 and often as late as the 1860s or 1870s.

But to return to the beginning of Scottish-made white dials about 1780, it is true to say that almost all were eight-day and were arched in shape, the round and square versions seldom appearing till after 1810. The style of early Scottish-made dials is very like that of their English contemporaries, usually copying the sort of decoration used by Osborne and Wilson. However there is a difference, which is difficult to define yet can usually be recognised.

DIAL STYLES

The artwork is usually a little heavier and not quite so well balanced as, for example, a Wilson dial, and often the flower corners lack the gold dot-dash border. Many of these early ones have no border at all, but when they do it is often a solid gold-lined border (see Colour Plate 24, Walter Scott dial) or a dot-dash border rather different from a Wilson dot-dash border (see Colour Plate 25, Wilkie dial). However, it is generally the case that a Period One dial on a Scottish clock will prove to be an English dial. Perhaps the only regular exception is a Dallaway dial, which is usually marked on its falseplate.

All japanned dials tend to show some signs of crazing on the white, japanned surface, not usually so obvious on the painted corners. On English dials this varies according to period and probably also according to the quality of the japanning and the conditions under which the clock has passed two centuries or so. On Scottish dials, however, this crazing is usually more obvious and the craze patterns seem to be often formed into larger pieces. This was probably because the japanning process was not of such high quality as with English dials.

Scottish-made dials are seldom less than thirteen inches wide, even in Period One. This may have been because by the time Scottish-made dials were under way the thirteen-inch size was coming into general fashion. Where a Scottish clock does have a twelve-inch dial, it will usually be found to have an English-made dial. I cannot recall having seen a dial on a Scottish clock (eight-day, of course) less than twelve inches.

As with English dials, some have falseplates and some do not. With Scottish-made dials falseplates seem to fall from use after about 1830. Some Scottish dials have unmarked falseplates, but some Scottish falseplate dials do carry the names of the dialmakers. 'Dallaway & Sons, Edinr.', 'H. Dallaway & Son, Edinr.', 'Patterson, Perth', and 'T. Smith & Stevenson, Edinr.' are known examples. A list of all known Scottish dialmakers appears on pages 39-40.

Some Scottish-made dials are lettered on the back in paint, sometimes with mysterious numbers, meaningless to us today, but at other times with what we know to be the dialmakers' names. 'Bell & Meudell, Edinr', 'Russel & Clark, Edinr.', 'Peter Bell, Edinr.' and 'D. Sinclair, Japr. Edinr.' are some examples. Some dialmakers added the words 'Best Fancy' or 'Finest Fancy', probably indicating a certain style or quality. Some of these 'fancy' dials (possibly even all of them?) are of the type with luminous colours, described later.

Many Scottish dials cannot be attributed to a particular dialmaker. Often we can deduce they are of Scottish make because they have features varying, as described above, from the English equivalent. With some, however, it is difficult to be sure whether they are of Scottish or English make, and if the experienced cannot be sure, then the beginner will probably be completely baffled.

Not very many Scottish-made dials date before 1800, and by this time the style of dialpainting has often acquired certain features which we can recognise as being distinctly Scottish in nature. Scottish dials did go through that phase of patterned, symmetrical corners often using fan corners. But solid corner paintings using 'fours' themes seem popular earlier in Scotland than in England. The Four Seasons were especially popular. The Four Continents and Four Countries too were popular, less so than the seasons yet more so than in England. Less popular but still met with are the Four Elements and the Four Virtues, and sometimes the Four Ages of Man (i.e. Infancy, Youth, Manhood, Old Age).

NUMBERING

Numbering patterns were similar to those on English-made dials, but one

PLATE 194. *Thirteen-inch eight-day dial of Scottish make, though an unknown dialmaker, from a longcase clock of about 1840-50 by Peter Feren of Dundee. A scene from the Lady of the Lake fills the arch. The corners show the Four Countries (England, Scotland, Ireland and Wales) featuring a female monarch, presumably Queen Victoria. The strong colours with metallic finish are typical of many later Scottish dials. Original hands in matching pattern in brass.*

variation used (perhaps exclusively?) by Dallaways was to number Period Two minutes as 60, 10, 20, 30, etc. instead of the usual English way of 60, 15, 30, etc. It is probably safe to say that dials numbering minutes in this way are likely to be Scottish-made, quite possibly by Dallaways. Some Dallaway dials also number seconds as 20, 40, 60, rather than 10, 20, 30, etc. (see Plate 192). Arabic hour numerals seem to have been far less common in Scotland than England, and when they do appear on a Scottish clock it is usually one using an English-made dial.

In late Period Two and Period Three some Scottish-made dials number the quarter-hour minutes, as was also done in England (i.e. 60, 15, 30, 45). However, a regular Scottish practice was to position these numbers *inside* the double minute

COLOUR PLATE 26. *Unrestored and rather worn eight-day longcase dial from a clock of about 1840 by Bain of Brechin, the dialmaker unknown but clearly Scottish. The Four Seasons corners are executed in a manner typical of Scottish dials. The arch is especially interesting showing a cabinetmaker at work with a half-finished longcase in the background. This arch scene is a one-off and must have been done at the specific request of the buyer. Calendar hand missing; other hands original in matching pattern in brass.*

COLOUR PLATE 27. *Thirteen-inch eight-day dial by an unknown Scottish dialmaker from a longcase clock of about 1850 by J. & G. Panton of Glasgow. The Four Seasons corners are in typical Scottish manner, each scene running into the next indicating a later period. The arch painting shows the 'Cotters' Saturday Night', being the family solemnly reading the Bible and an interpretation of a popular painting of the day. Original matching brass hands. The paints have a backing of silver leaf, giving a luminous effect to certain colours.*

track, whereas English positioning was almost invariably *outside* the track.

In late Period Two and Period Three many English-made dials have a gold line around the outside of the hour numerals. This gold line was sometimes used in Scottish-made dials too, but less often than in English ones. The absence of such a gold circle may therefore be an indicator towards a Scottish-made dial, though in itself is not proof.

PLATE 195. *Thirteen-inch Scottish-made dial by an unidentified dialmaker from an eight-day longcase clock of about 1840-50 by Robert Croal of Alyth. The Escape of Mary Queen of Scots fills the arch. The corners feature folk heroes Burns, Ramsay, Ferguson and Scott. Some colours are backed by silver leaf to give the luminous effect. The maker's name is often in a scroll at this time. Original matching hands in brass, the main hands of a most unusual pattern featuring a bird.*

THEMES

Scottish dials have a patriotic or nationalistic element to a far greater degree than English ones. Portraits of heroes of history and legend, literature and science often adorn the corners, with or without similar themes in the arch, and these heroic themes are far more common than in England, especially in Period Three.

Arch scenes often show scenes from Scottish literature, art or history and are often named: The Escape of Mary Queen of Scots, Robert the Bruce, Burns at the Plough, Burns and Highland Mary, The Lady of the Lake, Patie and Peggy, Auld

PLATE 196. *Unrestored eight-day dial of unmistakably Scottish origin, though the dialmaker is unknown, from a longcase clock by James Davidson of Airdrie dating about 1850. Wallace looks out from the arch between the figures of Justice and Scotland. The corners feature Burns, Ferguson, Ramsay and Scott (as in Plate 195 but differently represented). Luminous effects created by silver-leaf backing to certain colours. Hands are original (though here not polished) in brass in matching pattern.*

Robin Gray, Death of Marmion, The Cottar's Saturday Night, The Highlander's Return, Queen Victoria ('s coronation?). Some of these themes recur surprisingly often and the very popular ones are relatively few in number, and of course these subjects (Queen Victoria excepted) occur *only* on Scottish-made dials.

In Period Two we sometimes find patterned corners, akin to the English style, and sometimes these persist in a more flowery nature through Period Three.(see Plate 197, Sheddon dial).

At all periods we still find some English-made dials used by Scottish clockmakers and, after studying a few Scottish dials of this folklore type, an English dial

COLOUR PLATE 28. *Scottish-made eight-day dial, maker unknown, from a longcase clock of about 1840-50 by William Law of Linlithgow. The corners show one version of the Four Seasons, here with seated rather than standing ladies. The arch carries a scene entitled 'Domestic Happiness'. Note the unrealistic representation, especially obvious in the doll-like children. Original hands in matching pattern in brass of the crescent moon style.*

presents a very different and unmistakable appearance with quite different landscapes of rustic bliss.

The painting of these folk-art subjects, sometimes known in Scotland as 'couthy' subjects, is heavy and strong, often with bold, even dark, colours, heavily-draped curtains as surrounds and often with a silver-leaf base beneath certain colours, thus producing an almost luminous quality of iridescence. The people themselves

COLOUR PLATE 29. *Eight-day clock of about 1840 by Cameron of Dundee with a richly-coloured (silver-leaf backed) dial by an unknown Scottish dialmaker. In the arch is what appears to be Queen Victoria, and this may date the clock to soon after her accession (1837). The corners show the Four Countries. Quarter minutes marked inside the minute track. Original hands in brass in matching thistle pattern. The mahogany case has a most unusual hood style.*

PLATE 197. *Thirteen-inch dial from an eight-day long-case clock of about 1825-35 by Charles Sheddon of Perth, the dial unidentified but recognisable by style as made in Scotland. The patterned corners are of a busier nature than those on English dials and the arch is filled in the same busy manner as the corners. Numbering of quarter-hour minutes inside the double minute track is found not infrequently on Scottish dials, seldom on English. Original matching pattern hands in brass.*

are often painted as flat, cardboard pictures and are often misproportioned. Backgrounds are often crammed tight with small details and objects pertinent to the character or the theme. The painting quality and style of some of the later dials is akin to that of the fairground roundabout.

Some difference in taste between Eastern Scotland, centred on Edinburgh, and Western Scotland, centred on Glasgow, is apparent in dials as it is in casework. Edinburgh followed the English taste, using initially English dials, then Scottish dials in the English manner, then full-blown, 'couthy' dials, and dial size there remained restrained at first — twelve inches or thirteen inches, seldom more. In Western Scotland there was a taste sooner for the larger size of dial (often fourteen-inch dials by 1800 and often with a very high and therefore large arch area) and for the 'couthy' subjects.

After about 1830 this difference in dial style has largely disappeared. Restraint in dial style hereafter appears only in those square or round dials of the semi-Regulator style, which are totally devoid of any decoration.

Why the Scots should go for these heavier, more boldly coloured dials I cannot say. Perhaps the climate with shorter daylight hours in winter and generally drearier weather may have produced a call for a more colourful display indoors, and in the light of an oil lamp the brighter colours of these luminous dials would gleam in a more cheerful and eye-catching manner. It is likely too that some of these bright, even gaudy painted dials would be in poorer homes which might otherwise be devoid of any wall-hung paintings, which is perhaps all the more reason for their strong colours.

Although Dallaways offered their dials for export, it is interesting that we seem not to find American clocks with these strong and distinctive dials, but with those made on the English principles. These bolder dials were later in period than Dallaways anyway, but the same principle applies in that we do not see the 'couthy' dials used on American-made clocks.

Round dials lettered with numbering and name are found from about 1810 onwards. Most are plain white but some have a gold-painted 'chapter ring' area or a gold dial centre. Some London longcases of the Regulator and semi-Regulator type had these too (though not with the goldwork), and perhaps the Scots were following this London taste. Some round dial Scottish clocks do have a deadbeat escapement, and just occasionally they may have maintaining power, but they are not true Regulators. We often call these semi-Regulators and they have certain characteristics of them. Some will have a conventional anchor escapement, but with the teeth so cut as to produce little recoil and give an impression of a deadbeat.

Calendars on Scottish longcases are normally of the pointer type except where an English dial has been used, when they may still use the older mouth system. In fact I cannot bring to mind a Scottish-made dial with anything but a pointer calendar, which was certainly a more precise and reliable method but involved an extra wheel.

Scottish casework in longcase clocks is along the English lines but different. By the time the painted dial appeared in Scotland, longcase styles had already settled into established patterns, the great majority being based on the swan-neck hood. In Eastern Scotland the 'Edinburgh' school case of the eighteenth and early nineteenth centuries often has a neat little swan-neck pediment with often a distinctive small blind fret below the swan. In Western Scotland hoods and cases are often a little heavier (perhaps because of the wider dials?) and a style which we call the long hood developed there by about 1830. In this the pillars (where present) extend the full height of the arched hood door (see Plate 206, Gillies clock) giving the clock a much more top-heavy appearance. These long hoods originally had a cresting on top, now often missing.

Certain specialised styles occur in casework. The square dial clock was uncommon until after about 1830, after which this rather specialised style appeared, usually with a flat-topped hood originally surmounted by a crest (often now missing); see Plate 217 (Innes clock), which retains its crest, and Plate 216 (Muirhead clock), which has probably lost it. The square dial seems not to be found in small, oak, cottage-style clocks, as it was in England, though the flat-topped cottage case was sometimes made in arched dial form in cheaper woods such as pine (see Plate 214, Stobo clock). Pine would originally have been stained

COLOUR PLATE 30. *Dial from an eight-day clock of about 1800 by Jameson of Maybole showing an unusual version of fan style corners, which together with the heavy crazing suggests a Scottish-made dial, though unmarked. The five-minute numbering is also an unusual feature when combined with the double-track minute band.*

to resemble a more costly wood such as mahogany, though today we usually see pine in its presently-fashionable stripped state.

This type of square dial clock illustrated *was* small, but was usually in fine mahogany, was often made by prestigious makers, was often a high quality, precision clock, and was made more as a semi-Regulator type, probably for a gentleman's study.

Some later round dials (after about 1820 or 1830, and usually considerably later) have what we call 'drumhead' cases as in Plate 220 (Grey clock), this being a distinctive hood style only found in Scotland. Drumheads sometimes have the

COLOUR PLATE 31. *Eight-day clock of about 1840 by William Wylie of Stromness, clearly a Scottish-made dial with the Four Seasons corners and the arch scene showing the Cotters' Saturday Night theme. Matching pattern hands in brass – seconds hand may be a replacement.*

plain circular hood top, but others have a cresting piece atop this. Some drumheads have a bow door, that is a half-round door, as in Plate 220. Bow doors do occur on other styles of case too (see Plate 213). With most drumheads and some other Scottish round dial case styles too, the hood door is just a brass bezel, exactly as found on round dial wall clocks (Plate 219). The drumhead, like the square dial just mentioned, was probably also the sort of clock for the purist, for a gentleman's study or library or perhaps for the hallway of the sophisticated.

CHAPTER FIFTEEN

CASEWORK IN SCOTLAND

Before the introduction of the painted dial, clock casework in Scotland had more or less followed the English styles of the day. By 1770 the English models from which Scottish craftsmen took their styles were not those of London but of the English provinces and principally those of Northern England, presumably because those were the counties with which they had most contact. However certain aspects of Scottish clockmaking had a bearing on casemaking, most important of which was the fact that the great majority of Scottish longcase clocks at this time had arched dials. The square dial was then (1770) virtually unknown there and the round dial had not yet come into vogue there. So the fact that almost all longcase work had to suit the arched dial style has a considerable bearing on those English styles chosen as models. The other important factor is that Scottish clocks were rarely if ever of thirty-hour duration, so we are dealing exclusively with eight-day casework.

It could be argued that by this date traditional styles had already developed within Scotland on brass dial clocks, but as we are far more familiar with the much greater numbers of English longcases of the painted dial era than we are with brass dial Scottish clocks, it is probably easiest for the student to make comparisons against the English models.

Early painted dials in most of Scotland tended to be small, the twelve-inch arched dial being the norm, though in some parts of Western Scotland centred on Glasgow the thirteen inch dial came in early, usually earlier than elsewhere in that country. It is tempting to say that at this period (i.e. shortly after 1770) *the* style was long trunk, long door style with the swan-neck pediment. This is not entirely true as occasional examples will be seen with a flat-top hood, but as the reason for these flat-topped exceptions is usually because an applied swan-neck pediment has been removed later, it was probably true originally but later modification would make such a statement seem inaccurate.

Oak cases were not uncommon but by far the majority of Scottish painted dial clocks of all periods had mahogany cases, and this applied increasingly as time passed. Oak was most unusual after about 1830, when almost all cases were of mahogany. Pine (originally painted, of course) was little used, but an occasional example is seen. It is reasonably safe to say that these were the only woods used, but there is always an occasional exception to prove the rule, as, for example, the rosewood case illustrated in Plate 232.

A First Period Scottish painted dial longcase will normally resemble a small and neat English clock with a long door and swan-neck pediment – small because ceiling height may often have been lower in Scottish homes than in English ones, neat because the small dial kept case width down. The long door might occasionally have a flat top but far more often a shaped top or even a simple curve.

The swan-neck was usually small and neat. In eastern Scotland, based on Edinburgh, the swan-neck often had a distinctive shape and left a small space beneath the curve of the moulding, which space was often filled with either a fretted panel backed by cloth, or with a solid infill of veneer, which was sometimes in a quite different colour of wood for effect. I call these 'Edinburgh frets' or 'Edinburgh infills' for the sake of a term, though by no means all the clocks having them were made in Edinburgh, nor all the cases. They are most often found on mahogany cases but sometimes on oak ones too. These Edinburgh in-

PLATE 198. *Eight-day oak clock by James Anderson of West Haven, near Aberdeen, c.1785, standing only about 6ft.6in. Small and neat with classic East Scots features such as small swan-neck with pale mahogany 'Edinburgh infills' beneath, edged in stringing. Inlaid roundels for paterae. Long door with shaped top. Hood side windows occur on many such cases, as here.*

PLATE 199. *Small oak eight-day clock in typical East Scots style made about 1790 by John Smith of Pittenweem, on the east coast north of Dunfermline. Edinburgh frets beneath small swan-necks. Fluted quarter columns to long trunk with long, shaped-top door. Height 6ft.6in.*

fills were most common in Period One but sometimes continued to be used as late as Period Three.

In western Scotland, centred on Glasgow, a style of case had developed by 1770 also based on the swan-neck pediment but of a different concept in that here a flat-topped hood had a separate swan-neck piece glued on to the flat, appearing almost as an afterthought, although an integral part of the design. This was a type of swan-neck often used in north-east England in the counties of Northumberland and Durham, though why it should switch coasts in Scotland I do not know. Not all cases had this, of course, but those which did were principally from the west of Scotland. Most cases of this style were in mahogany rather than oak, but that may simply be because most Scots cases of this time were in mahogany anyway. As mentioned before, this applied swan-neck was often removed later to reduce height or on account of breakage, so that now we seem to have two styles: the flat-top case and the flat top with applied swan-neck. Both are really the same style.

Where a flat-top trunk door is used in Scotland there is a greater tendency for it to be found on this type of western flat-top case (with or without its applied swan-neck).

On some of these western Scots flat-top cases (with or without pediment) a style developed of making the hood door flat-topped too and taking the hood pillars up in height beyond the dial shoulder to a height equal to that of the hood door. These were therefore much longer pillars than on a normal arched dial case and gave the hood a long and sometimes top-heavy look. After about 1830 some of these long hood clocks ceased to have true pillars but had a mould run into the hood door frame in the manner of a pillar. The long hood case style is found from Period One through to Period Three, with or without the applied swan-neck.

By the time we reach Period Three other styles have appeared, a principal feature of some being what we call the bow door, that is a convex-surfaced trunk door, which might appear on arched-dial or round-dial cases but always on mahogany examples. Sometimes the bow door has a shaped and bowed top and sometimes also a matching bottom, but usually the top (and bottom) piece is fixed to the case, looking like part of the door but the true door being flat top and bottom. Bow door cases often have long half pillars at each side and sometimes the upper and/or lower trunk sections also have a half-round area like a large cushion mould. As far as I am aware the bow door is a feature found only in Scottish casework.

The square dial was occasionally used in Period Three in mahogany clocks which are often of a more formal type akin to a Regulator. They usually had a shaped top pediment, solid and carved rather than pierced. Flat-top arched dial cases also sometimes had such a pediment in Period Three instead of the true applied swan-neck found on earlier examples of this style.

Round dial clocks came into vogue during Period Two and initially their cases were based vaguely on the London round dial style, having a simple domed top rather than the swan-neck pediment found on northern English round dial clocks. One particular style of case became popular from about 1820 with round dials, and that is the style we know as a drumhead clock, a case style found only in Scotland. A drumhead case can take several forms but is identified by the fact that the topmost section of the case (above the trunk) resembles a mantel clock set on top of a longcase trunk, the hood itself being rounded like a drum. Drumheads may or may not have a bow door. Some have a pierced cresting above the drum top. One rather strange form of drumhead clock has a trunk of round section, often tapered wider towards its base and often fluted all round down its length,

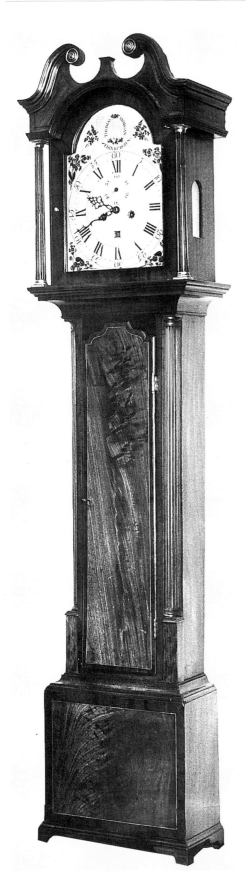

PLATE 201. *Hood detail of the mahogany eight-day clock by Thomas Morgan of Edinburgh dating from the 1780s. Typical narrow-waisted infills beneath the swan-necks are veneered in a different colour of mahogany for effect. Arched side windows to hood. Brass caps and bases to fluted pillars.*

PLATE 200. *Mahogany eight-day clock of about 1780 by Thomas Morgan of Edinburgh, standing only 6ft.8in. Classic Edinburgh proportions with long shaped-top door to long trunk and fluted quarter columns. Crossbanded outside a white stringing line. Side windows to hood are a common feature on these cases.*

PLATE 202. *Hood detail of a small mahogany eight-day clock of about 1790 by William Robb of Montrose (see Colour Plate 6), on the east coast south of Aberdeen. Edinburgh infills beneath the swan-necks, here in pale wood edged in stringing and 'matching' with inlaid roundels to the paterae. Similar pale cross-banding to hood door and shaped-top door. Three original finials. Shaped-top hood side windows. Fluted pillars here have unusually tiny brass Corinthian caps and bases, as have the rear quarter-pillars.*

not unlike a swelling tree trunk with fluting. These often sit uncomfortably on a normal square-shaped base. I have heard these described as resembling a fluted Doric column but the only name I know for them is a 'tree trunk' clock. They appear to be unique to Scotland, though some Scandinavian painted pine clocks are vaguely similar and this may be the source of influence.

The swan-neck pediment in relatively small and modest form remained in use on some clocks until the latter stages of Period Three. By this time occasional exotic or experimental hood forms appeared, some of which defy description.

PLATE 203. *Oak eight-day clock of about 1790 by Walter Scott of Lauder, south-east of Edinburgh. Classic East Scots case of the day with small swan-neck and Edinburgh narrow-waisted mahogany-veneer infills beneath. Long shaped-top door in long trunk with fluted quarter-columns. No hood side windows in this example. Height 6ft.10in.*

PLATE 204. *Mahogany eight-day clock of about 1810 by John Smith of Pittenweem, on the east coast north of Dunfermline, standing about 7ft.6in. Gilded wooden finials of 'flambeau' type are unusual for the area but believed original. Long curved-top door in long trunk with fluted quarter-columns. Hood side windows. Classic East Scots proportions but here without the Edinburgh infills to the neat swan-necks.*

PLATE 205. *All mahogany eight-day clock of about 1790 by D. Robb of Montrose on the east coast south of Aberdeen. Decorated with stringing, the oval to the base being unusual for the area. The Edinburgh infill area is simply outlined in stringing. Hood pillars and trunk quarter-columns here not fluted but inlaid with contrasting woods to resemble fluting, the lower one-third of each in a darker wood along the principles of London brass-piped pillars. Height a little over 7ft.*

PLATE 206. *Mahogany eight-day clock actually dated 1802 by Robert Gillies of Beith, near Glasgow. About 7ft. An example of the West Scots long hood style with flat-topped hood door and pillars extended its full height, these in fact projected forward on an extended mould and of an unusual twisted type. The flat-topped trunk door echoes the flat hood, on to which is attached a pierced swan-neck pediment, its upper sections broken away. Many such applied swan-necks have been removed completely.*

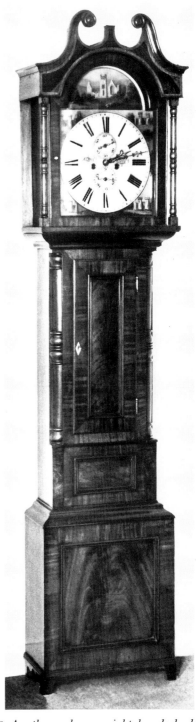

PLATE 207. *Mahogany eight-day clock of about 1840 in the East Scots style by Robert Croal of Alyth, just north of Dundee. Height 6ft.6in. Still displaying a type of Edinburgh infill below the swan-necks. Inlaid with satinwood cross-bandings and burr walnut panels. Shorter door in the shorter trunk is indicative of the later period.*

PLATE 208. *Another mahogany eight-day clock also by Robert Croal of Alyth in a different variation of the later East Scots case style and dating from about 1840-50. Shorter door and shorter trunk than earlier indicate period, as does the turning of the hood pillars and trunk quarter-columns. The recessed base panel with matching one below the door is a feature sometimes used at this time. The swan-necks still carry a form of Edinburgh infill below the moulds. Height about 6ft.10in.*

PLATE 209. *Mahogany eight-day clock of about 1850 by James Davidson of Airdrie, east of Glasgow, in the bow door style with half-round pillars often associated with this style and the cushion mould above and below the door. Panel effect in the base is simulated by a beading. Feet missing. Height about 7ft.*

PLATE 210. *Detail of the hood and dial of the clock by Davidson of Airdrie. The hood door frame sides are shaped to simulate flat-section hexagonal pillars. The dial features heroic subjects – Wallace, Burns, Ferguson, Scott, Ramsay. The cushion mould shows well below the top-of-trunk moulding.*

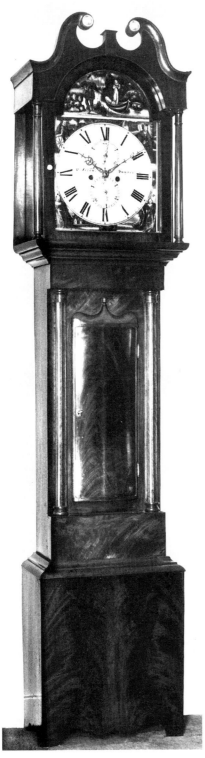

PLATE 211. *Mahogany eight-day clock of about 1840-50 by Peter Feren of Dundee on the east coast, standing 6ft.11in. An example of the bow door style, here with the accompanying half-pillars in fluted form. Relatively neutral in the swan-neck, though the whole style favours East rather than West.*

PLATE 212. *Mahogany eight-day clock of about 1840-50 by Melrose of Galashiels in southern central Scotland, standing about 7ft. Bow door style, here with turned half-pillars (which match those on the hood) and with the cushion moulds to top and base of trunk. Another version of the neutral swan-neck.*

PLATE 213. *Mahogany eight-day clock of about 1840-50 by William Law of Linlithgow, near Edinburgh. Bow door, cushion moulds, side half-pillars, sunken panel base running into semi-French feet, neutral swan-neck are all regular features of this case style and occur in varying combinations. No hood side windows in this style as a rule. Height about 7ft.*

PLATE 214. *Pine eight-day clock of about 1790 by Thomas Stobo of Strathaven, just south of Glasgow, standing 6ft.2in. Pine is unusual but the flat-top hood styling with flat-top trunk door suggest western influence. Dentil moulding along the hood topmould is a regular feature. The hood may once have had an applied swan-neck. Hood side windows are normal, but occasionally cloth-backed sound frets are used instead.*

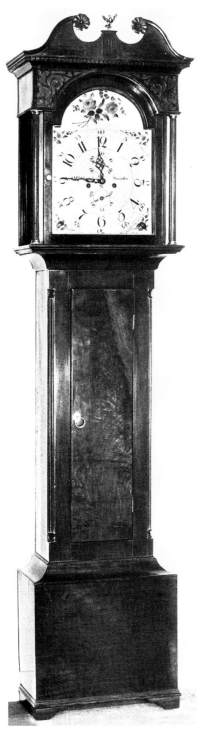

PLATE 215. *Eight-day clock in solid red walnut made about 1800 by Matthew Gemmel of Stewarton just south of Glasgow. An unusual wood for this period and often mistaken for mahogany. Typical West Scots style with flat top superimposed with a swan-neck and flat door top to match, still in the long door style. Shoulder-length hood pillars. Blind frets each side of the arch in what on some clocks is a blank area. Height 7ft.1in.*

PLATE 216. *Square dial eight-day clock in mahogany in the more formal style of a semi-Regulator made by James Muirhead of Glasgow about 1830-40 and standing 6ft.10in. High quality work with a few unusual features and perhaps made to match other furniture. Original bun feet.*

PLATE 217. *Square dial eight-day clock in mahogany by George Innes of Glasgow dating from about 1830. Flat-top hood with its original carved cresting piece. Matching flat-top door. Original tiny bun feet. Sound frets to hood sides. Height 6ft. 7in.*

PLATE 218. *Mahogany eight-day round dial clock of about 1820 by William Lithgow of Portobello (Edinburgh), standing 6ft. 6in. The dome top style follows the general London concept rather than northern English. Sound frets to hood sides. Still in the long door style. Finely figured wood with pale string lines.*

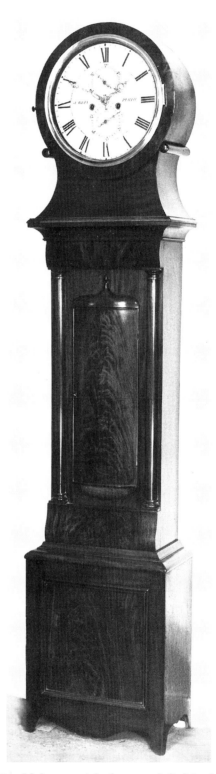

PLATE 219. *Mahogany eight-day round dial clock of the drumhead style made about 1820-30 by Brysons of Edinburgh and standing 6ft.8in. Three-quarter door with full side pillars and panel beneath matching the panel-effect base. The hood door has a brass bezel frame in the manner of a wall clock.*

PLATE 220. *Mahogany eight-day round dial in drumhead style made about 1820-30 by James Grey of Perth and standing 6ft.9in. This is of the bow door type with half-round pillars and the cushion mould above and below the door. Recessed panel base with semi-French feet.*

PLATE 221. *Mahogany eight-day round dial clock made about 1840 by Peter Penman of Dunfermline, north of Edinburgh. Bow door type with half-round trunk pillars, here echoed in the hood. The door top here is of a carved scroll pattern. Most unusual hood style, the two ball side finials missing. Height about 7ft.*

PLATE 222. *Mahogany eight-day clock in a case of most unusual cello shape with a hood style resembling that of the Penman clock, made about 1840 by Alexander Cameron of Dundee, on the east coast north of Edinburgh. Three-quarter length bow door type with carved scroll door top and panel below. Panel base and semi-French feet. Height about 7ft.3in.*

CHAPTER SIXTEEN

SPECIAL CLOCKS

My purpose in this chapter is to illustrate a few examples of unconventional clocks. Some clockmakers from the very earliest times were capable of making very complicated clocks; clocks which would chime or play tunes on bells or organs; clocks with moving figures; clocks showing times of sunrise and sunset, astronomical and even astrological conjunctions, moon phases and times of high tides, even, if need be, in numerous ports simultaneously; clocks showing simultaneous times in different parts of the world; clocks running to sidereal time, or even reading sidereal time and mean time simultaneously; clocks of intervals between windings as long as a year, and even at times much longer; calendrical clocks to show dates, days, months, Saints' Days, feast days, seasons and even the changing dates of Easter. At all times there were clockmakers quite capable of such work and this applies just as much during the period of painted dial clocks as at any other time.

Most clockmakers most of the time did not indulge in such things, not because they were incapable of them, but because there was no demand. Such clocks were complicated, costly, often impractical, and fraught with mechanical problems unless in the hands of a competent owner. A clock with complex calendrical readings, such as a perpetual calendar, might at first seem an interesting and useful idea, but had the problem that, if it should stop or run down, it would require the maker's attention to reset it. There were snags to many of these seemingly splendid options.

For example, in 1833 Job Rider of Belfast made a clock which was self-winding by changes in atmospheric pressure and ran for twelve years without attention whilst in the maker's own care. In practice such long duration was pointless, as any clock would need to be stopped for servicing before such a length of run was out. Sometimes a clockmaker might indulge his fancy by making a highly-complex clock for his own interest and amusement, really just to see if he could do it. But by and large the ordinary thirty-hour or eight-day longcase clock best fulfilled the householder's practical needs, and it is this type we meet in by far the largest numbers during the painted dial period. Nevertheless, there follows a series of clocks demonstrative of some of those unusual things which occasionally were done.

Whether or not a clock performs unusual functions, the rules we have so far observed in establishing period, and perhaps also locality, will still apply in both dials and casework. Dials may have additional sub-dials operating in places where otherwise decorative functions might assist us, which means they may offer fewer than usual of those features by which we establish period. All the same, adequate recognition points should remain for dating to be possible. Cases for special clocks might be built in a specific manner dictated by the clockwork, but most are simply variations on the theme of the day.

Illustrated in Plates 223-227 is a clock which runs for six months at one duration, made about 1820-30 by Benjamin Greening of Chepstow, Monmouthshire. This is an exceptionally rare item, and the only white dial clock I have ever seen with such a long run.

The clock by Thomas Lister junior (Colour Plate 32 and Plates 228-230) is unusual in several respects, particularly in the double-bell double-hammer striking of the hours. However the dial itself is of a most rare type showing the moon in an

PLATE 223. *Thirteen-inch dial by Walker & Hughes of Birmingham from a six-month duration clock by Benjamin Greening of Chepstow, c.1820-30. Calendar indication in the arch. Deadbeat escapement. Original hands in steel in matching style, very delicate with minute hand counterbalanced to reduce drag. Instructions on dial read 'Wind up Midsummer & Christmas Day'. The dial is seen here unrestored since new.*

PLATE 224. *Movement of the six-month clock by Benjamin Greening seen in dirty condition. Note deadbeat escape wheel, massive (solid) mainwheel and adjacent pinion, calendar shunt bar behind arch of dial. Even the gutline is unusually thick, as it has to carry exceptional weights. The clock also strikes the hours, and striking is unusual in such a long duration clock because of the problem of storing an adequate reserve of power.*

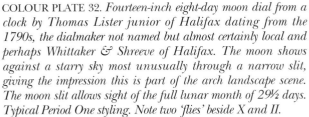

COLOUR PLATE 32. *Fourteen-inch eight-day moon dial from a clock by Thomas Lister junior of Halifax dating from the 1790s, the dialmaker not named but almost certainly local and perhaps Whittaker & Shreeve of Halifax. The moon shows against a starry sky most unusually through a narrow slit, giving the impression this is part of the arch landscape scene. The moon slit allows sight of the full lunar month of 29½ days. Typical Period One styling. Note two 'flies' beside X and II.*

COLOUR PLATE 33. *Fourteen-inch eight-day dial of about 1790 from a clock by Archer of Stowe, the dial made by Osborne, Birmingham, also with the very unusual slit moon, not unlike that of the Lister clock, the moon positioned as if part of the arch landscape. The visible sector, however, is two or three days short of the full 29½ lunar day span. Typical Period One styling. These two clocks have large dials to accommodate the wide moon span.*

COLOUR PLATE 34. *Thirteen-inch dial (by Hipkiss, Birmingham) from a clock of unique design, made about 1810 by William Porthouse of Penrith for the Revd. T. Clark of Rufford, Lancashire. The design, originating with Benjamin Franklin, was developed by James Ferguson as a pull-wind clock with a single hand rotating every four hours. The time in the photograph reads one minute past 4 or 8 or 12, so you need to know the approximate time within an hour or two to be able to use it. An interesting and novel idea, but it never caught on widely.*

PLATE 225. *The two lead drive weights of the Benjamin Greening six-month clock, each measuring 8in. by 5in. and each weighing an enormous 56lb. Hence the double-handled winding key for use with both hands during winding. The pendulum has a wooden rod to help avoid expansion with temperature change.*

PLATE 226. *The mahogany case of the Greening six-month clock is obviously of Bristol origin or style, many of its features being typical of the day. It has very sturdy feet, but at the front only. What at first sight appears to be the trunk door is in fact a panel to simulate a door (see Plate 227).*

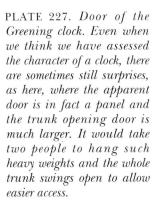

PLATE 227. *Door of the Greening clock. Even when we think we have assessed the character of a clock, there are sometimes still surprises, as here, where the apparent door is in fact a panel and the trunk opening door is much larger. It would take two people to hang such heavy weights and the whole trunk swings open to allow easier access.*

PLATE 228. *Detail of the Lister dial showing the two 'flies' (one fly and one wasp?). These cover the top two dial foot ends. Lister used the top two dial feet to carry a metal brace to which his moon gearing is fixed. He appears to have anticipated potential chipping from this extra strain, and therefore purposely had the flies positioned to camouflage this, though chipping did not in fact occur. This implies forward planning and liaison with the dial-maker.*

PLATE 229. *Movement of the Lister clock which strikes hourly on two bells simultaneously with two hammers, a most unusual method producing a more melodious sound. Note the name 'Lister' painted behind the moon wheel, which is cut with rounded teeth shaped for pinion drive.*

COLOUR PLATE 35. *Round japanned dial with silvered brass minutes ring and hours disc, a mixture of the two forms, made between 1772 and 1774 by William Thompson of Whitehaven, Cumberland, probably by way of experiment. The design is based on one by James Ferguson. Very rare if not unique. Case, of oak with mahogany trim, shows some Cumbrian features – bamboo effect pillars, run of three inlays beneath the hood – but not easy to identify for a beginner.*

COLOUR PLATE 37. *Sixteen-inch dial with twenty-four hour calibration made about 1790 by John Bolton of Chester-le-Street, County Durham. Sun face for an hour hand, counterbalanced minute hand. Moon dial. Subdial in arch registers calendar date (inner) and lunar date (outer). By using the central disc the clock will tell the time in any of the fifty named places around the world. Known as a world time dial. Despite the strange layout the numbering and painting styles help to assess the period.*

unconventional manner, which I had never before seen – until a few weeks later I was shown the clock by Archer of Stowe (Colour Plate 33), which has a very similar form of moon dial. The fact that Lister planned his moon gearing in advance of the dial being finished is most interesting, as the presence of the two flies to hide potential dial foot chipping (which never in fact occurred) implies that he was in close contact with the dialmaker/painter, so it was probably a Halifax-made dial.

The clock by Porthouse of Penrith (Colour Plate 34) is a variation on a theme developed by astronomer and mathematician James Ferguson, and is interesting as a novelty but was never a serious contender in the popularity stakes. It gives hours and minutes to the nearest five on a single hand which rotates every four hours. Q marks the quarters and H the half hours. The snag was that you had to know which four-hour sector you were in – as set here the dial reads roughly a minute past XII or VIII or IV! How you coped if disturbed from a deep sleep in the middle of the night I cannot imagine. Pull-winding systems such as this (and that of any thirty-hour clock) had built-in maintaining power, that is the clock did not stop during winding. It was simple mechanically, but personally I would have

COLOUR PLATE 36. *Astronomical clock dated 1830 by Ebenezer Henderson of Dunfermline made when he was only twenty-one. The mahogany case shows East Scots influences. Twenty-four hour dial with seconds from the centre. One of the two 'hour' hands reads the moon's age. Shows sunrise and sunset times, months and days of the month, signs of the Zodiac relating to the calendar, tide rise and moon phases, and much more. A very unusual dial and difficult to date by style. (Photograph by courtesy of Felix Hudson.)*

PLATE 231. *Detail of the arch of the Henderson dial, here seen unrestored. A ball moon revolves in the sky aperture showing the moon's phases. Between the cliffs is seen the surface of the sea, showing tidal water level and this rises and falls as the clock runs. These features were invented by James Ferguson and are usually known as the Ferguson tide and moon system, being exceptionally uncommon on painted dials.*

thought the ordinary thirty-hour single-handed clock did every-thing this clock does and in a way more easily understood.

From its dial style, even though of a very eccentric nature, we can assess the period – Roman hours and Arabic minutes, full corner paintings, hand of the diamond-tip type in steel as with a pair of matching hands of the day, falseplate giving the dialmaker as Hipkiss of Birmingham, all add up to about 1810.

Colour Plate 35 shows a round dial clock being a composite one with a japanned base sheet with silvered brass chapter ring on the surface to show minutes from a moving hand and a moving silvered brass inset disc for hours, read from a static pointer. The dial is a strange mixture of japanned and brass dial types. The design of the clock is an innovative one published by James Ferguson in 1771. The clock was made by William Thompson of Whitehaven about 1772-74; dial style alone would give a close indication of period. The clock was probably made by way of experiment rather than as a commercial clock. The case of oak and mahogany has some

PLATE 230. *Case of the Thomas Lister clock in oak with mahogany trim in the form of inset crossbanding (Leeds fashion) and mahogany borders to the door/base panel. Long door style but with high Northern base and overall a little broader than usual based on the large dial size. A relatively neutral style but Northern touches in the shaped door top, raised base panel and complex trunk-to-base mould. Shell and fan inlays are an unusual extra. Height 8ft.1in.*

PLATE 233. *Dial of about 1820 by James and John Thristle of Stogursey, Somerset, a conventional moon dial but lettered to show a separate subdial in each corner giving strike/silent option, month of the year, date of the month and day of the week. The arch is also lettered to show tidal times for a nearby tidal estuary ('High Water at Combewitch Pasage'), but the tidal time numerals are so worn as to be illegible.*

PLATE 232. *Eccentric three-train musical longcase in an all-rosewood case, believed to be Scottish, though with an English dial. Perhaps made to match other furnishings for a grand house of the day, dating from about 1840-50. Despite the overall bizarre nature we can still date the clock by those stylistic features which bear some resemblance to the normal. Height about 8ft.*

COLOUR PLATE 38. *Fifteen-inch dial of a clock adapted in 1849 by William Murray junior of Bellingham, Northumberland, when aged only twenty. Apart from centre seconds (counterbalanced hand) and centre calendar (serpentine hand) showing a full annual calendar, the clock also shows moon's phases and date. Above the moon is a sun rotating daily and showing times of sunrise and sunset, varied for different time of year by rising and falling shutters at each side. An experiment in clockwork by a very young man. Despite the odd layout the numbering pattern and painting style assist dating.*

features suggestive of Cumbrian work, but it would be difficult for the beginner to identify by virtue of its eccentric features.

The highly-complicated astronomical clock made in 1830 by Ebenezer Henderson of Dunfermline (Colour Plate 36 and Plate 231) is believed to be one he described himself in his *Annals of Dunfermline* and which he made as an experiment when he was only twenty-one years old. He was a scientist, not a regular clockmaker, but learned clockmaking from his father, who was a practising clockmaker. The clock shows solar time and sidereal time, annual calendar, times of tidal rise and fall, mood phases and lunar calendar, sunrise and sunset times with different lengths of day and night, the terms and degrees of the Ecliptic (Zodiac), has a deadbeat escapement and strikes the hours with rack striking. Henderson made other complicated clocks and orreries. This clock is

COLOUR PLATE 39. *Another clock by William Murray of Rothbury, known as the Apostle clock. The fifteen inch arch dial indicates all those things in the previous clock and additionally the sun, moon and stars, times of their southing and setting, the positions of the sun and moon in the ecliptic, and high and low water at Tynemouth. This was attached to a barrel organ (not pictured) playing six tunes and a chime on twenty-one bells, quarter-chiming on eight bells, either playable at any quarter. On the case below the dial was a figure of the Lord, and three times each day a small door opened as a procession of the Twelve Apostles marched round, each bowing his head in passing except Judas, who turned his head away. The maker moved from Bellingham to Rothbury about 1849.*

shown as a measure to which painted dial clocks could sometimes aspire.

Two complicated clocks are included by William Murray junior of Bellingham (Colour Plates 38 and 39), one made when he was only twenty. Such clocks are far from typical but show what could be done by even very youthful rural clockmakers when they had a mind to. The fact that few such clocks exist is principally because of lack of demand, not talent. Murray's 'Apostle clock' (Colour Plate 39), which he claimed to have spent five years of his spare time making, was apparently on display at their workshop for some years as a masterpiece in the 1880s. Its where-

PLATE 234. *The Thristle dial seen from behind reveals the linking work for the subdials, the day and date ones operated by a simple daily pin knock-on system, the month changes knocking on by a pin with every complete revolution of the date wheel. Not technically complicated but involving a lot of extra shunt work.*

abouts today are unknown, all that survives being a few photographs and an old description. It was in Newcastle upon Tyne till about 1910 but is believed to have been shipped to America some ten years or more ago.

The bizarre clock in Plate 232 is obviously a one-off special built in rosewood veneers, which is a very unusual wood for any longcase clock, largely because of the expense. The clock itself is a three train musical clock with a pointed arch dial, the case also having a pointed-top door to hood and trunk. We can guess the age of the clock at around 1850 by its period features, even though these are eccentric. The clock has no signature (perhaps worn away) and the dial is clearly English, though the clock is believed to be Scottish. The case is lavishly inlaid with brass and has finely-detailed brass caps and bases to the (six) pillars. I imagine this was made to match in with the style of other rosewood furniture, as some features resemble those on chiffoniers or sideboards of the day. Many features, such as the castellated pediment and the strange flambeau-type finials, are far from standard.

The clock by the Thristles of Stogursey, Somerset (Plates 233 and 234), uses each dial corner for a subdial, something which would need to be pre-ordered from the dialmaker. This shows strike/silent, then day of week, date and month. The moon dial is also lettered to read 'High Water at Combewitch Pasage' (a nearby tidal river mouth) but the tidal time numerals are worn and therefore illegible.

CHAPTER SEVENTEEN

SPRING-DRIVEN CLOCKS

Spring-driven clocks were of two types – those which hung on the wall and those which sat on a table or mantelpiece. Table clocks are usually known today as 'bracket clocks', arising from the fact that some had wall brackets on which they sat, though in fact it was always a small minority which had a bracket. So although it is really a misnomer, the term bracket clock seems to have stuck. Both bracket and wall clocks existed before the appearance of the japanned dial about 1770, but after this date they gradually became more numerous, reaching peak of production in the second quarter of the nineteenth century, after which both types were replaced by cheaper foreign imports which flooded the British market.

The essential difference between a spring clock and a weight-driven one is that the spring is a less efficient means of driving, and for two reasons. By its very nature a spring will sooner or later suffer from metal fatigue and will weaken or break with use. Secondly the spring has the inherent problem that it pulls strongly when fully wound and weakly when nearly run down, playing havoc with time-keeping. Spring clocks made in Britain were always of eight-day duration (or longer) so this varying power source was a decided problem.

THE FUSEE

A means was devised to try to overcome this unevenness of power. This was a cone-shaped intermediate gear known as a fusee (pronounced fuse-ee), often written as fuzzy in older times (see Figure 4). The word is of French origin, though oddly enough the fusee was not used in French clocks. The principle was that the fully-wound spring used its strongest energy in pulling against the narrow end of the fusee, and needed less pulling power against the wider end, when the spring power was running low. The fusee worked to some degree but could never totally remove the imbalance between weight and spring power.

One fusee gear was needed for each set of wheels, each 'train' of the clock. A non-striking clock, known as a timepiece, had a single train and hence a single fusee; a striker had two trains and is known as a 'double fusee'; three trains (and three fusees) were required for music or quarter-chiming; four trains (four fusees) would incorporate music and quarter-chiming. Five trains are hard to imagine, and I've never come across one.

INADEQUACIES

Other factors also made the spring clock less accurate than the weight clock. The movement was smaller and more subject to expansion from temperature change. The pendulum itself suffered much more from temperature change by its shorter length but also regulation was less fine than with the much longer pendulum of a longcase clock. Yet another problem was that, being more delicate, spring movements were less strong than weight movements and they were more subject to the problems arising from neglect such as dirt or rusting in damp conditions. So in many respects the spring clock was unable to compete with the weight-driven one.

It follows from the above that spring clocks have two extra ingredients not found in a weight clock – the spring and the fusee (three if we count the tiny drive chain). Springmaking was a very specialised craft and something which was always outside the skill of the clockmaker himself, who was obliged to purchase his

COLOUR PLATE 40. *Anchor escapement ebonised lancet style bracket clock of about 1810-20 by John Davidson of London with round (convex) japanned dial using Roman hour numbering without minutes. A two train (striking) clock with the unusual feature of pull-wind alarmwork – note the engraved brass alarm setting disc in the dial centre. Matching steel hands. Height 14in.*

COLOUR PLATE 41. *Mahogany bracket clock by Yeomans of Nottingham made about 1810-20 in the Egyptian taste. Matching steel hands. Height about 19in. Convex seven-inch dial. Chamfered and gadrooned top with pineapple finial. A very high quality case with applied brass sphinx-head figures.*

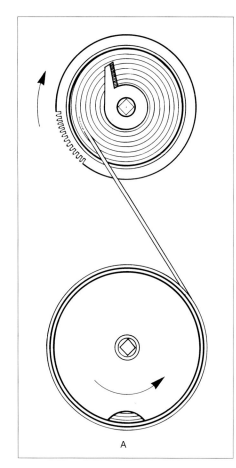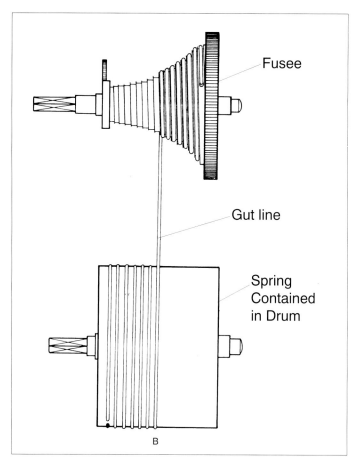

FIGURE 4. *The fusee principle. The fusee itself is the cone-shaped gear attached to the winding square. The arrow indicates the direction of winding. As the spring runs down it pulls against the wider end of the fusee, requiring less pulling power, an attempt at reducing the effect of power loss of an unwinding spring.*

spring from a springmaker. The fusee was an item which any clockmaker *could* make, provided he had a gearcutter known as a fusee engine, though most clockmakers had such little demand for spring clocks that it was not worth their while to own one. So again most clockmakers were obliged to buy their fusees. The extra cost of springs and fusees added to the price of a spring clock, which was in any event inferior in most respects to a weight one. Further items to be bought in were the fusee chains, which were also made by specialists. Gutline could be used but chain was stronger and was preferred. Yet another difficulty was the case, as this had to be made (with few exceptions) by a highly-skilled and sophisticated cabinetmaker or clock casemaker, and not just the local joiner or carpenter, who housed many longcase clocks.

VERGE AND ANCHOR ESCAPEMENTS

The escapement is a device designed to control the speed at which a clock runs. Without an escapement the wheels would spin round and the clock would run down in seconds. The spring or weight turns the wheels by pulling on them; the wheels in turn pull round the escape wheel, which is obstructed by the pendulum, which is pushed from side to side by the escape wheel, releasing the escape wheel tooth by tooth, one tick at a time. Thus the pendulum in its relationship with the escape wheel sets the speed of the clock, the rate at which it ticks.

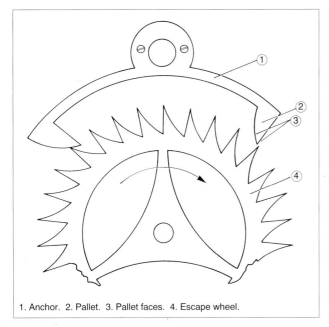

1. Anchor. 2. Pallet. 3. Pallet faces. 4. Escape wheel.

FIGURE 5. *The anchor escapement.*

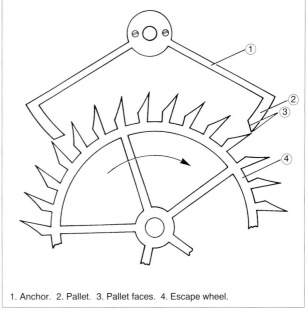

1. Anchor. 2. Pallet. 3. Pallet faces. 4. Escape wheel.

FIGURE 6. *The deadbeat escapement.*

The anchor escapement (Figure 5) was invented at a debatable date in the late seventeenth century and had long been the standard escapement in longcase clocks by the time the painted dial arrived. The deadbeat (Figure 6) escapement is a specific variation of the anchor, and is fractionally more accurate but, as it was prone to damage if abused, as it might be by a careless owner, the deadbeat was seldom used in domestic clocks, other than in clocks which showed seconds from the centre (known as centre-seconds clocks). The anchor escapement shows a recoil of the seconds hand at each beat, and an anchor escapement operating on a centre-seconds clock would have shown a ridiculously exaggerated recoil, whereas the deadbeat, as its name implies, showed no recoil at all. Because of its greater accuracy the deadbeat escapement was used in special clocks, such as Regulators, but in general it was not used in normal domestic longcase clocks where the standard anchor escapement was universal.

The deadbeat escapement was often used in combination with maintaining power (a supplementary spring system which kept the wheels driving during winding, partly to avoid winding time loss but also to avoid damage to the delicate escape wheel teeth). In centre-seconds clocks, however, maintaining power could not be used; a centre-seconds clock has to be stopped during winding or the long seconds hand would collide against the winding key! Though occasionally met with neither the deadbeat escapement nor maintaining power were normal in ordinary domestic clocks.

The original escapement used with the pendulum from the very start of pendulum clocks (1658) was the verge (Figure 7) escapement, which operated a short pendulum swinging in a wide arc, known as a bob pendulum. Because of its greater accuracy the anchor escapement had long before 1770 replaced the verge in weight-driven clocks such as longcases. In spring clocks, however, the verge was still in current use, as it was more tolerant of uneven levels than the anchor, even though the verge was known to be a less accurate timekeeper. This was another factor affecting the accuracy of timekeeping in bracket clocks; the advantage of the verge escapement was that the verge bracket clock could be moved from room to room and set down on any convenient surface – hence the carrying handle on most verge examples. By about 1790 the anchor had begun to replace the verge in bracket and wall clocks and by the first years of the nineteenth century had become standard.

COLOUR PLATE 42. *Drop dial single fusee white dial (twelve-inch) wall clock dating from about 1850, the dial style 'frozen' in the Roman hours style of almost half a century earlier, exactly as used on a round dial longcase. Maker Charles Hodson of Worcester. The unusual case is of papier mâché set with mother-of-pearl chips. Matching hands of blued steel.*

COLOUR PLATE 43. *Drop dial single fusee wall clock of about 1840 by Hunter of Clapham (London). The mahogany case has an unusual carved surround of oak leaves and acorns. The pendulum window has a brass-beaded rim. Matching steel hands. Twelve-inch dial with Roman hour numbering, as on a round dial longcase.*

COLOUR PLATE 44. *Octagonal single-fusee wall clock in rosewood with mother-of-pearl inlay made about 1850 by Abraham Fawcett of Mirfield, Yorkshire. Twelve-inch round dial with traditional Roman hour numbering.*

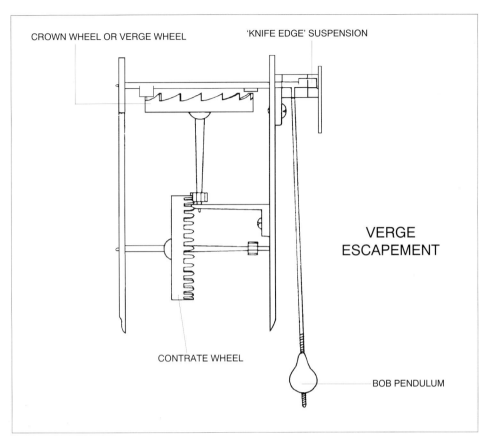

CROWN WHEEL OR VERGE WHEEL   'KNIFE EDGE' SUSPENSION

VERGE
ESCAPEMENT

CONTRATE WHEEL

BOB PENDULUM

FIGURE 7. *The verge escapement.*

THE MARKET

We might wonder who would want to buy a spring clock instead of a weight clock in view of all these disadvantages and the higher cost, and the answer for many provincial clockmakers was nobody. Numerous clockmakers are known whose output appears not to include a single spring-driven clock and spring-driven clocks formed a tiny fraction of the overall output of those provincial clockmakers by whom bracket clocks *are* known.

Until the mid-nineteenth century those who bought bracket clocks were largely the upper income groups, who could afford several clocks in their houses, who did not mind the expense, and who enjoyed the status of a more ostentatious type of clock. This was an exclusive clientele, who, when they did go in for such a status symbol, would in any event be likely to buy it in London, which explains why this was where the great majority of spring-driven clocks were made. There was a certain amount of one-upmanship in buying in London in the past, just as there still is today, the implication being that London goods were the best, and with bracket clocks there is some truth in that. To the provincial clockmaker spring clocks, especially bracket clocks, were a bit of a headache, and many never even attempted to make one. Others bought them from London specialist makers of spring clocks, lettered with their own name and town as 'retailers'.

LONDON SPECIALISTS

Even in London there was a handful of clockmakers who specialised in making spring clocks for the rest of the trade, both local and national. One such specialist who set up in the 1740s was Aynsworth Thwaites, later becoming John Thwaites, later Thwaites and Reed. Another was Handley and Moore who worked in

PLATE 235. *Anchor escapement bracket clock of about 1810 by Frodsham, Gracechurch Street, London, in mahogany case with brass inlay, seen before restoration. Here the dial has the full (unshouldered) arch, sometimes used in bracket clocks but rarely in longcases. Coloured artwork in the corners or arch were uncommon in London work. Matching brass hands. Height about 20in. Original pineapple finial.*

PLATE 236. *Anchor escapement ebonised bracket clock made about 1810 in the lancet style by Handley & Moore of London, spring clock specialists, using the very popular round (convex) japanned dial. Timepiece only. Height 14½in., dial 5½in. in diameter. Roman hours without minute numbering appeared earlier on bracket clock dials than on longcase dials.*

London in the early nineteenth century. Many bracket clocks bearing on the dial the name of even highly reputable and respected London clockmakers will be found to carry the initials or name or serial number on their movement frontplate of such a specialist spring clockmaker. This is a fact which is well known and accepted and such a clock is thought none the worse for it. Serial numbers used by Thwaites are listed in Ronald Rose's book *English Dial Clocks*, and these will often assist dating to the actual year.

Oddly enough those uncommon examples of provincial spring clocks made before about 1800 will often prove to be clocks *made* by that particular maker, as when a provincial maker obtained an order for such a clock, he often did the actual making. London-sold examples will more usually prove to have been made by other specialists in the city.

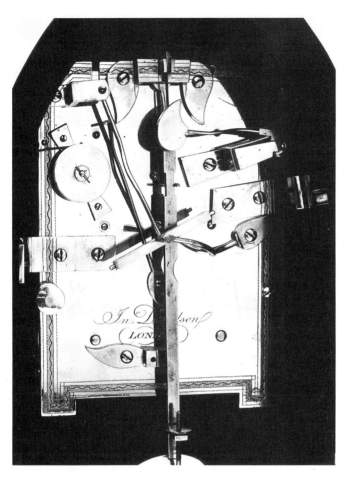

PLATE 237. *Engraved and signed backplate of the John Davidson bracket clock, the bell removed to show the double-headed alarm hammer. Note carrying screw in position in left engraved border. The pull-wind alarm mechanism is above the left fastening brace.*

PLATE 238. *Small mahogany timepiece bracket clock made about 1825 by James Smith of London, standing only about 12in. Full arch dial without shoulders. Scroll decoration in gold around the maker's name is restrained. Matching diamond-pattern hands in steel. This type of top is known as a gadrooned top.*

DIAL TYPES

The white dial came to spring clocks as it did to other types. A few verge escapement wall clocks had wooden dials early in our period, but the great majority of spring-driven (anchor escapement) wall clocks almost always had circular japanned dials, measuring anywhere from ten to fourteen inches in diameter, though twelve inches was the standard size before about 1830. Exceptional sizes were probably made for specific purposes, such as a gallery clock for a chapel, which might be much larger than standard. Weight-driven wall clocks such as hooded clocks sometimes had dials of arched or square shape, but spring wall clocks usually had round dials. British wall clocks appear not to have been made with dials of true enamel.

Most wall clocks have regular Birmingham japanned dials, white with the appropriate lettering and with no coloured decoration of any kind. Most were timepieces; striking wall clocks are unusual amongst British-made examples. Later imported ones from Germany and America were normally strikers.

Bracket clock dials went through a preliminary phase where some, though it seems very few, were made of true enamel, costly and fragile though this was. Anthony Theelke in his book *Faces of Mystery* and Richard Barder in his book *The*

PLATE 239. *Mahogany brass-inlaid single fusee (timepiece) bracket clock by Maple & Co. Ltd.,London, dating from the late 19th century (1870-80?) but in the style of about 1830. Six-inch round convex dial with Roman hour numbering, unchanged from fifty years earlier. Height 13in.*

PLATE 240. *Bizarre walnut-cased novelty bracket clock with circular white dial dating from the latter years of the 19th century, signed Dickinson, Preston. German-made with two trains but what would normally be the strike train here operates the automated figure. Instead of striking, the seated man lifts a spoonful of plums to his mouth, which opens and chews as his eyes roll. Wound from the front or back. Probably made as a feature for a coffee-shop window. The white dial retains the Roman hours styling.*

Georgian Bracket Clock seem to have recorded only seven between them. It was more usual to apply enamel discs (chapters) to a brass dial, a method which would combine the delicacy of the enamel with the strength of the brass dial. The use of true enamel is outside our scope here and in any event is very uncommon.

Small circular japanned dials (as well as other shapes) were supplied by the Birmingham dialmakers. However, many nineteenth century bracket clocks have small dials, from about four inches in diameter, with the japanwork on a tinned iron base, the tinning perhaps helping adhesion. These smaller dials may well have been made in London, though they seldom bear any maker's identification marks.

DIAL STYLES

Although the white dial took over rapidly in longcase work, it seems to have been slower to capture the bracket clock market during Period One (1770 - 1800). At this time many bracket clocks continue in the traditional brass dial form or with the silvered single-sheet brass dial. Japanned dial examples do occur, some very obviously in the Birmingham style of Osborne/Wilson with strawberry corners. Many in this period, however, have an all-white dial without decoration, perhaps because this resembled more closely the silvered dial. Dial shapes at this time were mostly arched, seldom circular, and square ones apparently unrecorded.

The circular dial seems to begin in bracket clocks at the very end of the eighteenth century, at first using the double numbers method, i.e. Roman hours and Arabic minutes marked 5, 10, 15, etc. Clocks of the balloon style seem to be amongst the few early types to have round dials.

Period Two (1800-1830) saw a continuation of the arched dial form, sometimes using the same numbering system as longcase dials, that is Arabic hour numerals with Arabic minutes, the minutes often marked only as 15, 30, 45, 60, but occasionally numbered every five minutes. However, if the Arabic hours form seldom seemed really popular on longcase dials, it must have been thought to suit bracket clock dials even less, if we are to judge by the relatively small number of Arabic-hour examples we see, as these seem to be unusual. The round dial came more regularly into fashion during this period, but again with only infrequent use of Arabic hours.

Instead the variant form of Period Two numbering seems to have been preferred for bracket clocks whereby Roman hour numerals were used sometimes with the minutes numbered at 15, 30, 45, 60 but more often and increasingly often over time without any minute numbering at all. In other words the form of Roman hours only numbering we associate with Period Three (1830-1870) in longcase dials was regularly used considerably before 1830 in bracket clocks. This may have been because the much smaller (than longcase) dials left little space for minute numbering. Another factor may be that these clocks were generally made for a more prosperous and educated clientele who did not need to have the minutes lettered on for them, but well understood that when the clock hands pointed at III past VI they indicated fifteen minutes past six.

Brass dials, now mostly of the single-sheet type, still appeared throughout Period Two and Period Three. Painted dials appeared increasingly regularly as time progressed, sometimes in arched form but increasingly often as round dials. Square dials now made an occasional appearance but seem not to have been widely popular. In Period Three the round dial is probably the most prolific.

Period Three japanned dials in arch form do exist of similar nature to longcase dials of the day, that is with painted cottage corner scenes and sometimes arch scenes, but this heavily-painted dial style was mostly on provincial clocks and was unusual. More often an arched dial would be all-white in the London style (perhaps because such clocks were supplied by the London-based specialist clockmakers to the trade elsewhere). Increasingly often, however, the arched shape gave way to the round dial, where there was no space for any decoration at all. What was the point, after all, of having the extra decorative space of arch and corners if it was to be left undecorated?

The distinctive and obvious styling of japanned dials as used on longcase clocks, and as outlined in the earlier chapters of this book, is of considerable help in dating and assessing spring clocks, both bracket and wall dials, but it will be seen from the above that it cannot be used so positively. More regard has to be taken of case styles in bracket clocks, and of makers' names (even if they are retailers rather than true makers).

HANDS

The styles of hands on bracket clocks and to some extent on wall clocks too

PLATE 241. *Mahogany drop dial single train wall clock made about 1830 by Keeling of London with thirteen-inch white dial and traditional Roman hour numbering. Note the 'ears', which are carved as bunches of grapes.*

PLATE 242. *Ebonised bracket clock with brass inlay dating from about 1830 by T. Hammond of Manchester, here using a square white dial. The square dial was not common in bracket clocks, most dials being round. Double fusee and anchor escapement. Matching steel hands. Total height about 15in. Gadrooned chamfer top with original pineapple finial.*

followed the same general trends as in longcase clocks. However, there was a tendency for brass hands (probably gilded originally) to become more widely popular in bracket clocks earlier than in longcase ones, perhaps because they looked more opulent than blued steel. We know they were more costly than steel, and perhaps it was thought fitting that these costly clocks should have hands which were appropriately luxurious.

Matching pattern hands gradually replaced non-matching pairs from the late eighteenth century both in steel and in brass. There was always a concern to keep these small hands delicate in appearance yet strong enough for use, and one does not see the heavier patterns of matching brass hands found on late longcase clocks. Wall clocks, usually made for a more mundane or workaday setting, tended to have plainer hands, usually in steel for strength.

CASEWORK

The styles of bracket clock cases are too varied to describe in detail here, but continued the progression of styles found on brass dial examples. Ebonised examples still occurred, often inlaid with brass or with applied brass mounts, but these were

PLATE 243. *Mahogany two-train bracket clock with convex round dial made about 1830 by Carley of Thetford, Norfolk, seen here in unrestored condition, the numbers rather worn. The case has considerable brass inlay and an unusual form of chamfer top with original pineapple finial. Height approximately 20 in., dial 8in. in diameter.*

PLATE 244. *Three-train dome top mahogany bracket clock, quarter-chiming on eight bells, made about 1800 by Perigal of Royal Exchange, London. This is the type with a brass dial and small subdials of true enamel, top left being fast/slow regulation, top right strike/silent. One dating feature is the five-minute numbering using single track minutes. Height 17 in.*

increasingly outmoded by mahogany with occasional fancy woods such as satin-wood being used in unusual styles such as balloon clocks. Rosewood was popular between about 1825 and 1845. Any of these might have brass string inlay. Ebonised cases made a small comeback with the more formal type of small square dial clock found in the 1840s and later. Oak was not used in British bracket clocks except perhaps for special clocks of an eccentric nature.

In wall clocks oak was sometimes used, usually for cheaper or humbler examples. Mahogany was probably the most popular wood, though rosewood had a certain following in its period. Ebonised examples do occur but seldom. Papier mâché inset with mother-of-pearl was sometimes used, but is uncommon.

CHAPTER EIGHTEEN

AMERICA

In America the longcase clock is sometimes known as a tall clock. Little has been written about this form of American clock during the painted dial period until very recently, and in the United Kingdom little has been written at all. Before 1770 the brass dial longcase took similar form to the English equivalent except that native American case woods differed. Pine and poplar were often used for cheaper clocks, walnut and cherry wood for middle grades, and mahogany for the finest.

The great majority (probably over seventy-five per cent) of all painted dial clocks in America consist of British-made clocks, either taken there complete by settlers or shipped there in the last thirty years by dealers. Sometimes emigrants would take with them just the movement (with dial) and re-case it in America in local woods. Owners of such clocks should refer to the British chapters. The following notes are for the benefit of those who own American-made tall clocks, which, of course, hardly ever appear in Britain. I have never seen a single American-made longcase clock in the United Kingdom, though I have often seen clocks from same name towns passed off as American. Many British towns have American equivalents, Boston and Bristol being the best known.

The British-made painted dial began to be produced about 1770 by the partners, Osborne and Wilson, who separated in 1777. It was not until about 1784 that British-made painted dials were imported by native clockmakers into America to fit on to the clocks they made. (This was probably on account of the Revolutionary War of 1775-83 between the two countries.) So, whilst American-made clocks are well known bearing dials by Osborne and Wilson independently, none seems to bear a dial by the two jointly during the partnership years. Painted dial clocks would therefore seem to begin in America about 1784. Other British dialmakers also exported to America and it seems that in the earlier years all American-made painted dial clocks had British-made dials. Many, though not all, would use the falseplate system (see page 19). As in Britain, falseplates were not used on American brass dial clocks, and those that have them are alterations or fakes.

It was suggested by Penrose Hoopes in an article in *Antiques* in 1931 that painted dials were not manufactured in America until after 1800. He quotes evidence of dials 'newly arrived from England' being offered for sale by local wholesalers in Baltimore in 1784 and in Philadephia in 1785. By about 1815 American-made dials seem to predominate and thereafter English dials seem very uncommon, perhaps on account of another war starting in 1812.

During the period when both were available, British-made dials are said to have been more popular in the urban areas (New York, Philadelphia, Baltimore) while American-made dials were used, even in eight-day work, by the more rural clock-maker.

Some American-made clocks with British dials fail to carry the name of the clockmaker (or retailer) on the dial. Opinions vary as to how commonly dials were supplied unnamed, but it is likely that if a batch of dials was being shipped to a wholesaler, it could not be known in advance who the purchasing clockmaker might be. These imported dials would need to be lettered locally or left unnamed, and it seems to me that this was far more likely to happen in America than in

PLATE 245. *Twelve-inch wooden dial of about 1815-20 from a wooden-movement clock by Silas Hoadley of Plymouth, Conn. The numbering pattern is not unlike that of a contemporary English dial, though the painting is of a more naïve nature. Fans were a popular corner motif in both countries. The dash method of minute marking differs from the English system.(Photograph by courtesy of Tom Spittler.)*

PLATE 246. *Wooden movement of wooden dial clock by Silas Hoadley of Plymouth, Conn. The plates are of quarter-cut oak, wheels of cherry and pinions of New England laurel. This is an eight-day clock, though the majority are thirty-hour. Countwheel striking. (Photograph by courtesy of Tom Spittler.)*

Britain, where the clockmaker's name was pre-known at the point of ordering. In fact we know that Samuel Deacon of Barton, Leicestershire, England, specified when ordering just how his name was to be lettered. There is evidence that some American clockmakers lettered their names on to their dials for themselves, but it is not known how widespread this practice was. Of course the thinly-lettered names on dials are often so worn as to be almost invisible, and, just as occurs in Britain, names on dials often escape notice when a careful examination would reveal them. The number of unnamed dials is therefore probably smaller than may first appear.

On the subject of clockmakers lettering their own dials, or even painting them fully, Stacy Wood advises me that in the inventory of clockmaker Christian Eby of Manheim, Pa., are listed:

> 3 painting books; 1 lot of painting bottles, pots, 'chares' [?=jars], & paints; 5 copper plates for 'pickters' [?=pictures]; 2 presses for preparing ditto; 1 'marvel' for grinding paint; 1 lot of painting pencils & pickters; 1 lot of pickturs without frames; 1 painting table with 3 drawers; 3 CLOCK FACES NOT FINISHED - 15s.-£2.5s.'

One suggestion is that, as English-made clocks could be bought in ready-made (or ready-to-assemble) form by the early nineteenth century, some American cabinet-makers may have imported these and sold them unsigned in cases of their own making. A number of unsigned clocks in Pennsylvania cases could be accounted for in this way.

The practice arose by about 1760 in America of making thirty-hour clocks with wooden movements, probably for cheapness and also on account of the scarcity of available metals, principally brass. Initially these were in small numbers in New England but by 1800 Eli Terry succeeded in mass-producing them. Wooden dials were used too. In Britain we occasionally see wooden dial longcase clocks, which are German-made (imported) clocks having wooden plates too with brass wheels. These British examples are mostly late (post 1840). American wooden dials are twelve-inch arched examples made with two pieces of dove-tailed poplar on the back to prevent warping. These date from about 1810 to 1835. The dials were painted on to the wood, but some (principally and perhaps exclusively ones made by Eli Terry) have a paper 'dial' stuck on to the wooden dial sheet. Many fakes are said to exist of these Eli Terry paper dial clocks, and apparently few genuine ones exist.

Eli Terry originated mass-production of wooden-movement clocks in America, setting up a factory in Plymouth in 1808, later run by Silas Hoadley (Plates 245 and 246) and Seth Thomas. It was Terry too who developed the shelf clock about 1815. After about 1830 the longcase clock fell from fashion in America in favour of the shelf clock, which also reached Britain in increasing numbers and ultimately aided the demise of the longcase clock here. Oddly the later American longcase dials tend to keep the same styling as was used about 1810, so there is not the sort of stylistic development found in England.

Early American-made japanned (metal) dials appear to imitate those by Osborne and by Wilson, and other English dialmakers whose work found its way to America – Keeling and Walker & Hughes for instance. It seems that the quality of the japanning on American-made dials at this time was usually inferior to British work, as also was often the quality of the artistry. Few early American dialmakers have yet been identified, though this is a subject receiving attention currently by American researchers.

Though it may not always be possible to determine who made an American-made dial, it is often possible to recognise one by its style. This requires some experience, and often even the experts are uncertain. Moon dials seem more common on these than on British-made dials, though even with British-made dials imported into America, there is a higher percentage of moon dials amongst them than amongst those sold in Britain. Centre seconds and centre calendar features too seem to have been more popular there than here. Some clocks had both features together, and although some British white dial clocks had centre calendars, few had centre seconds, this being a fashion which had largely passed here by the 1790s. Either or both of these features could naturally be called for by an American wholesaler ordering from England.

A feature sometimes claimed for American-made dials is that they were supplied undrilled, the winding holes being drilled by the clockmaker himself to suit his needs and any ragged edges being covered by what we usually call brass collets, known in America as grommets. English dial holes were invariably drilled before japanning and the white base paint can be seen spilling through them on to the dial back. The eccentric positioning of winding holes (for example one higher than the other) is not evidence of late drilling, as they occur sometimes on English dials too, and I am not sure how to explain these.

English-made eight-day dials usually had four *round* dial feet, thirty-hours usually three. Some American-made dials had *square* dial feet, something rarely if ever found on English-made painted dials. Moon dial click springs on English dials are

PLATE 247. *Fourteen-inch iron dial for an American thirty-hour clock. Dialmaker unknown but possibly Nolen or Nolen/Curtis. Raised gold dots outside the minute band are a typical American feature as is the gilt lyre in the arch. Unrestored dial with damage visible to two of the dial foot ends. Date about 1810. Numbering pattern similar to an English 'double Arabics' Wilson dial. Corner shells cruder than English. (Photograph by courtesy of Tom Spittler.)*

PLATE 248. *Fourteen-inch eight-day moon dial of about 1830-40, though the numbering system is little changed from a generation before. The figure 8 has thick sides and is formed of two same-size circles, a late feature on many American dials. Solid colour background is a late feature to the rather unrealistic seashells. Dialmaker unnamed. (Photograph by courtesy of Tom Spittler.)*

often attached to the dial or a top dial foot. American-made dials often have this attached to the falseplate, but so too do some English ones.

American dials often have falseplates which are thinner than English ones and with a larger surface area. Some American dials are considerably thinner than English ones, some being capable of being flexed with the fingers.

Moon 'humps' usually had the two hemispheres transfer-printed on them, normally with the Western hemisphere on the left and the Eastern on the right, but occasionally vice versa – whether by error or intent I do not know. A double-line border with hatching surrounds each. On some dials a further circle surrounds this, showing 0 degrees at the equator and 90 degrees at the north pole. American-made dials normally have the degrees marked: English ones rarely do. Some American dials (by Patton & Jones?) fail to show the ecliptic lines, which are normally present on English dials. The outline of Australia (named as New Holland) is usually very vague and box-like on American-made dials (see Plate 253) and more accurately outlined on English-made dials; why I cannot say. On British-made dials the British Isles are recognisable, but on American-made dials they may be a mere blob or at least very insignificant. American moon dials often show the sailing ship(s) flying the American flag.

By the 1780s white dials were sold through specialist trade and general suppliers. In 1785 John and Daniel Carell of Philadelphia advertised:

> Watch and Clock-Makers, Goldsmiths and Jewellers, In Front Street, seven doors below the Coffee-house; have for sale…eight-day and twenty-four hour clocks; clock dials, neatly japann'd, with or without moon-plates; cast clock work in setts; clock bells; clock pinions, ready slit….; and all manner of other trade supplies.

In 1791 Timothy Chandler of Concord, New Hampshire, advertised amongst other things 'warranted eight-day Clocks with enamelled moon or plain faces'. In 1798 H. & B. Penhallow, hardware dealers of Portsmouth, New Hampshire, offered clock dials for sale in their advertisement. In 1811 J. Pond of Portsmouth advertised in the *New Hampshire Gazette* that he 'expects by the first arrival from Boston, a handsome assortment of Clock Dials of every size, which will be sold by the dozen or singly at the factory price.'

Clockmaker Abel Hutchins of Concord, New Hampshire, offered in the *New Hampshire Patriot* of 23 November 1812 'warranted eight-day clocks of the newest fashion' but also all types of clock parts and case fittings including:

> clock balls – various prices [i.e. finials]; clock case capitals; quarter capitals; hinges; clock hands; clock pinions; clock bells and glasses; and clock faces with moon, plain and ship arches.

In Harrisburg, Pa., merchants Oglesby and Poole were dial distributors in the 1800-1840 period. Christian Eby of Manheim, Pa., was a clockmaker but also a dialpainter in the last fifteen years of the eighteenth century. Benjamin Whitman of Reading, Pa., advertised in 1799 that he was giving up clockmaking to 'carry on the clock dial manufactory in all its various branches'.

One of the best-known dialmaking concerns was Boston-based Willard & Nolen, 'clock dial and sign painters' (Spencer Nolen and his brother-in-law Aaron Willard), who are believed to have supplied most New England dials from about 1805 (see Plate 247). Their dials have marked falseplates. About 1809 the firm became Curtis and Nolen till about 1849, and they also had a Philadelphia branch and one in Pittsburgh. Spencer Nolen was born in 1784 and died in 1849. Curtis often used a paper label behind his dials reading 'Curtis Manufactory for Patton & Jones, Philadelphia', or 'Manufactured by Samuel Curtis'.

Patton and Jones (Plate 249) worked in Philadelphia about 1804-14 and also at Baltimore. They were ironmongers and distributors of clock parts but also made dials – some have falseplates marked 'Patton & Jones, Phila.' Some of their dials appear to have been sold undrilled and obviously some were supplied by the Curtis manufactory.

American researcher Stacy Wood points out that the Jones partner may have been the William Jones of whom Charles S. Grossman wrote in 1890 in *A Complete History of Watch and Clock Making in America*:

> William Jones was not a clockmaker, but was so closely connected with the trade and so well known to the Philadelphia clockmakers that he deserves mention. He certainly brought the art of painting and decorating clock dials to almost perfection. He even had an oven for baking after painting, so that when finished the paint on the iron dials was almost like a coat of enamel. For twenty years he had a shop in Strawberry Street, but did not do much after 1840 as his hands became paralysed, incapacitating him from work during the last years of his life.

American-made dials often use Arabic hour numerals, sometimes with the 5, 10,

PLATE 249. *Moon dial with falseplate of 'Patton & Jones, Phila' in a style which copies that of Osborne/Wilson. However: the dot-dash borders to the 'strawberry corners' have a double track; five-minute numbering is marked on a single track; the moon globes have degree numbers and a box-shaped New Holland – all very un-English. Date about 1805.(Photograph by courtesy of Stacy Wood.)*

PLATE 250. *Dial of an eight-day longcase clock of about 1805-10 by George Oves of Lebanon (Pa). The steel hands are original throughout – brass hands were not used on American longcase clocks. Gilt lyres are a common American theme at this period. Note tumbling Arabic for hours AND minutes. (Photograph by courtesy of Tom Spittler.)*

15 minute numbering but more often with the quarter minutes only (60, 15, 30, 45). Dial corners frequently carry shells or fans, sometimes flower sprays. This is the English dial style of about 1800-1810 and it seems that American-made dials did not progress beyond this style, so that fully-painted corners with landscapes as used in England are unknown. After about 1815 almost all American tall clocks have American-made dials, usually by now without falseplates.

Henry Nolen (relationship to Spencer Nolan, if any, is unknown) advertised in *The Western Spy* in 1817:

Clock Dial Establishment. Henry Nolen, clock dial manufacturer, in Wood between Fourth Street and Diamond Alley, Pittsburgh, keeps constantly for sale a regular assortment of dials, together with an assortment of Clock Movements and Materials, Patent Time Pieces, Looking Glasses, etc. which he will sell wholesale or retail at Philadelphia prices, including the cost of transportation. All orders from the states of Ohio and Kentucky punctually attended to.

A trade card of about 1830 reads:

Peter L. Grosch, sign, flag, masonic apron, letter, fancy and portrait painter, will attend to all orders in his line if left with Andrew Bear, Petersburg, or John Michael,

PLATE 252. *Fourteen-inch unsigned American-made longcase dial c.1815. The figure 8 has loops of uniform size, sometimes called an 'over-and-under' eight (shotgun barrel terminology), and appears on many later American dials. Shell corner motifs are common on American dials of this period and later. (Photograph by courtesy of Tom Spittler.)*

PLATE 251. *Cherrywood case of the George Oves clock, standing 8ft.2in., with original wooden finials. The lenticle glass is believed original but is not typical. Full hood pillars to front and rear. Original turned bun feet. Overall style not unlike some Southern English cases of the day. (Photograph by courtesy of Tom Spittler.)*

PLATE 253. *Eight-day dial from a clock by John Esterle of Maytown, Lancaster County, Pennsylvania. Unnamed falseplate. Believed to be an American-made dial. Note centre seconds and centre calendar used together. Date about 1815. Globes have degree-numbered borders and box-shaped New Holland. Otherwise not unlike an English dial with slightly odd corner designs.(Photograph by courtesy of Stacy Wood.)*

PLATE 254. *Eight-day dial from a clock by Samuel Breneisen of Reamstown, Pennsylvania, believed to date from 1834. Falseplate unnamed but thought to be an American-made dial. The shell corners are heavier than on English dials and have a strange wriggle-work background. (Photograph by courtesy of Stacy Wood.)*

innkeeper, Lancaster (Penn). NB CLOCK FACES MANUFACTURED AND PAINTED TO ORDER.

The business papers of Salem Community Store, Salem, North Carolina, include clock materials believed to have been for the exclusive use of the only local clockmaker, Ludwig Eberhardt. Letters between 1809 and 1812 to the Philadelphia wholesalers include several requests for 'Birmingham goods', including clock movements. A note to Patton and Jones in 1811 states:

be particular in the choice of faces, none but clear and round ones will answer ['round ones' seems to be a slip for 'sound ones']:
You will please be careful in packing the faces. Memo:
8 – 13inch moon clock dials
4 – 12inch solid arch – suitable for 8 day clocks
6 sett 8 day clock brass
1 doz sett pinions for 8 day clocks
1 doz brass minute pinions.

The same difficulties occurred here as in British dial supplying, namely the risk of damage in transit. It can also be seen that the stock of dials held always exceeded the stock of movements, as in Britain. Another letter of 1811 to Patton and Jones asks for the faces to be packed in a separate box: '8 – 13inch moon dials, net 6 dollars'. Another letter of 1812 asked for '1 doz 13inch moon dials, 4 with sec'd hand & date from the centre. ½doz 12 inch solid arch, 3 for 30 hour and 3 for 8 day'. This is interesting confirmation of the American fancy for centre seconds *and* centre calendarwork combined, as mentioned earlier.

Another extract from the Salem Store papers highlights the transport problem, and again mentions the centre calendar feature:

Messrs Patton & Jones   Salem
December 22 1812
Gentlemen,
Our last of 30th Ult. trust has reached you safe since we have received the clock faces lot [=bot?] of you, the wagon however that brot our goods had the bad luck to overset, by which the box containing the clock faces, not being hooped, burst open and whole of faces have thereby been considerable damaged, so as to render them entirely unsaleable, and not to loose the whole of them, have packed them up and shall send them back to you by first good opportunity to have them repaired, which have the confidence you will do, or have done for us on most reasonable terms, meanwhile please send us immediately the same quantity and assortment, some with the date by a hand from the center, well packed and hooped, by way of Baltimore & directed to Mr.Joseph Caldwell in Petersburg, not insured, & oblige your with esteem.'

PLATE 255. *Eight-day clock in walnut by John Conrad Heinzelman of Mannheim, Pennsylvania, dating from about 1800. This style is known as Lancaster County Chippendale, many features being reminiscent of North-western English work. (Photograph by courtesy of Stacy Wood.)*

The tall clock was replaced by the much cheaper shelf clock and by the 1830s the flow had diminished to a trickle, as it did later in Britain. Oddly enough square and round dials seem not to have been popular in American tall clocks, though many shelf clocks have square dials.

The following were dialmakers, suppliers or painters, or perhaps wholesalers:

Bond, William	Philadelphia	1829-33
Carell, John & Daniel	Philadelphia	1785
Curtis & Nolen	Boston & Philadelphia	c.1809-49
Eby, Christian	Manheim, Pa	c.1785-d1803
Grosch, Peter L.	Lancaster, Penn	c.1830
Hutchins, Abel	Concord, N. Hampshire	1812
Jones, William	Philadelphia	1820-40
Nolen, Henry	Pittsburg, Pa	1817
Oglesby & Poole	Harrisburg, Pa	1800-40
Patton & Jones	Philadelphia & Baltimore	c.1804-14
Penhallow, H. & B.	Portsmouth, N. Hampshire	1798
Pond, J.	Portsmouth, N. Hampshire	1811
Simpson, Alexander J.	Philadelphia	1849
Whitman, Benjamin	Reading, Pa	c.1799
Willard & Nolen	Boston	c.1805-09

Casework on American longcase clocks followed the basic English patterns but with variations. New England cases favoured the fretted top with pierced cresting and sometimes 'whale's tails'. New England was settled largely from the South of England, and cases from this area follow styles found in London and London-influenced Southern English counties, including East Anglia. Pennsylvania was settled more by Scots and Irish immigrants, who brought with them their taste for home styles, a principal feature of which was often the swan-neck pediment. Some early Pennsylvania cases have a very Irish look about them with Chippendale-influenced features to the hoods, exuberant swan-necks, and exaggeratedly long thin trunks. Later the taste for inlay and stringing developed along the Hepplewhite lines. The slim and graceful shape seems to persist longer than in England, and simple country-style cases still appear at all times. The heavier styling of later English cases does not occur in American casework any more than it does in dials.

PLATE 256. *Eight-day clock in cherrywood made about 1805 by John Eberman of Lancaster, Pennsylvania. Inlays and stringing of fancy woods are reminiscent of some turn of the century English work, as are certain of the other stylistic aspects. (Photograph by courtesy of Stacy Wood.)*

CHAPTER NINETEEN

IS IT GENUINE?

The pleasure found in the appreciation of the age and style of a clock is only valid provided the clock is genuine, and the enthusiast needs a method of approach to verify this aspect, which can appear totally baffling to a beginner. How do we begin to assess such things and what does 'genuine' mean anyway? Naturally over the years wear and damage will have taken place, accidents and breakages may have occurred. How do we assess what is a valid repair and what is an invalid alteration? As with any machine, we can all agree that if it is dirty, we clean it, if something is broken we mend it, if something is worn beyond use, we replace it. This is accepted practice and there is no shame in it. But where do we stop? If a clock has lost its hands, its dial or its case, do we fit replacements (new or old)?

NORMAL WEAR AND TEAR

The way I see it is to ask myself, if the 'clockmaker' (the man whose name appears on the dial) were alive today and could see the clock, would he recognise it as being the clock he originally sold in the case he sold it in? If so, then we have a genuine clock. Anything else is a fake, by which I mean a combination of un-related parts, whether done for deceit for money or from well-intended motives in an attempt at rescuing a neglected horological antiquity.

Normal restoration would include the replacement of such things as we expect to wear out, which would include gutlines, chains, ropes, fusee chains or guts, springs. Longcase weights and pullies get lost over the years, and replacements would not be regarded as a problem by most people. The same applies to pendulums, which may be broken or lost in auction rooms. The same would apply too to hands, which, by their fragile nature, are vulnerable, and it is accepted practice to replace broken or wrong-period replacement hands with new ones made in the appropriate style, as far as that can be established (though not with those terrible plastic reproduction hands sold for the purpose).

Pinions which are very worn may have to be replaced, which is a pity but some-times unavoidable, and surprisingly enough seldom necessary in clocks which are likely to be less than two centuries old. An occasional broken wheel can often be repaired rather than replaced, and repairing is usually cheaper anyway. Escape wheels in particular may be so worn as to need replacing. Even though a replaced wheel or pinion or hands or pullies would probably not put off a serious buyer, who would expect normal wear-and-tear replacements, it is obviously preferable for any buyer to find a clock without replaced parts, and if a clock has a considerable number of these sorts of quite honorable replacements, there comes a point where a buyer might rather choose one without them.

Clock casework too has often suffered through age and neglect, and again com-mon sense has to be applied. Replacement locks, catches, escutcheons, finials, paterae, even hinges are not unexpected. The feet of longcase clocks suffered from damp floors, and replacements are acceptable if in the correct style.

Cases which have been re-polished are a rather different story and would not appeal to the purist who seeks original colour and patina. Woodwormed back-boards in longcase clocks sometimes have to be replaced, and most would regard that as an acceptable necessity.

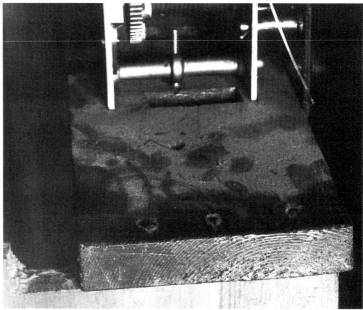

PLATE 258. *Original seatboard fitting correctly to its original case cheeks, here nailed in position. Note the marking-out lines where the overlength cheeks were cut by the clockmaker when he installed his clock. The casemaker often supplied the case to the clockmaker with overlength cheeks as he could not know in advance what height would be required by the movement.*

PLATE 257. *Thirty-hour painted dial clock with birdcage movement showing how the seatboard sits convincingly on to the cheeks without packings, as happened when the cheeks were cut to the correct height.*

UNACCEPTABLE ALTERATIONS

A clock in a non-original case would be unacceptable to many people, as would a clock in its original case but with a replaced dial, or a case with its original dial but a replaced movement – always supposing, of course, that we could recognise such things, and fortunately in the great majority of instances we can.

A clock made up in this way is normally known as a 'furnishing piece' or a 'marriage' or a 'married' clock. (A 'marriage clock' is a very different thing, the confusingly similar term used to refer to a clock made for the wedding of a particular couple, whose names it will probably also carry on the dial.) Auctioneers sometimes describe a married clock as 'composite' or 'associated' or even 'with restorations', which latter may well mean more than repairs. Fortunately most alterations of a serious nature were carried out in the past from pure expediency and not with intent to deceive. Therefore for the most part no attempt has been made to disguise them and the signs are there plainly enough if we look for them. But before we can attempt to spot such alterations we need to know what kind of thing to look for.

A CLOCK IN THE WRONG CASE

Perhaps the commonest kind of fake is a longcase clock housed in a non-original case, a situation which pertains to possibly as many as half of all the clocks I examine at auctions and elsewhere in the course of business. This is almost always apparent when we examine the way the clock fits (or fails to fit) the replacement case.

A very obvious giveaway is where a clock with, say, a thirteen-inch dial is housed in a case made for one of twelve or fourteen inches. Such discrepancy in the dial size and case size means that there will either be a gap between dial edge and the softwood masking inside the hood door, or that the mask will interrupt the dial design and/or numbering. In practice the mask is normally a fraction smaller than the dial, usually about adequate for the mask to overlap the white surround outside the coloured corners or arch. This is not always a precise factor and common sense needs to be applied when deciding. Some early country clocks never had such an internal mask, but by the time painted dials arrived almost all clocks had this with perhaps a very occasional exception in cruder country work.

Some alterations, usually those done in recent times to deceive, include rebuilding the mask itself to fit the new size of dial, so a buyer always examines the mask carefully for signs of alterations or replacement.

A clock movement, thirty-hour or eight-day, sits on a seatboard, sometimes loosely, but more usually being fixed to the seatboard by bolts, known as seatboard hooks. The seatboard itself rests on two end supports, one at each side, which are often extensions of the case sides protruding up into the hood area, but sometimes are separate support blocks glued or nailed into place. I usually refer to these as cheeks (see Plates 257 and 258). A non-original clock and movement can often be recognised by the fact that the introduction to a case of a non-original clock with its seatboard will have enforced changes in the cheek heights, causing them to be raised or lowered. Signs of such alterations are usually very obvious, even though sometimes the faker has tried to conceal new sawcuts or packing pieces by staining them to look old (Plate 259).

A further clue is usually found by looking at each end of the seatboard, where nails or screws may have been inserted at some past time to secure it safely down on to the top of the cheeks. Even though this was not necessary, it was often done by past owners out of caution, and occasionally by the original clockmaker. Holes (occupied or not) in the seatboard ends should line up with holes in the top of the cheeks. If not, then the seatboard is wrong to the case, and, if the clock sits on its original seatboard (usually obvious), so is the clock. A modern replacement seatboard has sometimes been fitted for two reasons; firstly it camouflages the fact that the cheek holes don't line up and secondly its thickness can be varied so that the cheeks do not need height modifications. A new seatboard, or one much newer than the rest of the case, may well be one clue towards a clock's not being in its original case.

Many clocks will show one or more rub marks on the backboard, where the pendulum has occasionally scuffed scratch lines – usually one made by the pendulum rating nut and one by the belly of the pendulum bob. If the present pendulum does not contact the backboard at the same height to line up with the scratches, it may be because the clock is not original to the case (see Plates 260 and 261).

The weights of a longcase may have rubbed to produce a worn area on the inner framework above and below the trunk door, though not every clock shows such wear marks. A thirty-hour would have produced one rub from its single weight, roughly in the centre of the case (Plate 262). An eight-day, having two

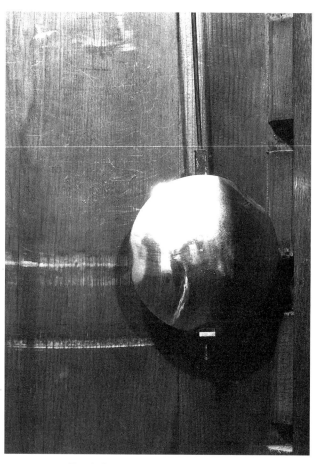

PLATE 259. *Obvious new and crude packings under a seatboard are usually signs of a clock which is not in its original case. In this instance old (original) packing had been used for the original clock to bring the cheeks level with the front blockwork, but the superimposed additional (new) packings are a giveaway.*

PLATE 260. *Pendulum of a longcase clock showing two rub marks, the upper and broader one caused by the rounded back of the pendulum bob, the lower and narrower one caused by the sharp edge of the rating nut. Adjustment of the rating nut for timekeeping has caused 'blurring' of the rub marks. This pendulum is correct for the case, the slight discrepancy caused by the angle of the camera.*

weights, would have scored two areas, each roughly equidistant from the side. Weights which do not now rub where the wear marks occur may indicate a non-original case. Also, of course, such wear marks reveal whether a case originally housed an eight-day or thirty-hour clock.

There can occasionally (and rarely) be quite genuine explanations as to why one or more of the above fitment aspects no longer tally even on a genuine clock in its original case. I will not specify what these are, as that would give every faker the excuses he needs. However, a combination of several such misfit features is fairly condemning, and very seldom have I been convinced by explanations for even a single one.

With experience the enthusiast can also draw on his knowledge of period styles of case and dial (and even movement) and also of regional styles. It is perfectly obvious that a clock made in London or Bristol or Norwich cannot be right in a Manchester style case. So even a smattering of knowledge of styles will add to the ability to form an opinion.

BRACKET CLOCK CASES
The problem of painted dial bracket clocks in non-original cases is very small, as

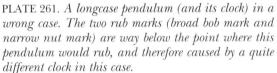

PLATE 261. *A longcase pendulum (and its clock) in a wrong case. The two rub marks (broad bob mark and narrow nut mark) are way below the point where this pendulum would rub, and therefore caused by a quite different clock in this case.*

PLATE 262. *Weight of a thirty-hour clock seen in position as it passes the lower door frame. Over the years it has worn a groove into the inner framework, proving that this case has always housed a thirty-hour clock. A thirty-hour weight runs just left of centre; two eight-day weights rub equidistant at each side.*

in my experience these are seldom met with. British bracket clocks vary greatly in dial size, shape and proportion, and it is no easy matter to fit one into another case, or for that matter even to come by a spare case. If such a clock were housed in a different case, it is quite likely that the pendulum might foul the case back, so watch for apparent cut-outs or alterations to allow pendulum clearance. Most movements are fixed into their cases by screwed side brackets, so look for alterations in bracket screw positions.

IS A WRONG CASE EVER ACCEPTABLE?
Most clocks in non-original cases have been so housed in recent years by dealers who sought to marry a pretty clock with a handsome case for commercial reasons, often encouraged by a public who cared much about appearances and nothing about originality. Some owners today console themselves by believing that a 'furnishing piece' may in any event be a combination of a 'suitable' clock and case, though often totally ignorant as to what might constitute 'suitable'. After all a clock was a combination of the work of two craftsmen, clockmaker and case-maker, so might not the clockmaker just as easily have opted for a case of this nature? Others argue that the case has contained the clock for many years anyway

– as if an ancient marriage is somehow not a marriage at all. Does the fact that the clock was married up years ago make it acceptable, when one married last week is not? And what about the clock married up last week and made to look as if it was done long ago?

Suppose we have a fine clock, even an outstanding clock of extraordinary nature by a foremost maker – caseless. Do we consign it to the scrapheap, make a new case, or try to find a period case we feel 'suitable', even if it means taking it from some other, perhaps less worthy or less valuable clock? Where do we draw a line?

Re-cased clocks almost always have cases newer than the clocks they contain, perhaps because age has taken greater toll of the older ones. It must sometimes have happened that a past owner of what might now be a two hundred year old clock had a fine 'new' case made for it a century ago to bring it into line with his other furnishings. The same principle lies behind many a late eighteenth century case which was carved in the late nineteenth to suit the taste of the day. It could be argued that a 1780s clock in an 1830s case was 're-cased' in 1830, phraseology regularly used by some dealers to explain away a marriage.

Each person will form his own opinion about non-original cases but I find it hard to imagine anyone deriving pleasure from the ownership of a Yorkshire clock of 1790 in a Norfolk case of 1840 if the owner is aware of the dual origin. People who buy such married clocks seldom set out with that intention but do so believing they are buying a genuine clock. Whatever individual attitude you choose to take, it seems to me that it is important to be able to recognise a clock as original or as a marriage before any attitude can be formed at all.

MOVEMENT WITH THE WRONG DIAL

The problem of movements with wrong dials is a considerable one in longcase clocks (much less so in bracket or wall clocks). However it is a problem mostly pertaining to brass dial clocks. It is not uncommon to find a white dial movement with its falseplate married behind a brass dial, but this is really outside our scope here.

If a different japanned dial were fixed to a white dial movement using a false-plate original to one or the other, there would be signs of alteration to either the falseplate or the dial feet holes. There might also be alterations (or lack of drivework) to any calendar and/or moon dial.

A replacement dial fitted to a non-falseplate movement would have involved alterations to the holes in the movement frontplate, which receive the dial feet. However, it is difficult to see the point of anyone having taken the trouble to do either of these types of dial change, as there is no profit in it for the faker. In my experience painted dial clocks very rarely have non-original dials.

AN OLD MOVEMENT RE-DIALLED

It occasionally happened that the owner of a reliable old brass dial longcase might decide to upgrade his clock by having one of the newer, more fashionable painted dials fitted to replace the brass one. Sometimes too he might decide to re-case it at the same time. In other words, rather than buy a complete new clock, the old movement was re-used with a new dial and case (see Plates 263 and 264). So it can happen that a movement may show signs of having had a previous dial, yet still be quite genuine. I've come across this occasionally, though not very often, and it can take considerable investigation to decide when a clock is a genuine example of this practice as opposed to a simple botched fake. This situation is a bit outside the grasp of the novice, who might find it safest to regard spare movement front-plate holes as highly suspicious (see Plate 265).

PLATE 263. *Hood and dial of a thirty-hour clock of about 1790 by Shakeshaft of Preston, Lancashire. 'Strawberry corner' dial of the Wilson type. Note unusual counterbalanced tail to minute hand of matching steel diamond pattern pair.*

PLATE 264. *Rear view of the thirty-hour movement of the Shakeshaft clock in the previous plate, showing it to be much older than the 1790s dial and case. Modifications have been made, including re-positioning the lower pillars, to enable it to be re-used to fit the present dial. Not a case of later faking but an instance where Shakeshaft used a good second-hand movement of perhaps 1740 (and of unusual skeleton form) for his new dial and case in the 1790s.*

RE-PAINTED DIALS OR NAMES

Sometimes white dials were re-painted, perhaps with some more attractive art-work. This is not a regular problem, however, and the few attempts at this I have come across were feeble and very obvious.

What is more of a problem today is the lettering of a more 'famous' name on a

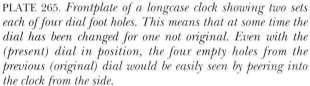

PLATE 265. *Frontplate of a longcase clock showing two sets each of four dial foot holes. This means that at some time the dial has been changed for one not original. Even with the (present) dial in position, the four empty holes from the previous (original) dial would be easily seen by peering into the clock from the side.*

PLATE 266. *Thirty-hour white dial of the late 18th century, obviously drilled crudely later to accept the winding squares of an eight-day movement. Apart from the extreme crudeness of the faking, the absence of a seconds dial often suggests a conversion. Inspection inside would supply confirmation of the conversion by revealing spare dial foot holes in the movement frontplate.*

dial instead of the original one, which was perhaps faded or deliberately erased by the faker. For instance, the younger Jonas Barber is today one of the few prestigious names from the painted dial era, and clocks do crop up here and there bearing that name, whose movements were not by Barber at all. These are usually sold at auction to catch the inexperienced, who ought to have more sense than to buy at auction anyway.

Dial restoration often involves cleaning the dial before re-touching, but does not normally involve re-painting the japanned ground (except to cover any small areas of damage). Beware clocks having a totally re-painted dial as you have no way of knowing whether it has been copied faithfully or invented, and the clockmaker's name with it.

False names of good makers are sometimes painted on to bracket clock dials. Beware total re-paints here, and hopefully check for the same name engraved on the movement backplate, though not all have this.

CHAPTER TWENTY

CARE, HANDLING AND RESEARCH

RESTORATION

After as much as two centuries or more of neglect many antique clocks need restoring. Dipping the movement in a can of paraffin and then rattling the wheels round by running it without the pendulum to 'thrash it into shape' is not the best way of going about this, though this passed as regular practice with some owners and dealers not very many years ago. Another remedy until recently was to hang on a heavier weight, which was the equivalent of putting a larger engine into a car with seized brakes. It may well have forced the clock to run, but probably hastened the end of many.

A clock restorer is not too difficult to find. A good one may be. If you do not already know one, then you have no way of knowing what sort of job to expect. One suggestion is to find someone with many years of experience, and perhaps examine the work he has in progress so that you can attempt to form some opinion of his skills and abilities.

Some professional associations will supply a list of their members. The British Horological Institute is one, located at Upton Hall, Upton, Newark, Nottinghamshire. Another is the Guild of Master Craftsmen at Castle Place, 166 High Street, Lewes, East Sussex. Not all good craftsmen join associations.

Many clocks may still run reliably despite many years without cleaning, and owners often content themselves to let well alone. This is akin to running your car without a service; it will probably keep running but such inaction is aggravating wear and building up more serious problems for the future, which might be nipped in the bud by a timely overhaul. When trouble does develop such an owner will frequently ask a restorer to have a quick look at it, suggesting there can't be much wrong as it has run for years without attention – which is of course precisely what is wrong with it!

Most dealers have their clocks restored thoroughly before sale, but even a clock bought in this way will need cleaning again in due time. After ten years a clock probably needs cleaning again.

The only real difference in the restoration of a white dial clock as against a brass dial one is the dial itself. Many have worn thin in the blackwork, especially the lettering, and sometimes to the point where the maker's name can no longer be made out. This is usually caused by past owners who have tried to 'clean' it by wiping the dial with a wet cloth dipped in kitchen cleaning fluid and have inadvertently erased much detail. Past owners have sometimes tried to re-letter in the numbers and name, making a real trembly mess of what should be crisply sharp detail. Sometimes a name has been incorrectly re-lettered by well-meaning owners unskilled at reading dial names. A good dial restorer has to remove past attempts at re-lettering before he can start work. (See Plate 267, Elgin dial.)

Dial restoration is a very skilled task. Specialist dial restorers can be found and they know what they are about. Problems with dials which are chipped, bent, or have the japanwork flaking off through rust, or bald patches where a loose dialfoot has moved can all be rectified. Very rarely otherwise does the white groundwork need to be re-done, and this should be avoided as it seriously impairs the originality of the dial.

If you do not know how to contact a dial restorer, or clock restorer, your local antique dealer will either refer you to one or have the job done for you. Using an

PLATE 267. *A very distressed painted dial of about 1800 from an eight-day clock by George Sutherland of Elgin, Scotland, but probably an English-made dial. Half has been cleaned and re-lettered. The white background on the right is original but has the dirt removed. This is an extreme example but shows what a good restorer can do using ultra-violet light for guidance with faint lettering.*

ultra-violet lamp a dial restorer can often see quite plainly lettering which may at first glance seem invisible. There are several kinds of UV lamp, and I am told it needs to be one with a mercury bulb.

However, even without such a lamp, an illegible name can often be deciphered by angling the dial against the light until the worn wording reveals itself letter by letter. It is possible to develop the knack of doing this, and it is one that dealers tend to have to learn early as they are often faced with apparently unnamed clocks in salerooms, where they don't have the same opportunity for table-top examination. A small pocket torch can help. Where a clock can be dismantled and the dial held horizontally, I find a fluorescent light can sometimes work where a normal light may not.

People sometimes ask whether or not the dial should be left in its 'original' state, that is unrestored. The problem there is that a dial carrying two centuries of dirt and faint lettering is anything but original. Most collectors, dealers and even museums seem today to take the view that sympathetic restoration of white dials is desirable. Commercially this is seen as adding to the value, not detracting, provided the restoration is done well.

Restoration of clock casework is the same process exactly as with any piece of antique furniture. It is vital not to remove patina, colour and/or age by stripping down the old surface and re-polishing, which unfortunately is what some people think of when they speak of restoration. The unevenness of colour arising from daily use over a century or two is an essential part of the appeal. Those who strip back to bare wood and re-polish end up with a case which looks new, because it is new.

Of course occasions will arise where the polish surface is perished, crackled or blistered, and in these cases there is little option but to remove such polish. A skilled restorer may be able to do this without also removing the colour and unevenness of shading, and then re-polish in such a way as to resemble original patina. This is the best compromise to be expected, but a case re-polished in this way will almost always be less valuable than one preserving a good original finish.

DISMANTLING A CLOCK

Moving a clock should be done in the correct manner, whether from room to room or on a long journey. With a longcase clock, or any other weight-driven clock, it is important not to attempt to lift the whole thing bodily in assembled state, as this may cause damage or at the very least disturbance of the beat setting. With an eight-day clock the weights should be removed after first winding the clock nearly (but not quite) fully to avoid long lengths of trailing gutline. Some like to let the gutlines fully down, but it may be difficult for a beginner to reach the release clicks on the barrels and if you handle a movement with long trailing lines it is awkward to re-hang the weights during assembly. With a thirty-hour clock wind it about two-thirds so that the pulley shows at a convenient height.

I find it a good idea with eight-day clocks to fix masking tape around the barrels to hold the coiled gutline in place during transit. This is a far easier operation than attempting to untangle gutlines which have come loose and wedged themselves between the wheels. If faced with gutlines which are much entangled, then it may be simplest to untie the end of the line and feed the whole thing out coil by coil to get a fresh untangled start. No taping is needed for thirty-hour clocks, as the drive rope or chain can be slipped into place easily by hand if need be.

With weight(s) and pendulum safely removed, lift the movement (with dial attached) out of the case. Most eight-day clocks are attached to the seatboard, which will then come out with the movement. With thirty-hour clocks the seatboard is sometimes a fixture to the case, in which cases lift the movement clean up from the fixed board.

The movement can be carried safely if rested in a box, dial down, at an angle of about 45 degrees in such a way that the hands cannot foul against the box side. The crutch (see Figure 8) is then safely out of contact with any obstacles which may bend it. Never lean a movement on its back, or the crutch will be bent or broken.

With spring-driven clocks such as bracket or wall dial clocks, there are of course no weights involved. Some bracket clocks have a carrying screw, which normally

270

fixes into a convenient section at the side of the backplate when the clock is in use. Remove this and screw it into the hole in the pendulum rod, thus fixing the pendulum firmly so that the clock can be carried safely. Verge clocks have a carrying hook on to which the verge pendulum is rested for carrying.

Those bracket clocks without a carrying screw, and all spring-driven wall clocks other than those with verge escapement, need to have the pendulum removed before transporting. If the clock is partly wound, as is usually the case, the escapement will begin running very quickly once the pendulum is removed, and this is not good for the clock. A small wedge of folded paper pushed gently between crutch and backplate will stop the clock running until re-assembled. A small piece of sellotape will achieve the same by taping the pendulum fast.

TRANSPORTING A CLOCK

Most bracket clocks will pack safely into a cardboard box with the pendulum screwed tight or removed. Always carry them upright. A spring wall clock is best carried lying on its back, again with pendulum removed.

Most longcase clocks can be carried quite easily in an ordinary family car, whether or not it is a hatchback. An estate is, of course, much easier but by no means essential. The hood has already been removed to withdraw the movement, and hood, weight(s), pendulum and movement will all be packed into the vehicle last, using what space remains after the main body of the clock is *in situ.*

Loading an estate is self-evident, though the length of the body section of the clock is often such that it will not lie in the space behind the passenger seat, especially with smaller estate cars. In this situation, load the estate as if it were a car, as described below.

The upper section of the body is just backboard, maybe an inch or so in thickness running a length of perhaps two feet. The aim is to load the body of the clock as if it were a sleeping passenger with the passenger seat backrest reclined (backwards of course, not forwards). In the foot well area will rest the backboard section, being thin enough to load right down into the foot well. The feet of the clock, which lies on its back, will reach about as far as, or slightly short of, the back seat backrest, which should be left in the upright position. It is a mistake to try to drop the backrest of the rear seats, even with those cars which allow this, and it is not necessary anyway.

With a hatchback car the body loads in through the hatch, passing between roof lining and back seat headrest till it reaches fully into the foot well. Cover the upholstery with cloths or a newspaper against damage from the rough outer backboard as some may have old nails standing proud.

With a non-hatchback a different method of loading is needed. Recline both front seats fully backwards. Feed the clock in on its back with upper backboard first through the driving side rear door, ease the backboard into the passenger foot well and lift the body across till it lies straight. Then raise the driver's seatback again to its normal position.

This system will work with most clocks and almost any car except a mini. It will not work in a small car with a very broad clock or a very tall one. Once the body of the clock is installed, the hood, movement (in box), weights and pendulum can be packed around it, mostly in the boot area. This method works better than a small van or small estate car and for most people involves less expense.

ASSEMBLING A CLOCK

Assembling a spring-driven clock is simply a matter of replacing the pendulum and winding the clock.

To assemble a longcase clock, first set the case where desired, in such a way that it leans against the wall, and if need be set packing pieces under the front feet to force it to lean slightly backwards and firmly against the wall. Try on the hood now and check for side-to-side level by using a spirit level horizontally on the small ledge in front of the hood door (almost all longcase clocks have a ledge there). Checking side-to-side 'level' in this manner is better than merely using a 'true eye', since if the clock is ever moved again later, or should bed itself down into a thickly-underfelted carpet, you have a positive measure of what 'level' you started with, making it easy to correct at any future time.

If the clock can wobble about from front to back or side to side, it is unlikely to run satisfactorily or may be subject to random stopping, so a firm wedging into position is essential. Having got the case level and firm, set the movement in its case, getting someone to hold it safely until the pendulum or weight(s) are in place. Many longcase clock movements are front heavy and may easily topple forward off the seatboard or side cheeks unless care is taken. Once weight(s) and pendulum are in place, they will hold it safely. Some seatboards screw down for greater security, but this is not essential. Nor is it essential to screw a longcase to the wall, though those who like to do so can hardly do any harm and it can help prevent a case from bedding down into the carpet pile later.

With the weight(s) safely hanging on the pulley(s), remove the carrying tapes. Your clock is then assembled and may run by simply giving the pendulum a push. However it may be out of beat and if so will probably stop after a few minutes, or a few seconds even, if badly out of beat.

SETTING A CLOCK IN BEAT

A clock which has not run for some long time or one which has been transported wrongly may not run for more than a few minutes or even a few seconds once assembled. Most such clocks are not in fact broken but are simply 'out of beat', which means not level. Use a spirit level to establish a measurable state. Level the case as described above (with a bracket clock, set it on a level surface) then make the clock run at this new, true, and checkable level setting. It may of course have run previously at a quite different 'level'.

Using our defined level basis we propose to alter the angle of the crutch to give an even beat side to side. First, however, ensure that the brass block of the pendulum sits neatly in the fork. It should not rub against the fork rim front or back and it should fit snugly enough at the sides of the fork to ensure it does not foul and that there is no slack. If it does foul, bend the crutch forward or back to find a central position for the brass block.

A clock in beat will tick regularly like someone walking. One out of beat will sound uneven, like someone limping. Even the beginner will soon get used to identifying this sound. The distance the pendulum swings *after* each tick (i.e. the overswing) will be further at one side than the other. If the clock ticks more heavily (or has more overswing) to the left (as you face the clock) than the right, bend the crutch towards the left, and vice versa. The crutch should be bent somewhere about the middle of its length using fingers and thumbs of both hands. Do not try to bend it against its top joint or you may loosen the joint without realising it, when the clock will keep running in and out of beat at random. (See Figure 8.)

If the pendulum should swing without giving any tick at all, the crutch is probably bent well out of place and may need bending half an inch or more. Normally, however, you will find it ticks but unevenly, in which case only a very small amount of adjustment is needed to the crutch, perhaps enough to move the fork by an eighth of an inch. Several attempts may be needed till the correct setting is

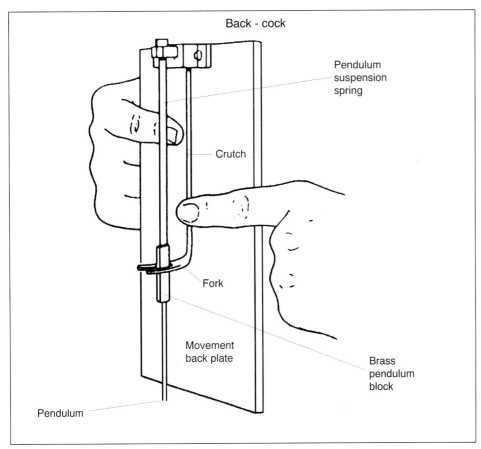

Back - cock

Pendulum
suspension
spring

Crutch

Fork

Movement
back plate

Brass
pendulum
block

Pendulum

FIGURE 8. *Setting a clock in beat. View of the crutch arrangement behind the backplate of a longcase clock showing how the crutch needs to be bent in its length (not at the top joint) for re-setting.*

found. The closer you get into beat, the longer the clock will run. A clock almost (but not quite) in beat will tend to stop about five minutes to any hour, as it struggles to lift the strike lever for warning.

REGULATION

To make a clock run faster or slower the rating nut below the pendulum bob needs to be turned. On some bracket clocks the rating nut is above the pendulum bob. To speed up the clock the pendulum needs to be shorter, to slow it down, longer. If you forget which, think that a very short pendulum would swing very fast.

The rating nut needs to be turned clockwise for shortening (faster) and vice versa, as seen from below. With a verge pendulum it is the bob itself which turns. Accuracy within a minute a week is not unusual for a longcase clock.

In setting the time it is always safest *not* to turn hands backwards. Most clocks will allow this between quarter to the hour back to a minute after the hour, but it is very unwise to try to take the hand of any striking clock back through the last hour position. When winding the hands forwards it is always safest to allow each hour to strike through fully.

There is no need to stop a clock during winding, even though the seconds hand on some eight-day clocks will be seen to turn backwards during the winding process. This is normal when the drive power of the weight is temporarily removed during winding, and is not a cause for concern.

OILING

Resist the temptation to drench the clock in oil as too much oil or oil in the wrong place is probably worse than no oil at all. An oil can is too generous. Special clock oil can be purchased but any light machine oil such as sewing machine oil will do. The idea is to oil those surfaces where friction arises, which means the points where the end of each arbor meets the plates (arbor is the horological term for axle). Take a six-inch length of thin wire such as a piece of coathanger, pick up a bead of oil and deposit it on the end of one arbor. Then repeat at the other end, covering every arbor in the clock. Do not oil the teeth of wheels or pinions, as this will cause dust to grind in. Do not oil the hands.

Oiling a longcase movement is easy, as it just means removing the hood. A bracket clock or a wall dial clock needs to be removed from its case. If you can't do it, get in someone who can. Occasional stopping for no obvious reason and with increasing frequency probably is the clock's way of telling you it needs oil.

RESEARCHING A CLOCKMAKER

Knowing something about the maker of your clock makes ownership far more interesting, whether he was famous or little known. You will already have been able to form a good idea of the age of your white dial clock from the information you have read so far. Knowledge of even a very few facts about the maker's life will enable you to confirm or change your assumed dating.

If your clockmaker worked in any of those fortunate few counties (or towns) whose clockmakers have been documented in book form, then you are lucky and these are your likeliest source of detailed information. Many of the county works are out of print today, but you may still obtain access through the libraries system.

Counties covered so far are: Buckinghamshire, Cornwall, Cumberland, Derbyshire, Devon, Dorset, Durham, Gloucestershire, Lanarkshire, Lancashire, Leicestershire, Lincolnshire, Oxfordshire, Northumberland, Nottinghamshire, Shropshire, Somerset, Sussex, Warwickshire, Westmorland, Wiltshire (part only), Yorkshire.

Individual towns covered separately are: Birmingham, Chester, Colchester, Dunfermline, Exeter, Hamilton, Hull, Leamington, Nantwich, Salisbury, Stamford, Stirling, Tiverton, Warwick.

Their titles in full are:

Chester Clocks and Clockmakers by Nicholas Moore (Chester Museum 1976)
Clock and Watch Makers of Buckinghamshire by Edward Legg (Bradwell Abbey Field Centre 1976)
Clock and Watchmakers of Nottinghamshire by H. Mather (Nottingham 1979)
Clockmakers of Northumberland and Durham by Keith Bates (Northumberland 1980)
Clockmakers of Warwick and Leamington by W.A. Seaby (Warwick Museum 1981)
Clockmaking in Oxfordshire by C.F.C. Beeson (Museum of the History of Science, 1989)
Clocks and Clockmakers of Salisbury by Michael Snell (Salisbury 1986)
Clocks and Clockmakers of Tiverton by Ponsford, Scott and Authers (Tiverton 1977)
Colchester Clockmakers by Bernard Mason (Country Life 1969)
Cornish Clocks and Clockmakers by H. Miles-Brown (David & Charles 1970)
Derbyshire Clock and Watch Makers by R.G. Hughes (Derby Museum 1976)
Devon Clocks and Clockmakers by Clive Ponsford (David & Charles 1985)
Devonshire Clockmakers by J.K. Bellchambers (Torquay 1962 but superseded by Ponsford above)
Dorset Clocks and Clockmakers (including Channel Islands) by T. Tribe & P. Whatmoor (Oswestry 1981)

Dunfermline Clockmakers by Felix Hudson (Dunfermline 1982)
Gloucestershire Clock and Watch Makers by Graham Dowler (Phillimores 1984)
Hull and East Riding Clocks by J.E.S. Walker (Hornsea Museum 1982)
Lancashire Clocks and Clockmakers by Brian Loomes (David & Charles 1975)
Leicestershire Clockmakers by John Daniel (Leicestershire Museums 1975)
Lincolshire Clockmakers by J.E.S. Walker (Lincolnshire Libraries, due 1995)
Marking Time in Hamilton by William Wallace (Hamilton 1981)
Nantwich Clockmakers by Alan A. Treherne (Nantwich Museum 1986)
Old Stirling Clockmakers (including St. Ninians) (Stirling 1990)
Samuel Roberts, Clockmaker by W.T.R. Pryce & T. Alun Davies (St. Fagans, 1985)
Shropshire Clock and Watch Makers by D. Elliott (Phillimores 1979)
Somerset Clockmakers by J.K. Bellchambers (Torquay 1969)
Stamford Clocks and Watches by Laurence Tebbutt (Stamford 1975)
Suffolk Clocks and Clockmakers by A.L. Haggar and L.F. Miller (Ticehurst 1974)
The Clockmakers of Cumberland by John Penfold (Ashford 1977)
The Clockmakers of Sussex by E.J. Tyler (Ashford 1986)
Time in Exeter by Clive Ponsford (Exeter 1978)
Watch and Clockmakers of Warwickshire by Joseph McKenna (Birmingham 1985)
Watch and Clockmakers of Birmingham by Joseph McKenna (Birmingham 1986)
Westmorland Clocks and Clockmakers by Brian Loomes (David & Charles 1974)
Yorkshire Clockmakers by Brian Loomes (Littleborough 1985)

Welsh clockmakers are documented in *Clock and Watch Makers in Wales* by Iorweth C. Peate (Welsh Folk Museum 1960). Scottish makers can best be found in *Old Scottish Clockmakers* by John Smith (E.P. Publishing 1975). However, a new work on Scots makers by Donald Whyte (*Scottish Clock and Watch Makers 1453 - 1900*) is due for publication in 1995 by the Scottish Genealogical Society and should update Smith considerably.

Unless local books exist you will need to refer to *Watchmakers and Clockmakers of the World* (Volume 1 by the late G.H. Baillie and Volume 2 by myself), containing brief details of over 80,000 clockmakers worldwide, but mostly British. You may also find there other Welsh and Scottish makers missed by Smith and Peate. Bear in mind that dates given in such works are not necessarily of birth and death but may be estimates or dates from trades directories, which were published only at irregular intervals. Always try to assess the age of a clock for yourself first and then use such books as a cross check to see how close you got.

If the maker you seek fails to appear in any of these works, you still have the option of trying to track down some details of his life for yourself. The museum or library of the town in question may themselves be able to help you, as some keep lists of local makers, or perhaps the County Record Office of the particular county.

Ultimately, however, you may have to get down to the genealogical task yourself, looking at local parish registers, etc. This can be a much easier task than you might imagine and can be enjoyable in its own right. To assist with just such a task I wrote *The Concise Guide to Tracing your Ancestry* published by Barrie & Jenkins in 1992.

LONGCASE CLOCK DIAL FEATURES

solid line = normal
dotted line = unusual

1770 1780 1790 1800 1810 1820 1830 1840 1850 1860 1870

NUMBERING
dotted minutes
mins numbered 5, 10, 15, 20, etc
mins numbered 15, 30, 45, 60 only
mins not numbered
hours in Roman numbers
hours in Arabic numbers
full minute band
single-handed clocks   (almost entirely Southern)

FALSEPLATE (eight-day clocks)
with
without

PAINTING OF CORNERS
spray of flowers or fruit
shells/fans/semi-geometrics
ruins, churches, landscapes
all-white, no corner painting
gold 'spandrel' corners

PAINTING OF ARCH
name only
birds/flowers on white ground
vignette inset on white ground
filled with painted scene
gold or silver background
luminous paints
swaying figures
moon dial
strike/silent feature   (largely Southern)

SHAPE/SIZE
arched
square
circular
width 10½in-13in
width 13in-15in

DATE INDICATOR
none
pointer, steel
pointer, brass   (unusual)
aperture, square box
aperture, curved

HANDS
non-matching steel (date and second hands may match)
matching steel
matching brass (rarely copper)
non-matching brass   (exist only as incorrect replacements)

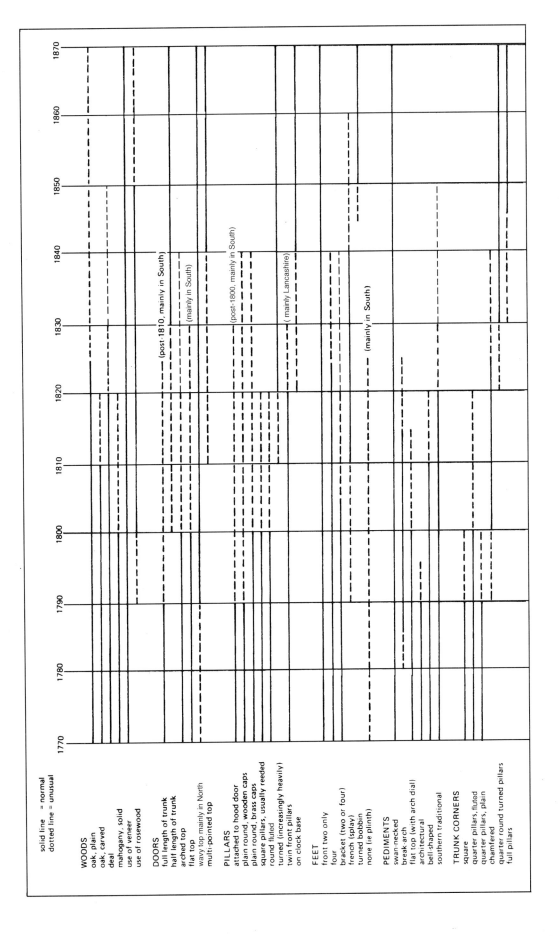

LONGCASE CLOCK CASE FEATURES

solid line = normal
dotted line = unusual

WOODS
oak, plain
oak, carved
deal
mahogany, solid
use of veneer
use of rosewood

DOORS
full length of trunk
half length of trunk
arched top
flat top
wavy top mainly in North
multi-pointed top

PILLARS
attached to hood door
plain round, wooden caps
plain round, brass caps
square pillars, usually reeded
round fluted
turned (increasingly heavily)
twin front pillars
on clock base

FEET
front two only
four
bracket (two or four)
french (splay)
turned bobbin
none (ie plinth)

PEDIMENTS
swan-necked
break-arch
flat top (with arch dial)
architectural
bell-shaped
southern traditional

TRUNK CORNERS
square
quarter pillars, fluted
quarter pillars, plain
chamfered
quarter round turned pillars
full pillars

277

INDEX

Ablitt, John, 106
Ainsworth, George, 40
Anderson, James, 69, 209
Arabic hours, 92
Archer of Stowe, 225
Armstrong, Thomas, 52
Astronomical clock, 229

Bain of Brechin, 198
Baker, John, 64
Baker of Newark, 92, 167
Barber, Jonas, 51, 60, 119
Barker, Thomas, 28
Barlow, William, 82, 145
Barnsdale, John, 96
Barron, John, 189
Barwise, Lot, 68
Bath, James, 95, 163
Beilby & Hawthorn, 42
Bellman of Broughton, 84
Benbow, Thomas, 93, 163
Benson, John, 53, 61
Bidlake of London, 101, 179
Bishop, John, 177
Blakeborough, Richard, 80, 116
Blakeway, Charles, 48
Blood, Richard, 58
Blow, Henry, 136, 137
Boyfield, Richard, 148
Braund, John, 108, 180
Breneisen, Samuel, 256
Brown, John, wheelwright, 100
Bryson of Edinburgh, 221
Buchan, Archibald, 74
Bulgin of Marshfield, 164
Bullock, William, 148
Burton, Samuel, 183
Burton of Kendal, 90, 157

Calendars, 75, 94, 109
Cameron, Alexander, 203, 222
Carell, John and Daniel, 252
Carley of Thetford, 247
Carved cases, 158
Casemakers named, 131, 134, 135, 136, 137, 138, 157
Casemakers' labels, 138
Casework terminology, 126
Chandler, Timothy, 252
Chapman, William, 33, 112, 136
Clock dresser, 44
Coates, J. & R., 146
Cock, William, 135, 182
Collier, J., 99
Countwheel, pinned type, 31
Croal, Robert, 200, 215
Crockett, John, 114, 182

Dallaway, William, 62, 188
Dallaway & Son, 192
Davidson, James, 201, 216
Davidson, John, 236, 243
Deacon, John, 123
Deacon, Samuel, 44, 50, 53, 54, 65, 124, 125
Dean, Thomas, 83, 147
Dials
    American borders, 42
    astronomical, 229
    Battersea enamel, 18
    Birmingham, 23
    black, 64
    border patterns, 42
    brass, japanned over, 63, 64
    chipping, 25
    colouring method, 31
    convex, 114
    couthy, 200
    dotted minutes, 74
    eight-day used for thirty-hour, 29, 47
    enamel (vitreous), 14, 15, 16, 17, 243
    fly, 85, 86, 225, 227
    gold corners, 66
    halo, 34
    job ticket, 31
    moon – see under moon
    oval, 84
    porcelain, 18
    prices, 48, 119
    printed from transfer, 33, 34, 110
    regulator, 116
    re-painted, 266
    restoration, 268
    silvered brass or one-piece, 13, 15, 62
    size, 80, 95, 113, 127
    strawberry corners, 42, 70
    twenty-four hour, 228, 229
    un-named, 248
    wooden, 14, 249, 250
    world time, 228
Dialmakers
    list of American, 258
    list of English, 35
    list of Scottish, 39
    punch marks of, 40, 41
Dickerson, Daniel, 15
Dickinson of Preston, 244
Donisthorpe, Joseph, 50
Dummy second dials, 47
Dummy winders, 29, 47

Eberhardt, Ludwig, 257
Eberman, John, 258
Eby, Christian, 252
Eggert, D., 167

Elliott, J.C., 115, 128, 184, 185
Elliott, William, 75
Engraved backplate, 243
Escapements
    anchor, 238, 239
    deadbeat, 239
    verge, 238, 241
Esplin, George, 110
Esterle, John, 255
Evans, John, 93, 162
Evans of Shrewsbury, 144

Falseplates, 19
    double names on, 43
    on brass dials, 46
Fawcett, Abraham, 240
Feren, Peter, 197, 217
Finials, 136
Fletcher, Celia, 83
Fly dials, 85, 86, 225, 227
Forster of Norwich, 154
Fothergill of Knaresborough, 180
Fox, Hudson, 92, 169
Frodsham of London, 242
Fuller, Robert, 70, 152
Fusee, 235, 238

Ganter, Paul, 183
Gemmel, Matthew, 219
Gillies, Robert, 214
Glover, Joseph, 79
Greening, Benjamin, 224, 226
Grey, James, 221
Grosch, Peter L., 253

Hallam of Nottingham, 114, 181
Hammond, T., 246
Handley & Moore, 164, 242
Hardaker of Salem, 63
Hargraves, Thomas, 72, 143
Harlow, Benjamin, 72, 156
Harlow, Samuel, 44
Harrison & Sons, 116
Heinzelman, John Conrad, 257
Henderson, Ebenezer, 229
Hepton of Northallerton, 31
Hewitt, George, 24, 73
Hewitt, Patrick, 58
Hewson, William, 107, 137
Hoadley, Silas, 249
Hodson, Charles, 240
Holmes, John, 84, 147
Hooded clock, 112
Howse, Thomas, 174
Hunter of Clapham, 240
Husband, Thomas, 77
Hutchins, Abel, 252

Innes, George, 220

Jameson of Maybole, 206
Japanned goods, 32, 190
Job tickets, 31
Johnson, Richard, 156
Johnson, William, 98

Keeling of London, 246
Keir, Peter, 193
Kelvey of Gainsborough, 128
Keys, Joseph, 172
Kirkland, Richard, 151

Laird, D.W., 111
Latches, 51
Law, William, 202, 218
Lawson of Wigan, 81
Lindley, Thomas, 53
Lister, Thomas, 225, 227
Lithgow, William, 220
Lomax of Blackburn, 84, 150
Low, Charles, 85
Lumley & Gudgeon, 153

Maltese Cross mark, 41
Manby, John, 121
Maple & Co., 244
Marriage clock, 88, 260
Married clock, 260
Marshall, Robert, 118
Mason, A. & E., 112
Mawman, George, 94, 170
Melrose of Galashiels, 217
Miller of Bedford, 108, 177
Milsome, John, 88, 159
Monkhouse of Carlisle, 174
Monkhouse & Son, 96
Moon dials, 77, 87, 94, 111, 251
  'scientific', 21
  unusual types, 21, 225
Moorehouse, William, 187
Morgan, Thomas, 78, 211
Morland, Richard, 184
Mortimore of Dartmouth, 97, 168
Movements
  birdcage, 27, 28
  posted, 27, 28
Muirhead, James, 219
Muncaster, William, 91, 170
Murray, William, 232, 233
Musical clocks, 57

Negative numbering, 102
Nicholas, William, 103, 105, 171, 181
Nicholas, William & Caleb, 14, 16, 17, 157
Nolen, Henry, 253

Northgraves, Denton, 105, 178
Novelty clock, 244
Numbering of clocks, 51, 52, 53, 57

Oglesby & Poole, 252
Osborne & Wilson, 19, 20
Oval dial, 84
Oves, George, 253, 254
Owen, Watkin, 79, 82, 144

Palliser, John, 173
Pannel, Joshua, 101
Panton, J. & G., 199
Pattison of Halifax, 158
Patton & Jones, 252, 253, 257
Pearson, Samuel, 91
Penhallow, H. & B., 252
Penman, Peter, 222
Perigal of London, 247
Phil(l)ipson, Henry, 119
Phil(l)ipson, John, 57
Pinney of Stamford, 111
Place, Thomas, 173
Place of Thirsk, 30
Pond, J., 252
Porthouse, William, 225
Prices (of clocks and dials), 119
Probert of Wigan, 158

Raymond, George, 27
Receipt, original, 123, 125
Reynolds & Earle, 15
Richards, Robert, 112
Richardson, Timothy, 68
Robb, D., 214
Robb, William, 73, 108, 212
Roberts, Owen, 185, 186
Roberts, Samuel, 48
Roberts, Woolston, 140, 141, 169
Robotham, Charles, 81
Rocking figures, 86, 101, 116
Rogers of Leominster, 70, 143
Russell, Edward, 145
Rust, William, 78, 151
Rutherford, William, 90, 134

Sagar of Skipton, 76
Salmon, Colin, 190
Schofield, Major, 159
Scott, James, 113
Scott, Walter, 194, 213
Seatboard fittings, 260, 261
Seconds dial, dummy, 47
Shakeshaft of Preston, 265, 266
Sheddon, Charles, 204
Sherwood, Thomas, 71, 155
Simpkin, John, 75, 109

Single-hand dial, 225, 228
Six-month duration clock, 224
Smith, James, 243
Smith, John, 209, 213
Snow, Richard, 172, 184
Snow, Will, 59, 60, 61
Snowden of Grimsby, 80, 152
Spendlove, John, 166
Stobo, Thomas, 191, 218
Stokes of Knutsford, 114
Stonehouse of Leeds, 102, 128
Stones of Blackburn, 171
Stott, Eli, 77, 131
Strawberry corners, 42, 70
Stuart, cabinetmaker of Kendal, 157
Stubbs, Peter, 120
Summerhayes, Robert, 27, 118, 187
Sutherland, George, 269
Symonds of Reepham, 165, 166

Tate of Winterton, 178
Terry, Eli, 250
Thompson, James, 94, 168
Thompson, William, 228
Thompson of Darlington, 30
Thorndike of Ipswich, 81, 150
Thorpe of Bath, 135, 182
Thristle of Stogursey, 231, 234
Tootell, John, 82
Tumbling numbers, 93

Usher, James, 137, 139

Waite, John, 117
Ward, Henry, 25, 74, 129
Waren, William, 67, 155
Webber of Ilfracombe, 130
Westmoreland, William, 131, 140
Weston, John, 95, 162
Whale's tail crest, 152, 153, 154
Whitehurst, John, 12, 13
Whitman, Benjamin, 252
Whittaker & Shreeve, 41
Wignall of Ormskirk, 146
Wilkie, Robert, 195
Willard & Nolen, 252
Wilson, James (Birmingham), 19, 22
Wilson, James (Belfast), 62
Wilson, John, 107
Wood, Peter, 78
Woods, 129
World time dial, 228
Worswick, Thomas, 88, 149
Wyatt, Robert, 109, 179
Wylie, William, 207

Yeomans of Nottingham, 237